"This is the best short introduction to Byron available. Stauffer steers us through a tumultuous life with poise and expert authority. The letters provide vivid snapshots of Byron at key moments across three decades and the biography that emerges is deeply absorbing."

Jane Stabler, author of *The Artistry of Exile:*
Romantic and Victorian Writers in Italy

"Framed around ten of Byron's most intriguing letters, Stauffer's lively narrative never loses sight of the poetry, reminding the reader of Byron's prodigious output even amidst the chaos of his domestic life. With many insightful observations on Byron's conduct, Stauffer does not hesitate to criticize when criticism is justified, but prefers to see in Byron not so much contradiction or hypocrisy but rather a synthesis of the light and dark sides of his nature, of the serious and the comic, of the ironic and the heartfelt. A delightful read."

Robert James Byron, 13th Baron Byron

"This new biography of Byron is a miracle of condensation; by putting the letters center-stage, Professor Stauffer manages to let his subject speak for himself in all the contradictory range of his moods and circumstances – at the same time as elegantly and unobtrusively shaping a narrative that leaps off the page."

Roderick Beaton, author of *Byron's War:*
Romantic Rebellion, Greek Revolution

"We have had many flings at a 'Life of Byron,' all of them more or less successful because all of them fail to hand over a dead man to us. This little book is as good as such a venture gets because it puts front and center what Shelley might have called the 'Life of the Life of Byron': his very self and voice in ten remarkable letters. They sketch the story of a life whose riches taught him poverty. 'I have spent my life both interest and principal, / And deem not, what I deem'd, my soul invincible.' A mortal life well spent."

Jerome McGann, author of *Byron and the Poetics of Adversity*

"Andrew Stauffer offers a fresh and intimate take on a prolific and notoriously ungovernable subject, through a handful of letters judiciously selected from over 3,000. Building on the poet's own voice, Stauffer beautifully evokes his world from Regency high society to the sordid whirl of Venice and political turmoil in Greece. Compelling, charming, and pleasingly scandal-packed – this is Byron, brilliantly distilled."

Emily Brand, author of *The Fall of the House of Byron*

BYRON

A Life in Ten Letters

Andrew Stauffer

 CAMBRIDGE
UNIVERSITY PRESS

Shaftesbury Road, Cambridge CB2 8EA, United Kingdom

One Liberty Plaza, 20th Floor, New York, NY 10006, USA

477 Williamstown Road, Port Melbourne, VIC 3207, Australia

314–321, 3rd Floor, Plot 3, Splendor Forum, Jasola District Centre,
New Delhi – 110025, India

103 Penang Road, #05–06/07, Visioncrest Commercial, Singapore 238467

Cambridge University Press is part of Cambridge University Press & Assessment,
a department of the University of Cambridge.

We share the University's mission to contribute to society through the pursuit of
education, learning, and research at the highest international levels of excellence.

www.cambridge.org
Information on this title: www.cambridge.org/9781009200165

DOI: 10.1017/9781009200134

First published 2024

Printed in the United Kingdom by CPI Group Ltd, Croydon CR0 4YY

A catalogue record for this publication is available from the British Library.

*A Cataloging-in-Publication data record for this book is available from the Library
of Congress.*

ISBN 978-1-009-20016-5 Hardback

For Jerry McGann
*a light to lesson ages, rebel nations,
and voluptuous princes*

CONTENTS

Contents

Plate sections will be found between pages 150 and 151,
and 246 and 247.

The Lord Byron I find there is our Lord Byron — the fascinating — faulty — childish — philosophical being — daring the world — docile to a private circle — impetuous and indolent — gloomy and yet more gay than any other — I live with him again in these pages.

Mary Shelley

INTRODUCTION

In April, 1824, news spread that Lord Byron, one of the most famous people in the Western world, had died suddenly in an obscure part of Greece. As would become the norm with celebrity deaths, people remembered what they were doing when they heard the news. A young Alfred Tennyson carved "Byron is dead" on a rock, recalling it as "a day when the whole world seemed to be darkened" and "everything was over and finished for every one." Sir Walter Scott wrote, "we feel almost as if the great luminary of Heaven had suddenly disappeared from the sky." Jane Welsh (the future wife of Thomas Carlyle) wrote that she heard the news "in a room full of people" and "if they had said the sun or the moon was gone out of the heavens, it could not have struck me with the idea of a more awful and dreary blank in creation than the words, 'Byron is dead!'" The poet's death seemed to many like a real-life enactment of Byron's apocalyptic poem "Darkness," which imagines a day when, without warning, "the bright sun was extinguished." To his contemporaries, the end of Byron felt something like the end of the world.

In the previous dozen years or so, Byron had become renowned for his poetry and notorious for the events of his personal life. His works and experiences were intertwined in ways that stoked curiosity and propelled him into the upper stratosphere of fame. In a series of narrative poems, lyrics, and verse dramas, he had all but invented the theatrically confessional style of modern celebrity, aloof yet mysteriously intimate. He seemed to be always sharing too much, and yet never enough. Rumors of blasphemy, adultery, sodomy, incest, and madness surrounded him, many of them mostly true. And the characters that populated Byron's poetry – the jaded pilgrim Childe Harold, the brooding romantic pirate Conrad, the self-tortured sorcerer Manfred, the heartbroken and vengeful Giaour, and many more – seemed to be projected versions of a man whom audiences grew to admire and condemn as the erotic arch-rebel of their days. And then suddenly, at age 36, he was gone.

A month after Byron's death, six men gathered solemnly around a London fireplace to shred and burn Byron's hand-written personal memoir, having judged the manuscript too scandalous for the public, or even for posterity. As the paper flared in the grate, the flames illuminated their somber faces: Byron's longtime publisher, John Murray; Byron's friend since their university days, John Cam Hobhouse; the Irish poet Thomas Moore, to whom Byron had entrusted the manuscript, and Moore's friend Henry Luttrell; and two other men representing the women in Byron's family, his wife Annabella Milbanke (Lady Byron) and his half-sister Augusta Leigh. Moore had told Byron he planned to leave the memoir as a legacy to his son, "who shall astonish the latter days of the nineteenth century with it." But the will of the others prevailed: the manuscript met the flames and the memoir passed into legend.

What we have instead are Byron's letters: approximately 3,000 of them, written to family members and lovers, to his publishers and bankers, and to the same friends who would one day torch his memoir. They offer the confessions, humor, lordly braggadocio, sordid details, and half-ironic self-mythologizing that surely characterized the lost memoir as well. The letters have long been admired as some of the most lively, witty, and readable in the language. Peter Graham nominates Byron as "one of the greatest letter-writers of all time," and Richard Lansdown places Byron's collected correspondence among the "great monuments of English Romantic prose." Leslie Marchand, the distinguished editor and biographer of Byron, praises the letters' "frankness and humanity," saying they provide "a clear mirror of his personality, of its weaknesses as well as its strengths," and "they reflect more accurately than any words left by his contemporaries the brilliance, charm, and wit of his conversation." Or, as Byron's friend Mary Shelley put it simply, "His own letters and journals mirror himself as he was, and are invaluable."

I had been reading and teaching Byron for a number of years before I held one of his letters, written in his hand, in my own. That moment of contact in the Reading Room of the Pforzheimer Collection at the New York Public Library converted me. I became first an editor of Byron's writing, and then a biographer devoted to unfolding the details of the curiously attractive records he left behind. When Byron's friend Thomas Moore produced the first full-length biography in 1830, he relied so heavily on Byron's correspondence that his book's title became *The Letters and Journals of Lord Byron, with Notices of His Life*. In this book, I have followed Moore's example, foregrounding the letters in my attempt to tell Byron's story. I have selected for closest attention ten of the most interesting and characteristic letters written between his teenage years and his last weeks in Messolonghi. Each chapter begins with Byron's voice on the page, as if we have opened a letter from the poet himself, followed by an account of the experiences and emotions it touches and its place in the poet's life. Accompanying illustrations of some of the actual letters convey their tactile, material aspects: the slanting scrawl of a paragraph written at sea, a red wax seal cracked upon opening, a tanned paper's edge worn away by time. Such details have a particular appeal now, when the art of handwritten letters is dying out. As Dwight Garner put it recently in the *New York Times*, "The age of proper correspondence has ended, and there's been no pan-ecumenical service to mourn its passing." Paper pages filled with Byron's rapid, mostly legible cursive hand offer windows onto that vanishing world.

A focus on Byron's letters also reveals the variable sides of his mobile personality, as he shifts his style and subject to suit the occasion and the correspondent. His friend Lady Blessington judged that "the chameleon-like character or manner of Byron renders it difficult to portray him," and she gave the opinion that "if ten individuals undertook the task of describing Byron, no two, of the ten, would agree in their verdict respecting him, or convey any portrait that resembled the other, and yet the description of each might be correct." Byron himself was well aware of his contradictions, and particularly of the contingent nature of his opinions and pronouncements. To Lady Blessington, he chuckled at the effect this would likely have on his "future biographers … as I flatter myself I shall have more than one": "Indeed, the more the merrier, say I. One will represent me as a sort of sublime misanthrope, with moments of kind feelings…. Another will portray me as a modern Don Juan; and a third … will … if only for opposition sake, represent me as an *amiable*, ill-used gentleman, 'more sinned against than sinning.'" To his friend Hobhouse, he expressed a similar idea in more worried tones: "Will not my life … be given in a false and unfair point of view by others? – I mean *false* as to *praise* as well as *censure?*" Letting Byron speak for himself to a wide variety of correspondents might give us our best chance of getting a composite view of his complex and evolving character.

Two centuries after his death, what aspects of Byron's life and work still resonate? Undergirding everything is his use of words, the seemingly endless capacity for verbal expression, adaptation, and invention evident in his poems, letters, and conversation. Byron himself wrote, "I twine / My hopes of being remembered in my line / With my land's language." Accordingly, this book is designed to amplify Byron's voice, animated by that lively, inventive, funny, disturbing, tortured, brilliant rhetorical force that readers hear in the poetry and letters alike. The stakes remain high. Byron railed against dishonest, hypocritical uses of language, which he called "cant" or "canting," and he aimed his own writing against "the *cant* which is the crying sin of this double-dealing and false-speaking time of selfish spoilers." In this light, the many contradictions and paradoxes of Byron's work can be seen as sallies in an unfinished war against dogma, cant, and false certainties. For Byron, this amounted to a struggle for liberty on both personal and global scales. He wrote in 1822, "it is necessary, in the present clash of philosophy and tyranny, to throw away the scabbard. I know it is against fearful odds; but the battle must be fought." As Jerome McGann has said, Byron's poetry "comes not to balance and reconcile opposite and discordant things and qualities. It comes to magnify their profusion" and thus break through to new possibilities. Byron's uncertainty, inconsistency, irony, and perversity remain useful postures of rebellion against the false, often oppressive, surfaces of the doctrinaire.

Despite his many privileges as a member of England's hereditary aristocracy, Byron was both insider and outsider. He was born physically disabled (with a deformed foot), suffered childhood sexual abuse, was raised by a volatile single mother in straitened financial circumstances, struggled with bipolar moods and disordered eating throughout his life, and was sexually interested in both men and women in a time when sodomy was still a capital crime in his native country. Accordingly, he produced work that traverses extremes of feeling with irony, energy, and a strong emphasis on individual liberty and resistance. Matt Sandler has demonstrated Byron's importance to generations of Black writers and his extensive influence on African American literature. Richard Cardwell and others have surveyed his pan-European influence, especially visible in adaptations of Byron's rhetoric of liberty and individuality as relevant to revolutions and national identity movements across the globe. His writing still speaks across class and racial lines to anyone who feels like a social exile or an alien to the status quo and embraces the power of that estrangement.

Some of Byron's championing of rebellion coalesces into the flawed masculine figures of his work through 1818. It would not be long before his name mutated into an adjective, Byronic, that signified a darkly charismatic and dangerous mode. As he describes the protagonist of *Lara*:

> There was in him a vital scorn of all:
> As if the worst had fall'n which could befall
> He stood a stranger in this breathing world,
> An erring spirit from another hurled;
> A thing of dark imaginings

Versions of this Byronic hero gave rise to a now-mythic cultural figure: the brooding, forbidding, charismatic rebel, "mad, bad, and dangerous to know" (as Caroline Lamb wrote of Byron), yet with the capacity for intense love, a gothic villain tempered by romantic sentiment somehow allied to tragic violence. Amplified by the *Frankenstein* summer of 1816 that also gave rise to *The Vampyre*, this character inspired the creation of many others like him, and their names are legion: Heathcliff, Mr. Rochester, Lestat, Edward Cullen, Angel, Dream, and more. Byron's life and candid letters give us an unusually clear view of the figure's origins and darkly seductive appeal.

Byron's other side is comedy, equally strong and particularly visible in his letters and his later poetry, such as *Beppo*, *The Vision of Judgment*, and *Don Juan*. In those works, as in Byron's letters, we hear the music of human experience in happier, funnier tones, even as darker ironies and more savage emotions await on other pages, or even lurk in the interstices of his brilliant, playful lines. Byron's friends and lovers often stressed how different he was in person from the tragic rebels of his early poetry – how convivial and high-spirited, witty and flippant, chatty and almost silly. That version of Byron oscillated with the depressive one, giving rise to Lady Blessington's observation about his chameleon-like nature. In the ten letters you are about to read, you will see examples of the many sides of Byron's temperament and be struck by a prose that is at once its vehicle and its mirror. In his ability to laugh at himself, wittily skewer the foibles of others, stress the comedy in unfortunate events, and, perhaps above all, to have fun with language itself, Byron models the vital pleasures of the comic worldview crucial for our sanity.

In its enumerative structure, this book resonates with a number of recent biographies of other poets, including Lucasta Miller's *Keats: A Brief Life in Nine Poems and One Epitaph*, Martha Ackman's *These Fevered Days: Ten Pivotal Moments in the Making of Emily Dickinson*, and Greil Marcus's *Folk Music: A Bob Dylan Biography in Seven Songs*. This arrangement prompts what we might call a stadial narrative of a life – a sequence of leaps between stepping stones across the breadth of that flowing river. At the same time, I've attempted to survey the overall territory, without any ambitions of replacing the previous full-length biographies of Byron, of which there have been many. Leslie Marchand's *Byron: A Biography* (1957) stands at the headwaters of all modern comprehensive biographical treatments, succeeded most recently and authoritatively by Fiona MacCarthy's *Byron: Life and Legend* (2002). Particularly valuable partial treatments of his life from a previous era include *Byron: The Years of Fame* and *Byron in Italy* (Peter Quennell), *The Last Attachment* (Iris Origo), and *Byron: The Last Journey* (Harold Nicolson). I have leaned heavily on the work of these biographers in my attempt to convey the complexities of Byron's character and the variety of his experiences.

In addition, since MacCarthy's biography, important new material has been presented in James Bieri's *Percy Bysshe Shelley: A Biography* (2004); the Cochran and Rees edition of Teresa Guiccioli's *Lord Byron's Life in Italy* (2005); Andrew Nicholson's *Letters of John Murray to Lord Byron* (2007); Edna O'Brien's *Byron in Love* (2010); David Ellis's *Byron in Geneva* (2011); Roderick Beaton's *Byron's War* (2013); Julia Markus's *Lady Byron and Her Daughters* (2015); Miranda Seymour's *In Byron's Wake* (2018); and Emily Brand's *The Fall of the House of Byron* (2020). Each of these first-rate books has informed this one in countless ways. Beaton's distinguished *Byron's War* was particularly crucial for my understanding of Byron's role in the Greek Revolution, and Stephen Minta's *On a Voiceless Shore: Byron in Greece* (1998) was an ongoing source of inspiration. My transcriptions of the letters themselves are taken (with some modifications based on my own examination of the originals) from Leslie Marchand's definitive edition of *Byron's Letters and Journals*, the single most important resource for this book. For those interested in reading more of Byron's letters, I recommend Richard Lansdown's judicious selected edition. I have also relied on the invaluable *Shelley and his Circle* volumes edited by Donald Reiman, Kenneth Neill Cameron, and Doucet Devin Fischer, on Peter Cochran's far-ranging editorial work on Byron, on Norman Page's *Byron Chronology* (my constant companion), and on the texts and information in Jerome McGann's authoritative *Complete Poetical Works*.

As even a partial list such as this suggests, a vast paper trail has followed Byron almost from the beginning. Two centuries on, his poetry and legend persist on the strength of that documentary record. As Auden writes of the posthumous Yeats, "he is scattered among hundred cities" across the world; like Yeats, Byron has become his admirers.

From the upper story of the Byron Research Center and Museum in Messolonghi, you can look out across the lagoon toward the mountains shrouded in mist and see something like Byron's last view of the world. Built as an homage to the Kapsalis house in which Byron lived and died, the Center stands as evidence of his ongoing influence both in Greece and around the world. Students, scholars, readers, and fans come here to make contact with Byron: it is a place, like Newstead Abbey in Nottinghamshire, that vibrates with the energy of his presence. And as an avatar of the Kapsa-lis house, it evokes a dark inflection point in the city's history. In 1826, two years after Byron's death, the long Turkish siege of Messolonghi had reached a crisis: starving and desperate, the surviving citizens determined to rush forth from the city gates. Most were cut down by the Ottoman soldiers or captured and sold as slaves. But there was a final, terrible moment of resistance. Sources say that the Kapsalis house was packed with barrels of gunpowder, and as the Turks entered the city, the depleted remnant of its residents (the sick and wounded, the women and children) fired the barrels and destroyed the house and themselves. The Center vibrates with that energy also.

But if Messolonghi is a city where things ended, it is also a place of beginnings. Byron's untimely death there imparted a sudden high seriousness to his efforts at nation-building. The "satanic" poet who had often been dismissed as a libertine, rake, dilettante, or dandy was in part redeemed. Byron wouldn't have thought himself lucky on that April night in 1824 in Messolonghi, as – feverish, bewildered, and exhausted by his doctors' regimen of purgatives and bloodletting – he felt death approaching. Yet he must have known that, despite the odds, he had managed for himself something like a hero's end. Byron would have been sarcastic about the whole situation, of course: he had already made jokes about dying "marsh-ally" from malarial fever rather than "martially," and he harbored few remaining illusions about himself or the Greeks by 1824. But he knew he had done *something*. And he may have dimly foreseen both the attention that his death would bring to the Greek cause and, relatively soon thereafter, the shift in British policy in the region. Two years after Byron's death, the combined forces of Britain, France, and Russia defeated the Ottoman navy at the Battle of Navarino, and modern independent Greece was born.

Up to the present day, the name of Byron still resonates across Greece, where he is grouped alongside the founders of the nation. The troubled little boy from Aberdeen, the overweight and bashful Southwell teen, the louche and scandalous libertine of Cambridge and London, the impassioned wanderer in the Mediterranean world, the Italianate lover in Venice and Ravenna, and above all, the Romantic poet – to this list of Byronic personae was added, finally, the Greek freedom-fighter. Poetical and martial glory, then: Byron would have treated that double legacy with heavy irony, but, ultimately, I think it would not have displeased him.

Messolonghi, Western Greece
May 2023

1

—— ◇ ——

A Spice of Every Thing

Trinity College, Cambridge
October 26th. 1807

My dear Elizabeth, —

Fatigued with sitting up till four in the morning for these last two days at Hazard [gambling], I take up my pen to enquire how your Highness, & the rest of my female acquaintance at the seat of Archiepiscopal Grandeur Southwell, go on. – I know I deserve a scolding for my negligence in not writing more frequently, but racing up & down the Country for these last three months, how was it possible to fulfil the Duties of a Correspondent? – Fixed at last for 6 weeks, I write, as <u>thin</u> as ever (not having gained an ounce since my Reduction) & rather in better humour, for after all, Southwell was a detestable residence; thank St Dominic I have done with it, I have been twice within 8 miles of it, but could not pre-vail on myself to <u>suffocate</u> in its heavy atmosphere. – This place is wretched enough, a villainous Chaos of Dice and Drunkenness, nothing but Hazard and Burgundy, Hunting, Mathematics and Newmarket, Riot and Racing, yet it is a

Paradise compared with the eternal dullness of Southwell, oh! the misery of doing nothing, but make Love, enemies, and Verses. –

Next January (but this is <u>entre nous</u> only, and pray let it be so, or my maternal persecutor will be throwing her Tomahawk at any of my curious projects) I am going to <u>Sea</u> for four or five months, with my Cousin Capt. Bettesworth. who commands the Tartar, the finest frigate in the navy. I have seen most scenes, and wish to look at a naval life. – We are going probably to the Mediterranean, or to the West Indies, or to the Devil, and if there is a possibility of taking me to the Latter, Bettesworth will do it, for he has received four and twenty wounds in different places, and at this moment possesses a Letter from the late Ld. Nelson, stating Bettesworth as the only officer of the navy who had more wounds than himself. – – –

I have got a new friend, the finest in the world, a tame Bear, when I brought him here, they asked me what I meant to do with him, and my reply was "he should <u>sit</u> for <u>a Fellowship</u>." – Sherard will explain the meaning of the sentence if it is ambiguous. – This answer delighted them not, – we have eternal parties here, and this evening a large assortment of <u>Jockies</u>, Gamblers, <u>Boxers</u>, <u>Authors</u>, <u>parsons</u>, and <u>poets</u>, sup with me. A precious Mixture, but they go on well together, and for me, I am a <u>spice</u> of every thing except a Jockey, by the bye, I was dismounted again the other day. – – –

Thank your Brother in my name, for his Treatise. I have written 214 pages of a novel, one poem of 380 Lines, to be published (without my name) in a few weeks, with notes, 560 lines of Bosworth Field, and 250 Lines of another poem in rhyme, besides half a dozen smaller pieces, the poem to be published is a Satire, apropos, I have been praised to the

Skies in the Critical Review, and abused equally in another publication, so much the Better, they tell me, for the sale of the Book, it keeps up controversy, and prevents it being forgotten, besides the first men of all ages have had their share, nor do the humblest escape, so I bear it like a philosopher, it is odd enough the two opposite Critiques came out on the same day, and out of five pages of abuse, my Censor only quotes two lines, from different poems, in support of his opinion, now the proper way to cut up, is to quote long passages, and make them appear absurd, because simple allegation is no proof. – on the other hand, there are seven pages of praise, and more than my modesty will allow, said on the subject. –

Adieu yours truly

Byron

PS. Write, Write, Write!!!

———○———

Once you pass through the massive sixteenth-century gate and emerge again into the light, the Great Court of Trinity College Cambridge unfolds in crisply manicured green squares, surrounded by the imposing stone walls of the chapel, the Master's lodge, the Great Hall, and the student residences. In late October, the air is chilly, the afternoon shadows fall long and steep, and the college hums with the bustle of students assembling for Michaelmas term. If you had been there in 1807, you might have seen the young George Gordon, Lord Byron walking stiff-legged across the paths, heading toward his "*Super*excellent rooms," most likely in Nevile's Court, the elegant inner sanctum of the College. There, he would be close to the airy colonnades of the Wren Library and, behind that, the tree-lined avenues and lawns of the Trinity Backs, the gardens leading down to what he called the "sedgy banks" of the river Cam. Byron had just returned after a year away from Trinity, and he was hurling himself back into the scenes of excessive sociability that occupied him there, writing to his Southwell friend Elizabeth Pigot (Figure 1.2) that he has been "sitting up till four in the morning" gambling with his friends, and hosting and attending "eternal parties" with other students and "a large assortment of *Jockies*, Gamblers, *Boxers, Authors, parsons,* and *poets.*" As Byron tells his correspondent laughingly, "I am a *spice* of every thing." He was still working out his complex identity as a disabled young man born an aristocrat in straitened financial circumstances, the title of Lord Byron less than ten years his own, newly thin since his "Reduction" through severe dieting, his first book just published, his youthful heart and body full of sexually fluid romance. The last of a series of high-spirited letters Byron wrote to Elizabeth, this one finds him in transition, on his way to becoming one of the greatest and most celebrated English poets of his age, a man who would transform his inherited family name into a universal adjective based on his passions, attitudes, and art.

In attending Trinity, Byron was in some ways following a predictable path for a young English nobleman of his era. Yet there had been twists. He was born on January 22, 1788 in rented lodgings in London's West End to Catherine Gordon Byron (Figure 1.3), a young Scottish lady who was by then probably questioning her choices. Like Jane Austen's heroine

Catherine Morland, Catherine Gordon, aged 20, had fallen in love in the Assembly Rooms of Bath, the fashionable resort town. John "Mad Jack" Byron had gone there seeking a second heiress to marry, after his first wife, Amelia Osborne, Marchioness of Carmarthen, died at age 29. Amidst public scandal, he had stolen the beautiful and intelligent Amelia from her marriage to the Marquis, a theft suggestive of the suave seductive powers that helped him make a rapid conquest of Catherine, who was well born and wealthy but unpolished, overweight, and relatively unprotected: both of her parents had died in recent years. "Mad Jack" swept in, and they married within a month. But, by the time of Catherine's pregnancy a few years later, John Byron had already run through her fortune of £30,000 and was hiding from his creditors in France. She returned alone to London to give birth and soon re-settled in her hometown of Aberdeen, where her husband joined them for a time. Within two years, he was in France again, and after a short period of penury and dissipation that included sexual affairs with actresses and (we now know) his own sister, John Byron died in Valenciennes, probably by suicide. As an adult, Byron the poet claimed to "remember him perfectly" and cherished an idea of him as a charming and glamorous figure, even while recalling scenes of him arguing bitterly with his mother. Byron later said to a friend that his father "seemed born for his own ruin, and that of the other sex." John Byron's death left Catherine to raise the boy alone, with little money. Yet, in spite of everything, she truly mourned the loss of her handsome former Captain of the Guards, writing to his sister, "notwithstanding all his foibles, for they deserve no worse name, I ever sincerely loved him. If I had only seen him before he died! Did he ever mention me? I am unable to say more."

Adding to Catherine's troubles, the infant Byron had been born with a deformed right foot: it was underdeveloped and turned inward, which made walking difficult all his life. His mother called in specialists who constructed various painful braces and boots for Byron, but none did much good. We catch a glimpse of him in early boyhood in Scotland: a nurse remarked on his leg, and his eyes flashed with anger as he struck out with a little whip, saying, "Dinna speak of it!" Much later, Byron's friend Edward Trelawny wrote that the deformity "was a curse, chaining a proud and soaring spirit like his to the dull earth," and that it "was always uppermost in his thoughts, and influenced every act of his life." Trelawny's view is extreme, but brings into focus Byron's conflicted relationship to his own body, and the complex corporeal self-image that would drive him to alternating fits of physical exercise and lassitude, of displays of athleticism and shy bookishness, of starvation diets and extreme indulgence, of manic sexual promiscuity and hermit-like withdrawal. At times, he thought of his disability as a punishment, a mark of Cain. But he was also stoic, very rarely mentioning his foot and doing so mostly facetiously. As an adult, he wrote teasingly to his friend Francis Hodgson about the Christian resurrection, "I hope … I shall have a better *pair of legs* than I have moved on these two-and-twenty years, or I shall be sadly behind in the squeeze into Paradise."

Before Cambridge, Byron had been first at Aberdeen Grammar School, next at Dr. Glennie's Academy in East Dulwich for a year, and then, moving upward in status, at the prestigious Harrow School just outside London. His ascent had depended on two losses: first, his father's untimely death in France; and second, the death of his second cousin William in the battle of Calvi in Corsica in 1794. Suddenly, little

George Gordon Byron was the heir apparent. And when the poet's grand-uncle, known as the "Wicked Lord," died in May 1798, the peerage fell to the 10-year-old boy: the title and estates of Lord Byron were now his. Right away, he noticed the new deference paid to him by the headmaster, and when George Gordon first heard the Latin words "Dominus de Byron" added to his name at morning roll call, he burst into tears. But that school year was drawing to a close, and so was Byron's time in Scotland, a place he would always remember with fondness. In *Don Juan*, he would write, "I am half a Scot by birth, and bred / A whole one." He had absorbed his mother's pride in her ancient Gordon ancestors, the violent, lawless, and suicidal Lairds of Gight. He had thrilled at the natural grandeur of the highlands, which he would celebrate in an early poem: "Oh for the crags that are wild and majestic, / The steep, frowning glories of the dark Loch na Garr." He had fallen in love for the first time (at age 7) with a distant cousin, Mary Duff, whom he idolized mostly from afar. And he had been shaped by the strict Scottish Calvinism of his schoolmasters and his nurses. From them, he imbibed a fatalistic sense of innate sinfulness that colored his imagination thereafter, and that was monstrously amplified when May Gray, one of those nurses, began seducing him when he was only 9: she "used to come to bed to him and play tricks with his person" until she was discovered and dismissed. But by then, these episodes had been occurring for two years, in alternation with Gray's teaching him pious lessons from the Bible and beating him when he rebelled. Small wonder that Byron learned to despise hypocrisy, to cherish memories of childhood innocence which was taken from him too soon, and to develop complex, divided attitudes toward female sexuality. By the time the coach containing him, his mother, and

May Gray completed its journey down from Aberdeen and crossed onto the grounds of Newstead Abbey in Nottinghamshire (Figure 1.4) in August 1798, the new Lord Byron must have felt much older than his mere decade of years.

Newstead Abbey itself was well adapted to Byron's imagination. A twelfth-century gothic priory converted to an ancestral estate by Henry VIII, the imposing house was in glamorous disrepair, parts of it derelict, its gardens overgrown, its atmosphere ghostly. As one historian puts it, "The great oaks surrounding the Abbey had been felled, the famous herds of deer were gone, and the Abbey had been stripped ... of all the furniture and property.... The East Wing was unroofed; the old monks' reception room and the grand refectory were full of hay; the entrance hall and monks' parlor were stables for cattle." Surveying the scene, Byron wrote in an early lyric on Newstead,

> Through the cracks in these battlements loud the
>   winds whistle,
>   For the hall of my fathers is gone to decay;
> And in yon once gay garden the hemlock and thistle
>   Have choak'd up the rose, which late bloom'd in the
>   way.

He would eventually use this imposing romantic ruin as a kind of lad's clubhouse, with pistol-shooting and fencing in the hay-strewn main hall, bouts of wine-drinking and spirited conversation, and sex parties with attractive young maids chosen for the purpose. As he wrote to Thomas Moore in 1813, it was "a thorough bachelor's mansion – plenty of wine and such sordid sensualities – with books enough, room enough, and an air of antiquity about all (except the lasses)." But Newstead Abbey also had significant symbolic power as the exterior manifestation of the title he had suddenly inherited. Ancient and noble, battered and dilapidated, Newstead would become for Byron at once an image of crumbling aristocracy in the wake of the French Revolution, an incarnation of the Byron family's decline from the heroic past he imagined for his ancestors, and an emblem of his own half-ruined self.

The years between Byron's arrival in Nottingham and this 1807 letter to Elizabeth Pigot were those of his adolescence and young manhood, from the age of 10 to that of 19. In that time, he had traversed a complex landscape of romantic and sexual experiences. Byron and his mother at first lived between Nottingham and London, visiting Newstead occasionally to see to what repairs could be managed. After May Gray's dismissal and a year of schooling in Dulwich, Byron entered Harrow, where he was surrounded by young male aristocrats and future prime ministers. Byron's early relationships at Harrow were central to his development. He had arrived wild and energetic, not particularly studious and struggling for acceptance from the older boys who mocked his lameness, his provincial manner, and his Scottish burr. But with the help of the patient and supportive headmaster Revd. Joseph Drury, Byron flourished as the years progressed. He had always been a great reader, and this continued at Harrow, despite his apparent insouciance: as he recalled later, "I was never *seen* reading but always idle and in mischief – or at play. – The truth is that I read eating – read in bed – read when no one else read."

Especially after his first year at Harrow, Byron grew to love a place he originally hated, and developed romantic and intimate connections with his favorites, including the Earl of Clare (perhaps his closest male friend), the Earl of Delawarr,

John Claridge, and the Hon. John Wingfield – all part of his cadre of junior admirers he called his "Theban band." That name alludes to the legendary Greek army of pairs of male lovers, over whom Philip of Macedonia shed tears when he finally defeated them at Chaeronea (338 BCE), saying "Perish the ones who suspect these men of anything base." To what extent Byron's relations with his "Theban band" were sexual, we can't know. Homosexual sodomy could be punishable by death in England at the time, so silence and circumspection were the order of the day. At the same time, passionately declared friendships between men (especially within the all-male worlds of the English public schools) were quite common: in an 1806 poem published in his early volumes, Byron wrote of Harrow as a place where "friendships were form'd, too romantic to last." And Byron's poems of this period to Clare, Delawarr, and others are warm and physical (heads are frequently laid on breasts), colored by idealizing emotions. Byron's Cambridge friend John Cam Hobhouse wrote in his diary that, in terms of Byron's "singularities," he "had nothing to learn when he came from Harrow," and it certainly seems reasonable to assume that Harrow's dawning glow for Byron was involved with an awakening sexual and emotional interest in boys. Accordingly, Harrow became a sacred spot for him, a place of safety and intimacy that, by the time he realized it, he would soon have to leave behind.

In 1803, on summer vacation, Byron had fallen distractedly in love with Mary Chaworth, the 18-year-old descendant of William Chaworth, whom the Fifth "Wicked" Lord Byron (the poet's predecessor) had killed with a short sword in a drunken duel. She lived at Annesley Hall, the estate adjoining Newstead, and Byron visited frequently, not insensible to the Romeo–Juliet overtones of a liaison between scions of the feuding families. "Those were the days of romance!" he remembered later; "She was the *beau ideal* of all that my youthful fancy could paint of beautiful." Although Mary was three years his senior and already engaged to another man, Byron was deeply and permanently affected by his feelings for her. Over a decade later, he was still dreaming of her and writing poems about that summer of 1803:

> The maid was on the eve of womanhood;
> The boy had fewer summers, but his heart
> Had far outgrown his years, and to his eye
> There was but one beloved face on earth,
> And that was shining on him: he had look'd
> Upon it till it could not pass away;
>
> ...
>
> But she in these fond feelings had no share:
> Her sighs were not for him; to her he was
> Even as a brother—but no more.

As is often the case with first love, Byron's for Mary Chaworth was amplified by being unrequited and doomed: "Her sighs were not for him." In an anecdote from Moore's biography of Byron (one that may have inspired the famous scene of Heathcliff's overheard rejection by Cathy in Emily Brontë's *Wuthering Heights*), Byron dashed angrily from Annesley Hall after hearing Mary saying with disdain to her maid, "Do you think I could care anything for that lame boy?" But Byron had invested heavily in his feelings, perhaps because he saw in Mary a pathway to, or emblem for, the mainstream English life that was expected of him. As Fiona MacCarthy writes, she was "the focus of his hopes for family and dynasty and sexual fulfillment within marriage: a future which Byron had half-begun to realise … was likely to prove impossible to him." Summer ended, and Byron was soon back among his "Theban band" at Harrow-on-the-Hill.

From this period through Byron's years at Cambridge, Mrs. Byron rented a small, elegant home, Burgage Manor, in the town of Southwell, about 12 miles from Newstead Abbey. Byron spent enough time there to develop strong opinions. He writes in this letter to their neighbor, Elizabeth, "Southwell was a detestable residence; thank St Dominic I have done with it, I have been twice within 8 miles of it, but could not prevail on myself to *suffocate* in its heavy atmosphere." Cambridge, according to Byron, "is a Paradise compared with the eternal dullness of Southwell, oh! the misery of doing nothing, but make Love, enemies, and Verses." His tone is telling: underneath this arch performance of detestation is a current of affection, not only for the place (where he wooed the local daughters and took part in amateur theatricals), but for Elizabeth herself, her "Highness," who was his favorite resident. Five years older than Byron, Elizabeth had become his friend and confidant, guiding him through his various love affairs with "the principal Southwell belles" and helping him get his first poems into print. As he wrote to her, "you gave yourself more trouble with me & my *manuscripts* than a thousand *dolls* would have done." Escaping from his mother's house, Byron spent lots of time with the Pigots, and he grew to depend on Elizabeth's frank and funny manner with him, calling her "my only *rational* companion." She remembered first meeting him at a party in 1804, when Byron was still "a fat, bashful boy, with his hair combed straight over his forehead," so shy that he barely spoke until she broke the ice by referring to him as Gabriel Lackbrain, a character from a popular comedy. So began the friendship that would make

Southwell a tolerable place for Byron to grow, making love, enemies, and verses – a preview of what would turn out to be the primary occupations of his lifetime.

Elizabeth and her brother John had been instrumental in the printing of Byron's early poems by Samuel and John Ridge of nearby Newark. She served as his amanuensis, making copies from Byron's rough manuscripts in the summer of 1806, correcting the pages, drawing the Byron family crest on copies of his first privately printed volume (*Fugitive Pieces*), and helping him scrap and rework it when some of the warmer erotic poems caused a flutter in Southwell. The poem "To Mary" (written not for Mary Chaworth but for a sexual partner about whom little is certain) was the worst offender, with its rakish, uncensored praise of the visual pleasures of sex: "'tis most delight / To view each other panting, dying, / In love's *extatic posture* lying." Byron turned to Elizabeth for help with a more formal volume, and ultimately, her copies were the foundation for *Hours of Idleness*, the book that brought Byron before the public eye in June, 1807. She thus became the first in a series of intelligent women who would manage Byron's poetic output, a group that includes Mary Shelley, Claire Clairmont, Lady Byron, and Teresa Guiccioli. In this October letter from Cambridge, Byron crows a bit over the critical reception of *Hours of Idleness*, telling Elizabeth, "I have been praised to the Skies in the Critical Review, and abused equally in another publication, so much the Better, they tell me, for the sale of the Book, it keeps up controversy, and prevents it being forgotten." What he didn't know was that Henry Brougham was sharpening his quill, about to deliver a crushing rebuke in the *Edinburgh Review*, the most influential literary periodical of the day. Byron here also gives Elizabeth a boastful accounting of his recent literary productivity: "I have written 214 pages of a novel, one poem of 380 Lines, … 560 Lines of Bosworth Field, and 250 Lines of another poem in rhyme, besides half a dozen smaller pieces." Most of this work is now lost (no novel, no Bosworth Field poem) and Byron may be exaggerating to impress his slightly older friend and collaborator. But the specificity of his enumerations suggests otherwise.

Byron would publish that poem of 380 lines in expanded form as *English Bards and Scotch Reviewers* in 1809, and in so doing emerge as a brash satiric talent. From his rooms at Cambridge, this precocious undergraduate was channeling Horace, Juvenal, and Pope, and penning rhyming couplets to convey his dim view of the current literary establishment, in a mood of what he later called "blind anger and boyish vivacity." His satire champions neoclassical aesthetics over what Byron saw as the childish decadence of poets such as Wordsworth (who writes "Christmas stories tortured into rhyme") and Coleridge (of "turgid ode and tumid stanza" who "takes a Pixy for a Muse"). And as Byron developed his poem, he would strike back at the Edinburgh critical circles that had poured scorn on his own lyrics. Although Byron affects carelessness in this letter to Elizabeth, he notes with satisfaction that *Hours of Idleness* had been praised in the *Critical Review* (which had opined that Byron's poems gave "ample evidence of a correct taste, a warm imagination, and a feeling heart"), without letting on that this praise was written by a fellow of Trinity College and likely a friend of Byron's. In this letter, we can see signs of his early, quite natural sensitivity to the reviewers. Against the "seven pages of praise" in the *Critical Review*, he counts "five pages of abuse," which were published in *The Satirist* and written by another Cambridge man, Hewson Clarke, who despised Byron. Of *Hours of*

Idleness, Clarke writes, "His preface, like his book, is stupid, but it is a dull stupidity"; the review gets worse from there. And this was before the Scottish critics had weighed in with their disapproval. Byron claims in this chapter's letter, "the first men of all ages have had their share, nor do the humblest escape, so I bear it like a philosopher." But that forbearance gave way when the *Edinburgh Review* (in a January 1808 review) called his poetry "stupid and tiresome," comparing it to "stagnant water." After getting very drunk and contemplating suicide, Byron poured his anger into his satire, calling out the Edinburgh reviewers as "young tyrants" who were "usurpers on the throne of taste." *English Bards and Scotch Reviewers* showed that, from the beginning, Byron cultivated an outsider position in relation to the Romantic-era mainstream. As he would later proclaim (in *Don Juan*), "I was born for opposition."

Byron's time at Cambridge was fragmentary and brief: he only spent three terms there between 1805 and 1808, broken up by sojourns in Southwell and London, not to mention holidays in Brighton, Littlehampton, and elsewhere. Yet Cambridge marked him indelibly as the scene of his first adult friendships, the place where childhood ended, for better and worse. He recalled years later, "When I went up to Trinity, in 1805, at the age of seventeen and a half, I was miserable and untoward to a degree. I was wretched at leaving Harrow … and consequently about as unsocial as a wolf taken from his troop." And he wrote years later, in his journal: "I was so completely alone in this new world that it half broke my Spirits … it was one of the deadliest and heaviest feelings of my life to feel that I was no longer a boy." His deeply nostalgic poem from 1806, "Childish Recollections," provides an index of this orphaned state of mind, the feelings of a troop-less wolf or shrine-less pilgrim that prefigure the Byronic persona he would soon begin to elaborate in his work:

> A Hermit, midst of crowds, I fain must stray
> Alone, though thousand pilgrims fill the way;
> While these a thousand kindred wreaths entwine,
> I cannot call a single blossom mine:
> What then remains? in solitude to groan,
> To mix in friendship, or to sigh alone?
> Thus, must I cling to some endearing hand,
> And none more dear, than Ida's [Harrow's] social band.

The Theban band had broken up, and, with it, Byron's sense of identity which had been forged within that well-loved community. In partial consolation, his Harrow friend Edward Long had come to Cambridge also, and the pair clung to one another in friendship, swimming in the Cam, reading poetry, and traveling down to the coast together. Their shared memories of Harrow helped Byron hold on to the last twilight rays of boyhood. He wrote in a poem addressed to Long, "you knew me in the days / O'er which Remembrance yet delays, / Still may I rove untutor'd, wild, / And ev'n in age, at heart a child."

But these descriptions paint in a single shade of blue what soon became a more particolored set of experiences. When he first arrived at Cambridge, Byron wrote to his business manager Hanson, "I will be obliged to you to order me down 4 Dozen of Wine, Port – Sherry – Claret, & Madeira, one Dozen of Each," saying "I … begin to *admire* a College Life." That admiration increased as his circle of friends expanded and the young poet realized that his title, wealth, talent, and personal charisma would draw new companions to him. "My table is constantly covered with invitations," he wrote, amidst a whirl of dining out, drinking, and general dissipation. Aristocrats were exempt from lectures and exams, and Byron had no great respect for the intellectual life of the university: "Study is the last pursuit of the Society: the Master eats, drinks, and Sleeps, the Fellows *drink, dispute* and *pun,* the *employments* of the under Graduates you will probably conjecture without my description" – to name them, drinking, gambling, and whoring, what Byron calls in this letter (written after staying out "till four in the morning" two nights in a row) the "villainous Chaos of Dice and Drunkenness," and in another of the same period, "the *monotony* of *endless variety.*" Even a "tame Bear" might "sit for a Fellowship" in such a place, where animal enjoyments seemed paramount and a scholarly position apparently bore no intellectual demands. Hedonism was the order of the day, only partially dispelling Byron's regret for lost youth. Another poem of his Cambridge years begins "I would I were a careless child" and continues:

> I lov'd—but those I lov'd are gone,
>> Had friends—my early friends are fled,
> How cheerless feels the heart alone,
>> When all its former hopes are dead!
> Though gay companions, o'er the bowl
>> Dispel awhile the sense of ill,
> Though Pleasure stirs the maddening soul,
>> The heart—the heart—is lonely still.

Spurred toward forgetfulness and escape, Byron later recalled that he "took the gradations in the vices – with great promptitude," shunning serious study and plunging into Pleasure while away from the small-town gossip of Southwell and the watchful eyes of his mother.

Writing to Elizabeth, Byron refers to his "maternal per-secutor," that phrase a glance at the combative relationship between a tempestuous mother and her mercurial teenaged son. Frequent arguments would turn to shouting matches, studded with recriminations and insults that included Cath-erine's mockery of Byron's disability, which he would later dramatize in an unfinished play:

> Bertha: Out, hunchback!
> Arnold: I was born so mother!
> Bertha: Out!
>   Thou Incubus! Thou Nightmare! Of seven sons
>   The sole abortion!

As Byron recalled later in life, "My poor mother was generally in a rage every day, and used to render me sometimes almost frantic; particularly when, in her passion, she reproached me with my personal deformity.... Those were bitter moments" that "destroyed a temper always disposed to be violent." His letters of these early years frequently refer to the oppres-sive atmosphere of Burgage Manor and his desire to escape from his overbearing "tormentor whose *diabolical* disposi-tion ... seems to increase with age." He wrote in late 1808 to his half-sister Augusta, "I never can forgive that woman, or breathe in comfort under the same roof. – I am a very unlucky fellow, for I think I had naturally not a bad heart, but it has been so bent, twisted, and trampled on, that it is now become as hard as a Highlander's heel-piece." Single mother to an only child, eager to see her son ascend even as he treated her haughtily, touched by the violent passions of the Gordons, Catherine Byron cared deeply and oscillated unpredictably between advocacy and attack: in rages mixed with love and regret, she would see the father in the son, calling him "a true

Byronne." We mostly have to imagine the moody, cutting rejoinders of a young man whose poetry would soon become a byword for dark passions and ferociously satiric wit. As he entered young adulthood, Byron took every opportunity to increase his distance from his mother: "her temper precludes every idea of happiness, and therefore in the future I shall avoid her *hospitable* mansion." A runaway's impulse for freedom was already driving him, setting in place the dynamics of self-exile that shaped so much of his life.

In his first year at Cambridge, Byron had come into the orbit of the well-born, wealthy, and brilliant William Bankes, "the father of all mischiefs" – a fellow student whom Byron called his "collegiate pastor, and master, and patron." Bankes would go on to become a celebrated traveler in the Near East, a collector of antiquities, a Member of Parliament, and, later in life, an exile escaping charges of homosexuality: he died in Venice in 1855, his life offering a close alternate history of Byron's own. While at Trinity, Bankes converted part of his rooms into a mock-chapel in which choristers performed, prompting at least one observer to inquire "what the devil does Mr Bankes do with those singing-boys?" It was likely at one of these performances that Byron first heard John Edleston's voice, "a voice whose tones inspire / Such soften'd feelings in my breast," as he wrote in a love poem of this period. A gentle, younger orphan from a modest background, Edleston sang in the Trinity choir but was not enrolled as a student. His voice, manner, and unprotected position called forth Byron's attraction and sympathy, and the two entered into a passionate romance. They exchanged rings: Byron received one with a small pink carnelian stone in the shape of a heart, and wrote in a poem that the stone "blushes as modest as its giver." Edleston presented the ring "with a downcast look / As *fearful* that I might refuse it," but Byron was deeply moved. Thereafter in his letters, he would refer to his shy protégé as "my cornelian." In another 1806 lyric, he wrote of the ring as a "toy of blushing hue" that "tells me of a Friend… / Who loved me for myself alone," at a time when "Both were open, Both were young." How far this relationship went physically we don't really know. Byron recalled their time at Cambridge in a later poem, disguised under the title "To Thyrza":

> Ours too the glance none saw beside;
>   The smile none else might understand;
> The whisper'd thought of hearts allied,
>   The pressure of the thrilling hand;
> The kiss so guiltless and refin'd,
>   That Love each warmer wish forbore—
> Those eyes proclaim'd so pure a mind,
>   Ev'n passion blush'd to plead for more—

Byron writes of shared glances and smiles, thrilling hands and "guiltless" kisses, and even passion herself blushing (like Edleston) to ask for anything more sexual. Whatever the case, Byron cherished the memory of these heady days of this intimate, erotic friendship, more intense than any he had experienced. Looking back almost fifteen years later, he recalled the "violent, though *pure*, love and passion" he had for Edleston as the "romance of the most romantic period of my life."

Not without a tearful parting, Edleston left for London in the summer of 1807: Byron told Elizabeth, "I write with a bottle of claret in my *head* and *tears* in my *eyes*; for I have just parted with my '*Cornelian*'" and "my mind is a chaos of hope and sorrow." A few months later, he began what would be his final term at Trinity. He had had a busy summer, not only publishing *Hours of Idleness* but, as he says in this chapter's letter, "racing up & down the Country for these last three months," including time in London where he "swam in the Thames through the 2 Bridges Westminster & Blackfriars," a distance he estimated at nearly 3 miles. Now he was to be "Fixed at last for six weeks" at Trinity, before leaving for good at Christmas. By this time, Edward Long and Bankes had also departed, and Byron was part of a new circle of friends, including the solid and cynical John Cam Hobhouse, the archly hilarious and eccentric Charles Skinner Matthews, and the witty gambler Scrope Davies, who both entertained and worried Byron with his heavy drinking and who, according to Richard Holmes, was "one of Byron's most important confidants." All three had literary leanings, and all evoked Byron's laughter by means of everything from pantaloon slapstick to razor-sharp bons mots. Matthews, whom he had met through Bankes and who had lived in Byron's Trinity rooms while he was away, was both freethinking and sexually interested in men. Byron remembered them talking at length on all subjects late into the night, alarming Hobhouse with the latitude of their remarks. The four of them were part of that "large assortment of *Jockies*, Gamblers, *Boxers*, *Authors*, *parsons*, and *poets*," the louche social circle that Byron cultivated and that moved freely among the Cambridge colleges, the high and low sets of London, and the racetrack at Newmarket. Interestingly, unlike at Harrow, no one in his close circle was a titled aristocrat. His "precious Mixture" included Henry Angelo, his fencing-master; John "Gentleman" Jackson, a former boxing champion; and the famous dandy Beau Brummel. The startlingly rich range of voices heard around those wine-soaked tables was to have a far-reaching influence on Byron's style.

And then there was the bear. A Cambridge prohibition on dogs forced Byron to leave his beloved Boatswain (a Newfoundland retriever) in Southwell. Supremely annoyed, he acquired a small tame bear, keeping him primarily in the college stables, feeding him on bread and milk, and telling all who asked that he should sit for a fellowship. The joke relies in part on Regency Oxbridge slang, in which students were referred to as "bears," and tutors, "bear-leaders." Edward Long joked that in bringing "a *bear* to Grantchester" (in Cambridgeshire), Byron was "carrying coals to Newcastle," equating students with their namesake while also punning on an older meaning of "bear" as an uncouth person. Hewson Clarke, who had mocked *Hours of Idleness* in print, also published a parodic poem, "Lord B–n to his Bear," which ends, "*What's felt by a* LORD *may be felt by a* BEAR!" To his poem, Clarke notes that Byron "has been seen to hug [this bear] with all the warmth of fraternal affection!" The scurrilous implication of bestiality, an obvious joke, conceals the deeper charge of homosexuality: the warm embraces between the Lord and his pet "bear," John Edleston. Byron wrote an icy letter to Clarke, "requiring an explanation" and demanding "an immediate & unequivocal disavowal" or else the satisfaction of a duel. But nothing came of it, so Byron took revenge with a pen rather than a pistol: in *English Bards and Scotch Reviewers*, he berates Clarke as "A would-be satirist, a hired Buffoon, / A monthly scribbler of some low Lampoon, / Condemned to drudge, the meanest of the mean, / And furbish falsehoods for a magazine." The weapons of satire were becoming sharper in the young poet's hands.

By January, 1808, the bear had been rusticated to Newstead Abbey, and Byron had moved to Dorant's Hotel in London, a residence he would maintain for much of the year.

Despite a few expeditions to Cambridge, he never returned as a student, though in July (thanks to his title) he collected a degree he had not earned. He had run through all of his ready money and amassed large debts to moneylenders, who were only too happy to advance funds to the nobility – at extortionate rates of interest. He confessed, "I am cursedly dipped; my debts, *every* thing inclusive, will be nine or ten thousand before I am twenty-one" – the equivalent of perhaps a million pounds in today's money. Yet he kept spending freely, giving generously to friends and also indulging his appetites for finery, for high living, and for the company of sexually available women. Much of this was sybaritic therapy that gave respite from depression but ultimately ended up deepening his despair. He wrote to Hobhouse in February, "I am buried in an abyss of Sensuality.… I am given to Harlots, and live in a state of Concubinage," boasting to another friend that "my blue eyed Caroline, who is only sixteen, has been lately so *charming*, that … we are commanded [by his doctor] to *repose*, being nearly worn out." As winter turned to spring, Byron wrote of having two or three women in his "own immediate custody," along with visits to "houses of Fornication," a pattern of "the most laudable systematic profligacy." For a time, Caroline Cameron remained a favorite. Byron kept her in a flat in Brompton near Hyde Park and traveled with her down to the sea at Brighton, where, accompanied by Hobhouse and Davies, he spent much of that hot summer, disguising Caroline as a boy and passing her off as his younger brother. This was done in part to avoid public censure and in part as gender-bending role play that spoke to Byron's sexual preferences. Later, an acquaintance reported that there was "a most ludicrous conclusion" to all of this, when "the young gentleman miscarried in a certain family hotel in Bond Street, to the inexpressible horror of the chambermaids."

Newstead Abbey beckoned again, as an escape from the feverish pleasures and expenses of London. Byron summoned workmen and began fitting up some of the rooms, though the state of his finances precluded any large-scale refurbishing of the decaying buildings. He was trying to sell his inherited properties in Lancashire to redeem some of his debts, but the legal knots around these arrangements seemed inextricable. That autumn, Hobhouse stayed at Newstead, and the two rode daily around the extensive park and grounds, swam in the lake, played with Byron's animals, attended local balls and masquerades in Nottingham, and even organized an amateur theatrical performance of Edward Young's *The Revenge* (which Byron had in part performed at Harrow). Meanwhile, Byron worked on *English Bards and Scotch Reviewers*, still smarting from the bad reviews of his lyrics and determined to get some of his own back. One night in early November, Byron summoned the courage to dine with Mary Chaworth (now Mrs. Musters) and her husband at Annesley Hall. Hobhouse came with him as support, but it still wasn't easy, and the sight of Mary's 2-year-old daughter sent Byron into a sharp melancholy. He wrote in a poem soon thereafter, "When late I saw thy favourite child, / I thought my jealous heart would break; / ... I deem'd that time, I deem'd that pride / Had quenched at length my boyish flame," but his feelings leapt up again, all the more strongly because they were hopeless – as they had in fact always been. Tellingly, five years later, when the Musters' marriage had failed and Mary was finally encouraging Byron (in increasingly urgent letters), he had no interest and avoided any reunion. Of course, by then, many things had changed.

In addition to his tame bear, Byron had three dogs with him at Newstead: Lyon (a bad-tempered half-wolf) and two Newfoundlands, Thunder and Boatswain. A tenant farmer recalled that Byron "would sometimes get into the boat with his two noble Newfoundland dogs, row into the middle of the lake" and then "tumble over into the middle of the water," whereupon "the faithful animals would immediately follow, seize him by the coat collar, one on each side, and bear him away to land." But in November, Boatswain, his favorite, was bitten by a rabid animal and died, as Byron "with his bare hand, wiped away the slaver from the dog's lips during the paroxysms." He wrote to Hodgson, "Boatswain is dead! he expired in a state of madness on the 10th after suffering much, yet retaining all the gentleness of his nature to the last." Byron buried the dog in the immediate back garden of the Abbey, in a vault large enough for his own tomb, intending to be buried next to him (Figure 1.5). Feeling for his friend's loss, Hobhouse composed an epitaph for "Boatswain, A Dog," "one who possessed Beauty without Vanity, Strength without Insolence, Courage without Ferocity, and all the Virtues of Man without his Vices." Byron went further, writing a bitterly misanthropic poem and having it cut in stone, along with the epitaph, on an imposing monument set above the tomb. The poem pays tribute to

the poor Dog, in life the firmest friend,
The first to welcome, foremost to defend,
Whose honest heart is still his Master's own,
Who labours, fights, lives, breathes for him alone,
Unhonour'd falls, unnotic'd all his worth,
Deny'd in heaven the Soul he held on earth;
While man, vain insect! hopes to be forgiven:

And claims himself a sole exclusive heaven,
Oh man! thou feeble tenant of an hour,
Debas'd by slavery, or corrupt by power,
Who knows thee well, must quit thee with disgust,
Degraded mass of animated dust!
Thy love is lust, thy friendship all a cheat,
Thy tongue hypocrisy, thy heart deceit,
By nature vile, ennobled but by name,
Each kindred brute might bid thee blush for shame.
Ye! who behold perchance this simple urn,
Pass on, it honours none you wish to mourn.
To mark a friend's remains these stones arise,
I never knew but one – and here he lies.

Ever the prankster, Matthews suggested that there was room on the other side of the monument "for another friend – and I propose the inscription be 'Here lies Hobhouse – a Pig &c.'" For his own part, Hobhouse suggested that Byron's final line be revised to read "here I lies" (meaning "here I tell a lie"), given the spirit of camaraderie shared among these young men. Hobhouse in particular would remain Byron's "firmest friend" and one of his most loyal defenders.

Matthews later recalled the hedonistic rhythms of these April bachelor days at Newstead, ones that impressed themselves firmly on Byron's imagination:

> Our average hour of rising was one…. It was frequently past two before the breakfast party broke up. Then, for the amusements of the morning, there was reading, fencing, single-stick, or shuttle-cock, in the great room; practicing with pistols in the hall; walking—riding—cricket—sailing on the lake, playing with the bear, or teasing the wolf. Between seven and eight we dined;

and our evening lasted from that time till one, two, or three in the morning. The evening diversions may be easily conceived.

Those "evening diversions" consisted primarily of drinking and cavorting with the female staff members, mostly local young women that Byron hired with all the *droit de seigneur* of his sex and class. In fact, around this time he impregnated one of his favorites, the maid Lucy, settling on her an annuity of £100 but otherwise taking no fatherly role. In a poem written soon afterward, he referred half-ironically to Newstead as a "Monastic dome! condemn'd to uses vile! / Where Superstition once had made her den / Now Paphian girls were known to sing and smile" – Paphos being the home of Aphrodite, goddess of erotic love.

Byron's own recollections of the 1809 house party at Newstead (with Hobhouse, Matthews, Davies, and James Wedderburn Webster all in temporary residence) tally with those of Matthews, including the details of monks' robes and a cup made from a skull – polished and set on a silver base – that Byron had found in the Abbey gardens (hearing of this macabre vessel, Wordsworth would refer to Byron as his "crack-brained skull-bearing Lordship"). Looking back later, Byron wrote,

We went down to Newstead together, where I had got a famous cellar, and Monks' dresses from a masquerade warehouse. We were a company of some seven or eight ... and used to sit up late in our friar's dresses, drinking burgundy, claret, champagne, and what not, out of the skull-cup, and all sorts of glasses, and buffooning all around the house, in our conventual garments. Matthews always denominated me "the Abbot."

As with those choirboys in his faux chapel at Cambridge, Matthews encouraged theatrical, half-ironic gothic scenes, drafting Byron in the role of "Abbot" as the master of Newstead Abbey. Matthews reported, "A set of monkish dresses ... with all the proper apparatus of crosses, beads, tonsures, &c. often gave a variety to our appearance, and to our pursuits." At one point, Matthews hid in a stone coffin in darkness and waited, rising up suddenly to blow out Hobhouse's candle.

These Newstead nights would return in Byron's poetry throughout his career, from *Childe Harold's Pilgrimage* to *Manfred* to the English cantos of *Don Juan*, the latter set largely at "Norman Abbey." But his congenital restlessness was growing, and soon his thoughts turned more resolutely to going abroad for an extended tour. In this chapter's 1807 letter to Elizabeth Pigot, Byron had shared his plan of "going to Sea for four or five months ... probably to the Mediterranean, or to the West Indies, or to the Devil." By the spring of 1809, such a trip was finally in the offing – not with the frequently injured Capt. Bettesworth but in the company of Hobhouse. Their itinerary would take them to the Iberian peninsula, just skirting the clashes of Napoleon's army with the allied British–Spanish forces, and then to the European borderlands under the control of the Ottoman Empire: Albania, Turkey, and Greece. It was to be a time of adventure and self-discovery, and it would give rise to Byron's first masterpiece, leading him to sudden celebrity and international fame. For now, his pugnacious *English Bards and Scotch Reviewers* was out, ruffling the feathers of the British literati, and, although he had nominally accepted his seat in the House of Lords, Byron was ready to shake the dust of what he called "that tight little island" from his shoes. By early summer, he and Hobhouse (along with valet William Fletcher and young servant Robert Rushton) were poised to depart. To his mother, he wrote (casting himself in the role of a contemptuous Adam exiting Eden), "The world is all before me, and I leave England without regret." He echoed this sentiment in a letter written from Falmouth while waiting for the tide to turn, "I leave England without regret – I shall return to it without pleasure. I am like Adam, the first convict sentenced to transportation, but I have no Eve, and have eaten no apple but what was sour as a crab; – and thus ends my first chapter. Adieu."

2

——◇——

The Air of Greece

Salsette frigate. May 3ᵈ. 1810
in the Dardanelles off Abydos.

My dear Drury, –

When I left England nearly a year ago you requested me to write to you. – I will do so. – I have crossed Portugal, traversed the South of Spain, visited Sardinia, Sicily, Malta, and thence passed into Turkey where I am still wandering. – I first landed in Albania the ancient Epirus where we penetrated as far as Mount Tomerit, excellently treated by the Chief Ali Pacha, and after journeying through Illyria, Chaonia, &c, crossed the Gulph of Actium with a guard of 50 Albanians and passed the Achelous in our route through Acarnania and Ætolia. – We stopped a short time in the Morea, crossed the gulph of Lepanto (i.e. Corinth) and landed at the foot of Parnassus, saw all that Delphi retains and so on to Thebes and Athens at which last we remained ten weeks. – His majesty's ship Pylades brought us to Smyrna but not before we had topographised Attica including of course Marathon, and the Sunian Promontory. – From Smyrna to the Troad which we visited when at anchor for *a fortnight off the Tomb of Antilochus, was our next stage, and now we are in the Dardanelles waiting for a wind to proceed to Constantinople. – This morning I <u>swam</u> from <u>Sestos</u> to <u>Abydos</u>; the immediate distance is not above a mile but the current renders it hazardous, so much so, that I doubt whether Leander's conjugal powers must not have been exhausted in his passage to Paradise. – I attempted it a week ago and failed owing to the North wind and the wonderful rapidity of the tide, though I have been from my childhood a strong swimmer, but this morning being calmer I succeeded and crossed the "broad Hellespont" in an hour and ten minutes. – –*

Well, my dear Sir, I have left my home, and seen parts of Africa & Asia and a tolerable portion of Europe. – I have been with Generals, and Admirals, Princes and Pachas, Governors and Ungovernables, but I have not time or paper to expatiate. – I wish to let you know that I live with a friendly remembrance of you and a hope to meet you again, and if I do this as shortly as possible, attribute it to anything but forgetfulness. – Greece ancient and modern you know too well to require description. Albania indeed I have seen more of than any Englishman (but a Mr. Leake) for it is a country rarely visited from the savage character of the natives, though abounding in more natural beauties than the ~~more~~ classical regions of Greece, which however are still eminently beautiful, particularly ~~about~~ Delphi, and Cape Colonna in Attica. – Yet these are nothing to parts of Illyria, and Epirus, where places without a name, and rivers not laid down in maps, may one day when more known be justly esteemed superior subjects for the pencil, and the pen, than the dry ditch of the Ilissus, and the bogs of Bœotia. – The Troad is a fine field for conjecture and Snipe-shooting,

*and a good sportsman and an ingenious scholar may ex-
ercise their feet and faculties to great advantage upon the
spot, or if they prefer riding lose their way (as I did) in a
cursed quagmire of the Scamander who wriggles about as
if the Dardan virgins still offered their wonted tribute. The
only vestige of Troy, or her destroyers, are the barrows supposed to contain the carcases of Achilles, Antilochus, Ajax
&c. but Mt. Ida is still in high feather, though the Shep-
herds are nowadays not much like Ganymede. – But why
should I say more of these things? are they not written in
the <u>Boke</u> of Gell?* and has not Hobby got a journal? I keep
none as I have renounced scribbling. – I see not much difference between ourselves & the Turks, save that we have
foreskins and they none, that they have long dresses and
we short, and that we talk much and they little. – In England the vices in fashion are whoring & drinking, in Turkey,
Sodomy & smoking, we prefer a girl and a bottle, they a
pipe and pathic. – They are sensible people. Ali Pacha told
me he was sure I was a man of rank because I had <u>small
ears</u> and hands and <u>curling</u> <u>hair</u>. – By the bye, I speak the
Romaic or Modern Greek tolerably, it does not differ from
the ancient dialects so much as you would conceive, but
the pronunciation is diametrically opposite, of verse except
in rhyme they have no idea. – I like the Greeks, who are
plausible rascals, with all the Turkish vices without their
courage. – However some are brave and all are beautiful,
very much resembling the busts of Alcibiades, the women
not quite so handsome. – I can swear in Turkish, but except
one horrible oath, and "<u>pimp</u>" and "bread" and "water" I
have got no great vocabulary in that language. – They are*

---

* Sir William Gell, *The Topography of Troy* (1804).

extremely polite to strangers of any rank properly protected, and as I have 2 servants and two soldiers we get on with great eclât. We have been occasionally in danger of thieves & once of shipwreck but always escaped. – At Malta I fell in love with a married woman and challenged an aid du camp of Genl. Oakes (a rude fellow who grinned at something, I never rightly knew what,) but he explained and apologised, and the lady embarked for Cadiz, & so I escaped murder and adultery. – Of Spain I sent some account to our Hodgson, but I have subsequently written to no one save notes to relations and lawyers to keep them out of my premises. – I mean to give up all connection on my return with many of my best friends as I supposed them, and to snarl all my life, but I hope to have one good humoured laugh with you, and to embrace Dwyer and pledge Hodgson, before I commence Cynicism. – Tell Dr. Butler I am now writing with the gold pen he gave me before I left England, which is the reason my scrawl is more unentelligible than usual. – I have been at Athens and seen plenty of those reeds for scribbling, some of which he refused to bestow upon me because topographer Gell had brought them from Attica. – –

But I will not describe, no, you must be satisfied with simple detail till my return, and then we will unfold the floodgates of Colloquy. – I am in a 36 gun frigate going up to fetch Bob Adair from Constantinople, who will have the honour to carry this letter. – And so Hobby's <u>boke</u> is out, with some sentimental singsong of mine own to fill up, and how does it take? eh! and where the devil is the 2d Edition of my Satire with additions? and my name on the title page? and more lines tagged to the end with a new exordium and what not, hot from my anvil before I cleared the Channel? – The Mediterranean and the Atlantic roll between me and

Criticism, and the thunders of the *Hyberborean Review** are deafened by the roar of the Hellespont. – Remember me to Claridge if not translated to College, and present to Hodgson assurances of my high consideration. – Now, you will ask, what shall I do next? and I answer I do not know, I may return in a few months, but I have intents and projects after visiting Constantinople, Hobhouse however will probably be back in September. – On the 2d. of July we have left Albion one year, "*oblitus meorum, obliviscendus et illis,*"† I was sick of my own country, and not much prepossessed in favour of any other, but I drag on "my chain" without "lengthening it at each remove". – I am like the jolly miller caring for nobody and not cared for. All countries are much the same in my eyes, I smoke and stare at mountains, and twirl my mustachios very independently, I miss no comforts, and the Musquitoes that rack the morbid frame of Hobhouse, have luckily for me little effect on mine because I live more temperately. – I omitted Ephesus in my Catalogue, which I visited during my sojourn at Smyrna, but the temple has almost perished, and St. Paul need not trouble himself to epistolize the present brood of Ephesians who have converted a large church built entirely of marble into a Mosque, and I don't know that the edifice looks the worse for it. – –

My paper is full, and my ink ebbing, Good Afternoon! – If you address to me at Malta, the letter will be forwarded wherever I may be. – Hobhouse greets you, he pines for his poetry, at least some tidings of it. – I almost forgot to tell you that I am dying for love of three Greek Girls at Athens, sisters, two of whom have promised to accompany me

---

* The Edinburgh Review; Hyperborea was a mythical northern land.
† "Forgetting my friends and being forgotten by them"

to England, I lived in the same house, Teresa, Mariana, and Kattinka, are the names of these divinities all of them under 15. – your ταπεινοτατοσ δουλος *[most humble servant]*

Byron

——●——

Late afternoon light on calm water, and on the teak decking of a small British warship at anchor in the Dardanelles, the narrow Turkish strait connecting the Aegean to the Sea of Marmara. Several hours earlier, a 22-year-old Lord Byron and Lieutenant William Ekenhead had been ferried to the northern European shore, just above the site of the ancient Thracian city of Sestos, for a second attempt at swimming across, diagonally and down, to the Asian coast. They had first tried in early April, but the wind had been contrary and the current too strong. Now Byron sat aboard the *Salsette* and wrote expansively to Henry Drury, his friend and former tutor and housemaster at Harrow, to report his success and also to give a glancing overview of his travels since he left England ten months before. It's a joyful letter, written in a confident hand on both sides of four large sheets of paper that was made by the firm of James Whatman in England in 1806. Byron would have brought writing materials with him on his travels, including the "gold pen" he writes with, a gift from Harrow headmaster, George Butler. Pen and paper were thus both tangible links to England, a means of making contact with home.

Today's triumph had been both physical and imaginative. Though his deformed right foot limited his athletic success on land, Byron was a prodigious swimmer. As a young man, he swam 3 miles "in the Thames from Lambeth through the bridges, Westminster and Blackfriars," and, on this journey, had traversed the Tagus river in Lisbon, arguably a more difficult challenge than the Hellespont. Here in Ottoman Turkey he had completed the swim in just over an hour, covering almost 4 miles in icy spring-thaw water, driven by the current across to what once was Abydos, near the site of ancient Troy. It was not quite the "broad Hellespont" of Homer's *Iliad* – that would presumably have been the upper end of the strait – but the narrow opening near the Aegean was also loaded with legend. The Persian king Xerxes had built a pontoon bridge across it to invade Greece in 480 BC, and, more important to the occasion, the mythic Greek lover Leander swam this same route each night in his visits to Hero, a priestess of Aphrodite, until he was drowned in a storm and she followed him in a suicidal leap from her tower. Byron was only half-ironically enjoying the sense of communion with the ancient past, writing as his limbs ached in the aftermath of effort, "I doubt whether Leander's conjugal powers must not have been exhausted in his passage to Paradise."

Somewhere below decks, hiding from the mosquitos, was John Cam Hobhouse, Byron's loyal Trinity College friend and traveling companion (Figure 2.1). With Byron's funds, they had toured "part of Africa & Asia and a tolerable portion of Europe" since embarking from Falmouth in July. Enthusiastic explorers of other cultures, both Byron and Hobhouse had met their changing surroundings with a mixture of facetious humor, genuine wonder, stoic acceptance, and outright enjoyment, solidifying their friendship into a lifelong bond. The war with Napoleon meant France and northern Italy were closed to them; and besides, Byron said that he aimed to avoid "the common *Turnpike* of coxcombs & *virtuosos*," the predictable European itinerary of the gentleman's Grand Tour. Instead, Byron and Hobhouse had followed a less well-traveled, half-improvised route through Albania, Greece, and Turkey, all part of the Ottoman Empire at that time. In addition to mosquitos, they had endured lice and fleas, illness, thieves, wretched lodgings, long days and nights on horseback, and storms on land and sea. As Byron had written in an earlier letter, "Comfort must not be expected by folks that go a-pleasuring." But these challenges were interspersed with rewards: luxuries in places such as the Governor's residence at Malta and the splendid court of Ali Pasha at Tepelene; scenes of intense natural beauty loaded with historical associations; glances of martial excitement aboard warships; and flirtations and seductions of various kinds. Byron would write to Francis Hodgson two days later,

> We have undergone some inconveniences and incurred partial perils.... a few alarms from robbers, and some danger of shipwreck in a Turkish Galliot six months ago, a visit to a Pacha, a passion for a married woman at Malta, a challenge to an officer, an attachment to three Greek girls at Athens, with a great deal of buffoonery and fine prospects, form all that has distinguished my progress.

The "married woman" was Mrs. Constance Spencer Smith, who became "fair Florence" and "sweet Florence" in the poetry Byron was writing, an object of passionate and unconsummated attachment. For his part, Hobhouse was keeping an extensive travelogue that would be published as *A Journey through Albania and other provinces of Turkey* in 1813.

Mentioning that "Hobby" has "got a journal," Byron tells Drury, "I keep none as I have renounced scribbling."

In fact, no statement could have been more misleading. Two weeks before he boarded the *Salsette*, Byron had finished drafting the poem that would make him famous: *Childe Harold's Pilgrimage*. He had started writing it the previous fall, eventually producing almost 200 stanzas of descriptions, reflections, and set-pieces, tied to the perspective of a world-weary, alienated young nobleman amid the landscapes of the Mediterranean. As he would reflect later, those stanzas "were written as if by a man – older than I shall probably ever be." This was something far different than Hobhouse's dry record of observations, and something more exciting than a traditional topographical poem. Byron had developed a persona and a voice that would soon become his signature and would rage through England and Europe as readers devoured and writers were influenced by his work. True, Byron had not written much since late March, not even letters, being content after finishing the second canto of *Childe Harold* to, as he writes here, "smoke and stare at mountains, and twirl my mustachios very independently." But he must have known, as he composed this playful letter to Drury, that he had already accomplished something more important than the Hellespont swim. You can hear his self-confidence, his sense of easy languor as he considers what is behind and ahead of him, even as he plays the part of the misanthrope, saying he intends to "give up all connection ... with many of my best friends as I supposed them, and to snarl all my life." He compares himself to the "jolly miller" of the old folk song who rejoices in his freedom from commitments, signaling an enthusiasm for life as it was unfolding before him. Young, strong, aware of a newly amplified poetic power, buoyed by erotic possibilities, surrounded by near-mythic landscapes: you could make a case for this being the happiest period, and one of the happiest days, of Byron's entire life.

Byron's expansive letter to his former tutor Drury (who was only ten years his senior) connects his itinerary to his classical reading: he and Hobhouse have "topographised Attica," moving simultaneously through "Greece ancient and modern." In the pile-up of geographic names in this letter, we see Byron's philhellenic pride in journeying to the sites of classical antiquity, paraded before Drury with a studied insouciance. He calls Albania, for example, "the ancient Epirus," "Illyria," and "Chaonia," names familiar from Virgil and Strabo (and Shakespeare); and the river Scamander "wriggles about as if the Dardan virgins still offered their wonted tribute" – that is, their virginity, according to ancient Greek sources. Byron had written in December after he and Hobhouse "landed at the foot of Parnassus," sacred to Apollo and the Muses,

> Oh, thou Parnassus! whom I now survey,
> Not in the phrenzy of a dreamer's eye,
> Not in the fabled landscape of a lay,
> But soaring snow-clad through thy native sky,
> In the wild pomp of mountain majesty!

Behind the braggadocio lies a deep sense of encounter, this direct overlay of real and ideal, as Byron's attention is captured by the sacred sites of the Greek past: the Hellespont, Parnassus, Marathon, Delphi, Mount Ida, and the plains of Troy. Sir William Gell's "Boke" or book, *The Topography of Troy* (1804), was Byron's guide as he made daily trips from the *Salsette* to the Troad for "conjecture and Snipe-shooting," and for imaginative communion with the heroes of Homer's

Iliad: "Achilles, Antilochus, Ajax, &c." Byron was finding his element, and finding himself as a poet. As Fiona MacCarthy observes, "There is a dreamlike quality in Byron's writing of his travels as the real scenes before him merge with scenes imagined, scenes already in his mind from his reading, his immersion in the history of the place." This sojourn in Greece and the Ottoman world changed everything, catalyzing something in his imagination and breeding a permanent, life-changing affinity for the Greek people. He would later tell his friend Edward Trelawny, "If I am a poet … the air of Greece made me one." Byron inhaled this atmosphere, full of natural beauty, heavy with history and myth; the resulting poetry blended sublimity with irony, romance with tragicomic farce.

A few days after writing this letter to Drury, Byron composed a short poem on his Hellespont swim, catching something of the letter's tone:

1.

If in the month of dark December
  Leander, who was nightly wont
(What maid will not the tale remember?)
  To cross thy stream, broad Hellespont!

2.

If when the wintry tempest roar'd,
  He sped to Hero, nothing loth,
And thus of old thy current pour'd,
  Fair Venus! how I pity both!

3.

For *me*, degenerate modern wretch,
  Though in the genial month of May,

My dripping limbs I faintly stretch,
    And think I've done a feat to-day.

4.

But since he cross'd the rapid tide,
    According to the doubtful story,
To woo,—and—Lord knows what beside,
    And swam for Love, as I for Glory;

5.

'Twere hard to say who fared the best:
    Sad mortals! thus the Gods still plague you!
He lost his labour, I my jest:
    For he was drown'd, and I've the ague.

That final double-syllable rhyme – "plague you / ague" – is facetious in precisely the manner of Byron's masterpiece, *Don Juan*, still many years ahead of him. Byron didn't really catch an ague (a cold), but the poem depends on the ironic clash between romantic myths and the real claims and limitations of the body. If Leander indeed swam across the strait "when the wintry tempest roar'd" according to "the doubtful story," Byron writes, then he pities both lovers. A long swim in icy water would have been quite the cold shower for anyone who came "To woo—and—Lord knows what beside" (that sexually suggestive feint is also pure *Don Juan*). Leander's conjugal powers must have been exhausted, he tells Drury; and Byron's own swim for "Glory" ends with a common cold. Yet Byron knows that's not the whole story, as he makes sure to publicize his accomplishment, telling various correspondents about the swim and then including this poem in the *Childe Harold* volume, published when he returned home. The "majesty" of Parnassus and the "jest" of Byron's Hellespont swim met the public eye together in this best-selling book, the one that inaugurated his legendary persona.

Byron was moving through long-imagined landscapes of Greece, with ancient names and schoolboy associations rising before him at every turn. We can see in his reactions the Romantic movement's deep, paradoxical roots in an idealized classical age. As he wrote in *Childe Harold*, "one vast realm of wonder spreads around, / And all the Muse's tales seem truly told / Till sense aches with gazing to behold / The scenes our earliest dreams have dwelt upon." At the same time, he was encountering Ottoman Turkish culture up close in the Ottoman Empire, which at that time spread from North Africa to Baghdad to the Austro-Hungarian border. Britain had recently been supporting Russia against Turkey, but now the *Salsette* was headed for Constantinople to retrieve Robert Adair, the British ambassador who had just signed the treaty that put an end to hostilities. Ten days after the Hellespont swim, Byron saw from aboard ship "the white minarets of Sultan Achmed and Santa Sophia looking" (wrote Hobhouse in his diary) "like Kings College Chapel at a distance." For the next two months, the two men toured the city and the surrounding countryside, dining at the British embassy, exploring the bazaars and kebab houses, visiting the mosques by special permission due to Byron's rank, and even having an audience with Sultan Mahmoud II, resplendent in yellow satin edged in sable, with diamonds encrusting his turban and ceremonial dagger. They marveled at the "immense triple battlements covered with Ivy, surmounted by 218 towers" of the Seraglio, even as they recoiled from the sight of dogs gnawing dead bodies in the street. They watched lascivious male dancers in wine houses of Galata, toured the docks and shipyards, and rode their horses out to the former palace of

Sultan Selim III, who had been deposed in a recent rebellion. Describing the ruins to Annabella Milbanke, Byron wrote of "the grandeur of desolation in their aspect – – Streets in ashes – immense barracks (of a very fine construction) in ruins – and above all Sultan Selim's favourite gardens round them in all the wildness of luxuriant neglect – his fountains waterless – and his kiosks defaced but still glittering in their decay." He would later recast this scene in *The Giaour*, the best of a series of narrative verse romances we now call his Turkish Tales. Greece was leaving its mark on Byron's imagination, but so was Ottoman culture and its richly layered contrasts of dark and bright.

Byron had been fascinated by the Ottomans since he was a boy: he later said that Richard Knolles's *Turkish History* was "one of the first books that gave me pleasure when a child," and that it "had much influence" on his life and work. Drawn to the exoticism of Turkey, Byron also came to appreciate Turkish sexual mores that made allowance for relations between men, particularly the pederasty that Byron favored. He had written to a like-minded friend just before leaving England of "a handsome Bouquet" of Hyacinths (beautiful young men) that were mere prelude to "the exotics we expect to meet in Asia." And he writes with studied casual humor to Drury, "In England the vices in fashion are whoring & drinking, in Turkey, Sodomy & smoking, we prefer a girl and a bottle, they a pipe and [a] pathic." As Byron headed into the Ottoman territories, he sent his young page Robert Rushton back to England, worried that he might be seduced or assaulted. Although Byron's own sexual activity with men during his Eastern tour was apparently confined to his months in Athens, the possibilities were visible all around him. He tells Drury he has learned the Turkish word for "pimp," suggesting that, like Hobhouse at the brothels, he transacted with local sex workers; it's possible that some were male. When Byron visited his first Turkish bath, Hobhouse says they were both too shy to enter the inner room where patrons were washed by young men – but Byron, years later, described such a bath as a "marble paradise of sherbet and sodomy."

Early in their travels, Byron and Hobhouse visited Ioannina, viewing the elegant domes and minarets of "what was then the finest, most cultured city in Greece." Yet one of the first things they saw was the quartered arm and shoulder of a rebellious Greek patriot, hanging from a tree. The Albanian chieftain Ali Pasha was in control of the region, with Ioannina as his capital, and his brutal methods of suppression were in evidence. The travelers were given a lukewarm welcome by the British resident, Captain William Martin Leake, the leading authority on Greece at the time, who seems to have thought of these two young visitors as irritating dilettantes. But they were both charmed by the city, and the flattery of Ali Pasha's secretary: the pasha himself had left word for the visiting Englishmen to come to Tepelene – the birthplace and mountain stronghold of the already-legendary outlaw chief – where he had gone to pursue "a little war" against a rival. In Ioannina, they also met Ali's grandsons (ages 10 and 12), who enchanted Byron with their formal manners, "painted complexions," and "large black eyes."

Byron and Hobhouse were being drawn into the little-known region of Albania, riding through the craggy, gorgeous landscapes of the Pindus range, through "Monastic Zitza" perched above ravines and cataracts, and arriving at the walled city of Tepelene in mid-October. Byron's description of his reception by Ali Pasha is worth quoting at length:

The next day I was introduced to Ali Pacha, I was dressed in a full suit of Staff uniform with a very magnificent sabre &c. – – The Vizier received me in a large room paved with marble, a fountain was playing in the centre, the apartment surrounded by scarlet Ottomans, he received me standing, a wonderful compliment from a Mussulmen, & made me sit on his right hand.... He said he was certain I was a man of birth because I had small ears, curling hair, & little white hands, and expressed himself pleased with my appearance & garb. – He told me to consider him as a father whilst I was in Turkey ... Indeed he treated me like a child, sending me almonds & sugared sherbet, fruit & sweetmeats 20 times a day. – He begged me to visit him often, and at night when he was more at leisure.... His highness is 60 years old, very fat & not tall, but with a fine face, light blue eyes & a white beard ... He has the appearance of any thing but his real character, for he is a remorseless tyrant, guilty of the most horrible cruelties.

Byron and Hobhouse often dressed in British military uniforms to ease their path as they traveled in the East, and Ali took note admiringly of Byron's "garb" and "magnificent sabre." He also praised Byron's aristocratic features, flattering and flirting with him. The meeting had a quasi-diplomatic aspect: Ali was hoping to cultivate an alliance with Britain, and, overestimating Byron's political clout, played upon his vanity. But there also was a barely concealed current of feminization and seduction in Ali's attentions. Byron was never interested in older men, but the scene suggested opportunities he would find elsewhere as he adapted himself to life in the Ottoman Empire. As he writes in this letter to Drury, "I see not much difference between ourselves & the Turks, save that we have foreskins and they none, that they have long dresses and we short." Around this time, he bought a handsome Albanian costume that he would wear for the famous portrait by Thomas Phillips (Figure 2.2). And when he left Tepelene to return to Ioannina in late October, he started writing *Childe Harold's Pilgrimage*.

Now, on the deck of the *Salsette*, with Albania behind him, Constantinople ahead, and beyond that a return to Athens, Byron had his first real inclination in months to send a letter to England. Full of boyish pride after his heroic swim, his thoughts turned to Harrow and the scenes of the previous summer, when he had visited his old school to attend Speech Days and socialize with residents, including his former tutor. This letter has something of that spirit of reconnection, as Byron asks to be remembered to Dwyer, a tutor with "flame-coloured whiskers"; Francis Hodgson, a close friend from Cambridge (who would marry Drury's sister-in-law); Dr. Butler, the Harrow headmaster whom Byron had mocked as "Pomposus" in an early satire but had come to admire; and Claridge, one of Byron's "juniors and favourites" whom he had "spoiled with indulgence." As Byron had written in 1806, already nostalgic for a place he had left only a year ago, "Ye scenes of my childhood," "Where … friendships were form'd, too romantic to last,"

> Where fancy, yet, joys to retrace the resemblance,
>   Of comrades, in friendship and mischief allied;
> How welcome to me, your ne'er fading remembrance,
>   Which rests in the bosom, though hope is deny'd.

As we have seen, Harrow would always be a kind of paradise lost in Byron's imagination: a place and a time of romantic teenage male companionship, more or less erotic.

Drury likely shared Byron's letter, perhaps reading it aloud to a small group of eager listeners at Harrow, to whom Byron had already become a local hero after the success of *English Bards and Scotch Reviewers*. Byron had first written it as a light Horatian poetical essay on the current literary scene, but had pushed the poem toward pugnacity in the wake of scathing reviews of his early lyrics. In the second edition that Byron mentions, *English Bards and Scotch Reviewers* achieved its definitive "caustic" form, meant to cure "the present prevalent and distressing *rabies* for rhyming" and also "bruise one of the heads" of the "Hydra" of criticism he calls here the "Hyberborean Review." Despite his assertion that all critical "thunders" are "deafened by the roar of the Hellespont," Byron was eager to hear how this new version was going down, asking "where the devil is the 2d Edition of my Satire with additions? and my name on the title page? … hot from my anvil before I cleared the Channel?" In fact, the new, more acidic edition had appeared in May 1809 just before Byron left England, but he had not seen it. He had written to his publisher Cawthorn from Lisbon last July, but the replies missed him. By now, the poem had already gone into a third edition and Cawthorn was preparing a fourth, as the poem grew in popularity and notoriety. A reviewer for the *Poetical Register* wrote, "The luckless wights who have brought upon themselves the hostility of Lord Byron have ample cause to regret their rashness. He wields the scourge of satire with a vigorous and unrelenting hand." In his absence, Byron was gaining a literary reputation as an *enfant terrible*. He would return to become, with the publication of *Childe Harold*, a near-literal Hot Young Turk.

Hobhouse, or "Hobby," was also eager to hear about the reception of *Imitations and Translations*, published in 1809;

Byron writes to Drury, he "pines for his poetry, at least some tidings of it." This was a miscellaneous collection of lyric poems by Hobhouse and his Cambridge friends, including Byron, who calls his own contributions "sentimental singsong." The *Critical Review* (December 1809) had praised the volume, but they warned that the book contains indecent imitations from the classics, which women "had better not read." Of Byron's lyrics, the reviewer confessed that "we have seldom read … verses of more tenderness and real feeling." Byron had given Hobhouse a drinking song, the elegy for Boatswain, and several poems that lamented the end of romance, especially the loss of Mary Chaworth. All of this sentiment seemed far away now, as Byron surveyed the coast of Turkey and reflected on his experiences since leaving England. He quotes Horace – "oblitus meorum, obliviscendus et illis" – and disclaims the lament of Goldsmith's *Traveller* (1764): "Where'er I roam, whatever realms to see, / My heart, untravelled, fondly turns to thee … / And drags at each remove a lengthening chain." Yet we know Byron's assertion of chainlessness was mostly a pose. He worked hard to assert a casual distance from past attachments and past wounds, both romantic and literary. In a passage he would write in Athens the following year, Byron alluded to this Goldsmith passage again, admitting that his anger at the *Edinburgh Review* (figured here as Holyrood) was quite present during his Eastern travels:

> Is it for this on Ilion I have stood,
> And thought of Homer less than Holyrood?
> On shore of Euxine or Aegean sea,
> My hate, untraveled, fondly turned to thee.

Mary Chaworth haunted him also, if only as a figure for youthful love and that lost path of domesticity that he might have taken. For all his irony and cynicism, Byron had a deep streak of sensitivity, even sentimentality, that never really went away. Like many rakes, he was also a true romantic.

When Byron and Hobhouse had first stayed in Athens, from the previous Christmas until early March, they had explored the monuments, and rode out to see – and carve their names on – the Doric temple at Suonion, what Byron would call "Sunium's marbled steep / Where nothing, save the waves and I, / May hear our mutual murmurs sweep." They also visited the plain of Marathon, site of the legendary Greek victory over the Persians, which would inspire Byron to write the lines so persistently associated with his commitment to the Greek struggle for independence:

> The mountains look on Marathon –
> And Marathon looks on the sea;
> And musing there an hour alone,
> I dream'd that Greece might still be free.

Athens was at that time a small, walled town of about 10,000 people, many of them Turks, most of them poor. The marble temples and monuments were either neglected or repurposed for contemporary use. The archeological rediscovery of ancient Greece was in its very early phases, with Lord Elgin pulling down sections of the Parthenon and shipping them to the British Museum, a practice that filled Byron with disgust. He was simultaneously disillusioned and charmed by the Greek people, whom he calls "plausible rascals, with all the Turkish vices without their courage. – However some are brave and all are beautiful." This doubled attitude would come to characterize his feelings toward the Greeks, as he oscillated between romantic visions of their past, dismay at their present state, and a kind of wild hope or dream that they might yet be free.

During these ten weeks, Byron and Hobhouse had taken rooms in the house of Mrs. Tarsia Macri, the Greek widow of the former British vice-consul. In this letter, Byron informs Drury that the Greek women are "not quite so handsome," but admits that he is "dying for love of three Greek Girls at Athens." These were Teresa, Mariana, and Katinka, the young daughters of Mrs. Macri, "two of whom," Byron assures Drury, "have promised to accompany me to England." The youngest, Teresa, was only 12 years old, yet she was the one Byron singled out for immortality as his "Maid of Athens," composing one of his best-known love poems in her honor (Figure 2.3):

> Maid of Athens, ere we part,
> Give, oh, give me back my heart!
> Or, since that has left my breast,
> Keep it now, and take the rest!
> Hear my vow before I go,
> Ζώη μου σάς άγαπώ. ["My life, I love you."]

Like Mrs. Bennet of *Pride and Prejudice*, Mrs. Macri was keen to get her daughters married, especially to an English nobleman. Since the death of her husband, she and the girls had survived on the produce of sixty olive trees and the rental of rooms in their house to English visitors. Byron's arrival was an opportunity, and, noting his interest in her youngest, Mrs. Macri colluded to push Teresa toward him. Hobhouse noted in his diary on March 3 that Teresa was "brought here to be deflowered, but Byron would not." Byron wrote later that he was "near to bringing away Theresa, but the mother asked 30,000 piastres." Whether it was Byron's delicacy, diffidence, or debts that prevented it, nothing came of these rather sad negotiations. In any case, his passion for the Macri girls seems to have been transitory. When he returned to Athens after visiting Constantinople, he moved into the Capuchin monastery rather than staying in the Macri house again. As he wrote to Hobhouse, "the old woman Teresa's mother was mad enough to imagine I was going to marry the girl, but I have better amusement."

That amusement involved young men of Greece whom Byron adopted as companions and protégés, pursuing male sexual relationships away from British hypocrisies that deplored homosexual practice while remaining enamored of homoerotic ancient Greece. Hobhouse had returned to England in mid-July, "dividing with [Byron] a little nose-gay of flowers" as he said a tearful goodbye to "this singular young person." His departure left Byron at more liberty: he wrote to a friend, quoting Milton, "I feel happier, I feel free. 'I can go and I can fly freely to the Green earth's end.'" He was soon touring the Morea with his bisexual college friend the Marquis of Sligo, and romancing his "dearly beloved" Eustathius (Efstathios) Georgiou, a young Greek with "ambrosial curls hanging down his amiable back." Eustathius was "as froward as an unbroken colt," and he embarrassed Byron by carrying a parasol; Byron confessed, "I never in my life took so much pains to please any one, or succeeded so ill." That relationship, probably both farcical and sexual, ended as Byron settled back in Athens, at a monastery at the foot of the Acropolis, where six young men were in residence at a school run by the abbot. "These Sylphs," Byron wrote, caused "nothing but riot from Noon till night." For Byron, the scenarios with these young students reminded him of Harrow: "my lessons … are sadly interrupted by scamperings and eating fruit and peltings and playings and I am in fact at school again, and make as little improvement now as I did then, my time being wasted in the same way." In one of the many ironies of Byron's experience, he was reconnecting with the sexually liberal environment of the British private school in a monastery in Athens.

Byron was learning Italian from one of the "Sylphs," a Greek-born French teenager named Nicolo Giraud, who also became his lover. The pair had sex "above two hundred" times, and by October, Byron confessed (in coded language, to Hobhouse) to being "almost tired" of it. But Nicolo nursed Byron through a serious attack of malarial fever in Patras, waiting on him "day and night" until Nicolo caught the disease himself. Byron had half-expected to die, and he later would tell a "ghost story" about himself: as he suffered in Patras, he was seen on the streets of London by Sir Robert Peel and at least two other people, causing Byron to speculate that "we may be *two* by some uncommon process" of the body and spirit. The idea of the double or doppelgänger fascinated Byron, and would become part of the conversations with Percy and Mary Shelley that led to the creation of *Frankenstein* and informed Byron's gothic play *Manfred*, as well as his prose fragment that became the basis for John Polidori's *The Vampyre*. For Byron, the double self seemed symbolic of his mobile personality, and an instability of character that at times would trouble him. But some of this reflects his bisexual identity, and becomes coded language for that double life. The Nicolo Giraud relationship may have been Byron's first complete sexual experience with a male, or at least his first extensive one. As a measure of his attachment and gratitude, soon after he returned to England, Byron made a will that named Nicolo first and bequeathed him the princely sum of £7,000. But that will was later canceled.

Byron and Nicolo swam daily in the Aegean, riding out to Piraeus to escape the summer heat. Byron was also writing, working in the monastery's small circular library located inside the base of the ancient monument to Lysikrates (Figures 2.4a and 2.4b). Finding a copy of Horace there, he embarked on a sequel to *English Bards and Scotch Reviewers*: it was a satire conveying poetic guidelines (modeled on Horace's *Art of Poetry*) entitled *Hints from Horace*. He also wrote *The Curse of Minerva*, an angry attack on Elgin's depredations of the monuments of Athens. Finally, he added to *Childe Harold's Pilgrimage*, composing additional stanzas and augmenting the lengthy notes that would accompany the poem, including considerations of the present political and cultural state of Greece. He was immersed in the classical world, or rather immersed in contemporary editions of the ancient authors, while also awash in the daily experiences of Athens itself. Out of this, he developed an imaginative outlook that blended the formal structures of Greek and Roman literary art with the passionate spontaneity of Romanticism. He was also learning more about modern Greece, aided by a tutor, Ioannis Marmarotouris. As he did so, he moved further toward understanding and supporting the Greek cause of freedom, suggesting "the interposition of foreigners" to "emancipate the Greeks, who, otherwise, appear to have … small … chance of redemption from the Turks." During these months, he was laying the emotional and intellectual groundwork for the journey that would bring him back to Greece near the end of his life.

By April, Byron was weary and ill, and his finances were in total disrepair: he was still trying to sell his property in the Lancashire coalfield but it was tied up in legal knots. Leaving Nicolo at Malta, he departed for home, landing back in England, just over two years since he and Hobhouse had embarked. As he wrote to Hodgson from the frigate *Volage*, "my prospects are not very pleasant, embarrassed in my private affairs, indifferent to public, solitary without the wish to be social, with a body a little enfeebled by a succession of fevers, but a spirit I trust yet unbroken, I am returning *home*, without a hope, & almost without a desire." He had contracted a "severe" case of gonorrhea in Greece, and (he told Scrope Davies) picked up another one shortly after his arrival back in London. Yet, he confessed, "I have written some 4000 lines of one kind or another on my travels," and he was soon working to get both *Hints from Horace* and *Childe Harold's Pilgrimage* into the hands of a publisher.

But before Byron could make much progress, or begin to untangle his complicated finances, a series of deaths shook him. Most importantly, his mother died on August 1, only one day after he heard she was ill and before he could get to Newstead to see her. He had just heard of the death of a close Cambridge companion, John Wingfield, and then, a week after his mother passed away, he learned that Charles Skinner Matthews, Hobhouse's best friend and a confidant of Byron's, had drowned in the river Cam after becoming tangled in the weeds. Byron was reeling, "bewildered with the different shocks." He wrote to Hobhouse, "I have lost her who gave me being, & some of those who made that Being a blessing," and to Hodgson, "The blows followed each other so rapidly that I am yet stupid from the shock." By later August, he was threatening to go abroad again, as soon as he could repair his finances – perhaps, as he wrote to his half-sister Augusta, by marrying "any thing inclined to barter money for rank … after which I shall return to my friends the Turks." His homecoming was already looking like a mistake, and Byron had a strong urge simply to flee these scenes of pain and responsibility, to "leave England & all its clouds for the East again."

Two things changed Byron's mind. First, he returned to Newstead Abbey and began "to gather my little sensual comforts together," in the form of attractive female servants, including Lucy, the one whom he had impregnated before his tour of the Mediterranean. As during his earlier period of depression after he left Cambridge, sexual command over multiple young women assuaged him. As he wrote to Hodgson,

> I am plucking up my spirits … some very bad faces have been warned off the premises, and more promising substituted in their stead…. As I am a great disciplinarian, I have just issued an edict for the abolition of caps; no hair to be cut on any pretext; stays permitted, but not too low before; full uniform always in the evening; Lucinda to be commander … of all the makers and unmakers of beds in the household.

Turning his home into a small harem, Byron was overcompensating for the chaos of his personal life. At a time when he was feeling buffeted by fate and the consequences of his own financial recklessness, he took pleasure in asserting control over these pliant "Girls on the Manor," with Lucy as his majordomo. They even make an appearance in the opening stanzas of *Childe Harold's Pilgrimage* as "Paphian girls" who now "sing and smile" in Harold's "vast and venerable" ancestral hall. In a letter to Hobhouse, Byron wrote that, although he has "Lucy, Susan a very pretty Welsh girl, & a third of the Nott[inghamshire]'s breed … all under age [i.e., under 21], and very ornamental," he was able to "carry on nothing carnal" due to his severe dieting.

Second, Byron was working to get *Childe Harold* published, having given it to the man who would enable Byron's literary fame: John Murray. Murray was an influential figure, the publisher of Walter Scott and eventually Jane Austen, and a centre of the London literary scene. He immediately recognized the power of Byron's poem, and by early September was sending Byron the proofs, urging his careful attention to them: "it were cruel indeed not to perfect a work which contains so much that is excellent – your Fame my Lord demands it – you are raising a Monument that will outlive your present feelings." Seeing *Childe Harold's Pilgrimage* through the press would partially occupy Byron for the ensuing months, tethering him to England. Yet he was at that time unstrung by news of another great loss: his former Cambridge protégé and idealized romantic friend, the choirboy John Edleston, had died of consumption. He was, Byron wrote to a friend, "one whom I loved more than I ever loved a living thing." His grief over Edleston made its way into *Childe Harold*, whose narrator mourns "thou loved and lovely one! / Whom youth and youth's affection bound to me," "ever loving, lovely, and belov'd!" Two poems "To Thyrza" lamenting the loss of Edleston were included at the back of the volume, and, in another lyric of this period, Byron remembered, "a Lip which mine has prest, / But none had ever prest before," "a bosom all my own" that "pillow'd oft this aching head," and "two hearts" that beat "pulse to pulse responsive still." Byron's Childe Harold persona was thus deepened, made more directly yet mysteriously personal, by the erotic bereavement that colored the poetry. When the book appeared in early spring of 1812, the effect was immediate and "electric," with Byron's fame springing up, "like the palace of a fairy tale, in a night": as he later recalled with half-ironic awe, "I awoke one morning and found myself famous." For now, the wanderer was home and, like Leander in the Hellespont, he had committed himself to the treacherous path of glory.

3

———◇———

Mad, Bad, and Dangerous to Know

[Aston Hall, Rotherham, Yorkshire]
<u>*Octr. 8th. 1813*</u>

My dear Ly. M[elbourn]e—

I have volumes—but neither time nor space—I have already trusted too deeply to hesitate now—besides for certain reasons you will not be sorry to hear that I am anything but what I was.—Well then—to begin—& first a word of mine host—he has lately been talking at me rather than <u>to</u> me before the party (with the exception of the women) in a tone—which as I never use it myself I am not particularly disposed to tolerate in others—what <u>he</u> may do with impunity—it seems—but not suffer—till at last I told him that the whole of his argument involved the interesting contradiction that "he might love where he liked but that no one else might like what he ever thought proper to love" a doctrine which as the learned Partridge observed—contains a "non sequitur" from which I for one begged leave as a general proposition to dissent.*—This nearly produced a scene—with me as well as another guest

---

* Partridge, a character in Henry Fielding's *Tom Jones* (1749), speaks in *non sequiturs* while also pointing them out in others.

who seemed to admire my sophistry the most of the two—&
as it was after dinner & debating time—might have ended in
more than wineshed—but that the Devil for some wise purpose
of his own thought proper to restore good humour—which has
not as yet been further infringed.— — — — —

In these last few days I have had a good deal of conversation with an amiable person—whom (as we deal in
letters—& initials only) we will denominate Ph.[Frances]—
well—these things are dull in detail—take it once—I have
made love—& if I am to believe mere words (for there we
have hitherto stopped) it is returned.—I must tell you the
place of declaration however—a billiard room!—I did not
as C[aroline] says "kneel in the middle of the room" but like
Corporal Trim to the Nun—"I made a speech"*—which as
you might not listen to it with the same patience—I shall not
transcribe.—We were before on very amiable terms—& I
remembered being asked an odd question—"how a woman
who liked a man could inform him of it—when he did not
perceive it"—I also observed that we went on with our game
(of billiards) without counting the hazards—& supposed
that—as mine certainly were not—the thoughts of the other
party also were not exactly occupied by what was our osten-
sible pursuit.—Not quite though pretty well satisfied with
my progress—I took a very imprudent step—with pen &
paper—in tender & tolerably turned prose periods (no poetry even when in earnest) here were risks certainly—first how
to convey—then how it would be received—it was received
however & deposited not very far from the heart which I
wished it to reach—when who would enter the room but
the person who ought at that moment to have been in the

---

* Laurence Sterne's *Tristram Shandy* (1759–1767), book 8, chapter 22.

*Red sea if Satan had any civility—but <u>she</u> kept her coun-
tenance & the paper—& I my composure as well as I
could.—It was a risk—& <u>all</u> had been lost by failure—but
then recollect—how much more I had to gain by the reception—if not declined—& how much one always hazards to
obtain anything worth having.—My billet prospered—it did
more—it even (I am this moment interrupted by the <u>Mar-
ito</u> [husband]—& write this before him—he has brought
me a political pamphlet in M.S. to decypher & applaud—I
shall content myself with the last—Oh—he is gone again)—
my billet produced an <u>answer</u>—a very unequivocal one
too—but a little too much about virtue—& indulgence of
attachment in some sort of etherial process in which the
soul is principally concerned—which I don't very well understand—being a bad metaphysician—but one generally
<u>ends</u> & <u>begins</u> with Platonism—& as my proselyte is only
twenty—there is time enough to materialize—I hope nevertheless this spiritual system won't last long—& at any rate
must make the experiment.—I remember my last case was
the reverse—as Major O'Flaherty recommends "we fought
first & explained afterwards."*—This is the present state of
things—much mutual profession—a good deal of melancholy—which I am sorry to say was remarked by "the Moor"
& as much love as could well be made considering the time
place & circumstances.— —*

*I need not say that the folly & petulance of — —[J.
W. Webster] have tended to all this—if a man is not con-
tented with a pretty woman & not only runs after any little*

---

* Richard Cumberland's popular sentimental comedy *The West
   Indian* (1771): "what need is there for so much talking about the
   matter; can't you settle your differences first, and dispute about 'em
   afterwards?" (Act v, sc. i).

country girl he meets with but absolutely boasts of it—he must not be surprised if others admire that which he knows not how to value—besides he literally provoked & goaded me into it—by something not unlike bullying—<u>indirect</u> to be sure—but tolerably obvious—"he would do this—& he would do that—if any man["] &c. &c.—& <u>he</u> thought that every woman "was <u>his</u> lawful prize nevertheless["]—Oons! who is this strange monopolist?—it is odd enough but on other subjects he is like other people but on this he seems infatuated—if he had been rational—& not prated of his pursuits—I should have gone on very well—as I did at Middleton*—even now I shan't quarrel with him—if I can help it—but one or two of his speeches has blackened the blood about my heart—& curdled the milk of kindness—if put to the proof—I shall behave like other people I presume.—I have heard from A[nnabella]—but her letter to me is melancholy—about her old friend Miss M[ontgomer]y's departure &c.—&c.—I wonder who will have her at last—her letter to you is gay—you say—that to me must have been written at the same time—the little demure Nonjuror!†— — — —

I wrote to C[aroline] the other day—for I was afraid she might repeat the last year's epistle & make it <u>circular</u> among my friends.— — —Good evening—I am now going to <u>billiards</u>.—

ever yrs,

P.S. 6 o'clock—This business is growing serious—& I think <u>Platonism</u> in some peril—There has been very nearly

---

* Middleton Park in Oxfordshire, the seat of the Earl of Jersey and Lady Jersey.

† A clergyman who refused to take the oath of loyalty to William III and Mary II in 1689.

a scene—almost an <u>hysteric</u> & really without cause for I was conducting myself with (to me) very irksome decorum—her <u>expressions</u> astonish me—so young & cold as she appeared—but these professions must end as usual—& <u>would</u>—I think—<u>now</u>—had "l'occasion" been <u>not</u> wanting—had any one come in during the <u>tears</u> & consequent consolation all had been spoiled—we must be more cautious or less larmoyante.— — —

P.S. second—10 o'clock—I write to you just escaped from Claret & vociferation—on G-d knows what paper—my Landlord is a rare gentleman—he has just proposed to me a bet "that <u>he</u> for a certain sum wins any given <u>woman</u>—against any given <u>homme</u> including <u>all friends</u> present["]—which I declined with becoming deference to him & the rest of the company—is not this at this moment a perfect comedy?—I forgot to mention that on his entrance yesterday during the letter scene—it reminded me so much of an awkward passage in "the Way to keep him"* between Lovemore—Sir Bashful—& my Lady—that embarrassing as it was I could hardly help laughing—I hear his voice in the passage—he wants me to go to a ball at Sheffield—& is talking to me as I write—Good Night. I am in the act of praising his pamphlet.—I don't half like your story of Corinne†—some day I will tell you why—If I can—but at present—Good Night.

———•———

* *The Way to Keep Him* (1760), a comedy by Arthur Murphy (1727–1805).
† Germaine de Staël, *Corinne; or, Italy* (1807).

It's like something out of a novel or a play – this indiscreet, moment-by-moment letter, with James Webster as
the overconfident, fatuous husband, Lady Frances as the
pale but passionate wife, and Byron as the sly rake, half-
ironically pursuing and narrating the "business" of seduction. Throughout, Byron makes it clear that he feels like he is
living in a romantic fiction or erotic farce, comparing himself to literary characters (Corporal Trim, Major O'Flaherty)
and asking rhetorically, "is not this at this moment a perfect
comedy?" He's also clearly stage-managing the proceedings,
both in this letter and in real life. Not only does he write
to his confidante Lady Melbourne in ways that amplify the
hothouse theatricality of Aston Hall, but Byron also seems
to be consciously playing a role among the Websters, doing
and saying things in large part that he may write about them.
Indeed, like the heroine of Samuel Richardson's *Pamela*, he
writes about some of them *while doing them*. The double
postscripts and interruptions ("[Webster] is talking to me as I
write") convey a risky immediacy, and the letter itself unfolds
to reveal a second ragged sheet added at the end to contain
Byron's rapid-fire, time-stamped updates. It is an immoral,
conspiratorial, wildly entertaining letter, one that evokes
the spirit of Valmont's correspondence with Madame Mer-
tueil in *Les liaisons dangereuses*, which Byron probably had
read by this time. As in that novel, the dupes – here, James
Webster and Lady Frances – are pawns in a larger game, one
extending well beyond mere billiards and its "hazards," and
even beyond the seduction of the lady.

To understand the stakes, we need to look back over the
previous year-and-a-half of Byron's life. Since the publication of *Childe Harold's Pilgrimage* in early March 1812, he had
moved from the fringes of Regency high society to its center.

Suddenly famous, he was attracting gossip, fan mail, reviews, and portraits, including the sketch by Augustino Aglio that appears on the cover of this book (Figure 3.2). His poem had been a smash hit, selling out in a few days and making him a sought-after guest at the balls, routs, formal dinners, and opulent soirées of the leading families of the Whig party, to whom he gave his political and poetical allegiance. Despite his aristocratic title, Byron had up to this point felt himself something of an outsider: born in near poverty, lame, relatively unpolished, a latecomer to the glittering world of the *bon ton*. Every coterie of privilege has gradations that are only visible from the inside: there is always one more inner circle, and the lines of social rank in the Vanity Fair of Byron's England were very finely drawn. But the fame of Childe Harold propelled his creator like a meteor, and soon Byron (aged 24) was socializing with the Prince Regent, visiting the great London homes and country estates of the upper reaches of Whig society, and conducting love affairs with women of distinguished parentage, wealth, and high social position. Many of these women, like Lady Frances Webster, were married already, a fact that may say as much about the sexual conduct of the Regency aristocracy as it does about Byron himself. Particularly among the nobility, marriages were made as alliances of names, property, and money, and adulterous affairs on both sides were a frequent and expected part of that system. Appearances needed to be preserved – and yet, predictably, discretion and concealment gave way often enough to make this era one rich in sexual and domestic scandal.

Byron's correspondent, Lady Melbourne (Elizabeth Lamb, Viscountess Melbourne), had smoothly weathered several scandals of her own, including well-known affairs with the Prince of Wales and Lord Egremont, both of whom fathered some of her children (Figure 3.3). She was an extraordinary woman, intelligent and beautiful, the close friend of Georgiana, Duchess of Devonshire, and one of the most influential and celebrated hostesses of the later eighteenth century. She was also an incorrigible gossip with a sharp tongue that earned her the nickname "The Thorn." By 1813, she was in her sixties, still formidable, one of the "Queen Mothers" of High Whiggery, and someone who knew where all the bodies were buried. Jonathan Gross writes, "In her letters, as in her life, she often traded on the private lives of well-placed individuals. The comfort she provided to others as their confidante became the political coin she minted when she needed a favor returned." To the young Byron, she was a figure of vintage glamour: power broker, trader in confidences, advisor on female psychology, and message-carrier to various women with whom he was involved. Around this time, at the height of their relationship, Byron called her "the best friend I ever had in my life, and the cleverest of women." His love of gossip and his keen interest in the passions and habits of his fellow humans made Lady Melbourne an ideal correspondent. Byron's letters to her are full of scandalous reports and flirtatious repartee. Receiving his praise of her "Magical influence," Lady Melbourne replied, "it always appears to me that when you are describing my influence over you, you mean yours over me": the woman who wrote thus to Byron was nobody's fool.

Her love of erotic machinations aside, Lady Melbourne had her reasons for encouraging Byron's seduction of Lady Frances (Figure 3.4). When this letter reached Lady Melbourne at Brocket Hall in Hertfordshire in October 1813, Byron was enmeshed in intense, problematic affairs with two other married women. One of them – let this sink in – was the wife of Lady Melbourne's own eldest surviving son (William Lamb), and the other – even more problematic – was Byron's half-sister, Augusta Leigh. Both women mattered far more, and would cost Byron far more, than his "proselyte" in the billiards room in Yorkshire. Caroline Lamb was Lady Melbourne's mercurial daughter-in-law (slim, elegant, creative, headstrong) who pursued Byron with a near-mania of attention, causing scenes both public and private, while he fed the flames with his own passionate declarations of love (Figure 3.5). Augusta Leigh, daughter of "Mad Jack" Byron by his first marriage, had known Byron since his Harrow years; and, in the summer of 1813, the two had begun a sexual affair that compelled and troubled him deeply. Both of these relationships would determine the course of Byron's life and reputation and would exert immediate and far-reaching influence on his poetry. And both form the subtext of his reckless and essentially comic pursuit of the lady of Aston Hall, lying just beneath the surface of Byron's vivacious narrative of events. Lady Melbourne wanted him to make use of Lady Frances as a transition away from these two damaging liaisons; and Byron himself knew that he had to find a way out, by either leaving England or marrying a wife of his own. Within a year, he was engaged to one of the women he mentions in this letter.

The story of Byron and Caroline Lamb has been told so often that it threatens to become a series of well-worn vignettes, the same stack of scenes shuffled and slipping through the biographer's hands. Clara Tuite calls it "one of the most celebrated but banal love affairs of Romanticism," an *amour fou* that left many traces and witnesses as the two high-profile lovers performed their devotions and agonies for one another, for their circle of intimates, and for the public.

As can be seen in this letter about Lady Frances, "scenes" were central to Byron's experience of romance, even as he claimed to hate histrionics; in another letter to Lady Melbourne, he wrote, "there is no comedy after all like real life." Caroline generated overheated scenes instinctively, whether slicing her hand open at a waltzing party after he snubbed her or (recalling the cross-dressed Caroline Cameron that Byron took with him to Brighton) smuggling herself into Byron's rooms disguised as a pageboy. Of this later episode, Byron recalled, "My valet, who did not see through the masquerade, let her in; when, to the despair of Fletcher [his valet], she put off the man, and put on the woman. Imagine the scene: it was worthy of Faublas!" Again, Byron is charmed by moments in which life imitates art – here a French libertine novel, *Les Amours du Chevalier de Faublas*, with its cross-dressing hero who seduces wives while dressed as a woman. Caroline Lamb was the ideal co-conspirator for a man who needed experiences to shimmer with the heightened reality of theatre or fiction; and her boyish looks and instinct for breeches-roles also spoke to the multiple channels of Byron's libido. Both of them pursued artifice so fervently, with such reckless commitment to its consequences, that they pushed through to the other side of the looking-glass and found themselves violently in love.

Caroline had cast herself in the role of romantic heroine from the outset, writing in her journal after meeting Byron that he was "Mad, bad, and dangerous to know," even as she summoned him to her with the follow-up notation, "That pale beautiful face is my fate." No stranger to acting a part, Byron readily took up the role of rakish and brooding lover, giving her a rose and a carnation with "a sort of half sarcastic smile" and the words, "Your Ladyship, I am told, likes all that is new and rare – for the moment." Their whole relationship at times seems to exist in quotation marks, constituted by the melodramatic, self-aware discourse of these two highly literate sophisticates. And yet, even at this distance, one can feel the heat of their brief union. Its urgency is perhaps most evident in the silences, the lack of words describing the long afternoons that they spent together in Caroline's private room on the second floor of Melbourne House, when their performances were only for themselves.

But for Caroline, romantic passion meant defying convention, exposing self, lover, and family to embarrassments that proved how far she was willing to go. A daughter of highest privilege, with much better family connections than Byron, the unstable Caroline was brought up to cultivate her own impulses, often damaging herself in her pursuit of extremity and abjection. As she wrote to Byron, "I lov'd you as no woman ever could love … more like a beast who sees no crime in loving & following its Master – you became such to me – Master of my soul." Her husband, William Lamb, was complaisant and had lovers of his own; but Caroline courted scandal by flaunting the affair with Byron, clinging to him in public, insisting she be driven in his carriage, and even waiting for him outside in the street at parties to which she hadn't been invited. Buffeted by her indiscreet performances, Byron soon was the one urging prudence, "tiresome enough but one *must* maintain it." As he wrote to her, "Then your heart – my poor Caro, what a little volcano! that pours lava through your veins…. You know I have always thought you the cleverest, most agreeable, absurd, amiable, perplexing, dangerous, fascinating little being that lives now, or ought to have lived 2000 years ago." That list of adjectives is mostly complimentary, but it foreshadows Byron's exhaustion, his sense that he was losing control of the narrative and didn't like it. Amid their ongoing power struggle, he demanded that Caroline swear she loved him more than her husband. When she refused, he exploded: "My God, you shall pay for this. I'll wring that obstinate little heart." He was tangling with the volcano.

In August 1812, worried that she was losing Byron, Caroline returned a golden locket in which she enclosed clippings of her pubic hair and a note telling him, "I will kneel & be torn from your feet before I will give you up," and signed "Caroline Byron … your wild antelope." A few days later, she fled from Melbourne House after being chastised by her father-in-law for her ongoing shameful conduct. Her mother and Lady Melbourne immediately sought her at Byron's apartments, but she had not come there. Promising to help find her, Byron wrote later that day to Lady Melbourne to accept his leading role in this act of the tragicomic romance: "As I am one of the principal performers in this unfortunate drama, I should be glad to know what my part requires next?" When Caroline sent him a letter, Byron followed the messenger to find her hiding in a surgeon's house in Kensington, with plans to leave the country. Through a combination of entreaties and force, he returned her to her forgiving husband and relieved family, who left with her for Ireland soon thereafter. Shaken by these events, Byron determined to end the affair for good; but it wasn't so easy. In his letter of farewell, he assured her that he "would with pleasure give up all here & all beyond the grave for you." And by the breathless postscript, he had talked himself back into the role of Caroline's true love: "I was and am *yours*, freely & most entirely, to obey, to honour, love – & fly with you when, where, & how you yourself *might & may* determine." And so the relationship spiraled on at a distance, as these two dangerous romantics provoked one another in letters and messages.

Many of these letters were triangulated through Lady Melbourne herself, who was corresponding with both Caroline and Byron and enjoying her role as devious confidante and double agent. In part, she was pulling the puppet strings in an attempt to orchestrate an end to the affair. But she also relished drama for its own sake: she would purposefully leave Byron's confidential letters in Caroline's way, knowing Caro would read them and become enraged at Byron's news of his latest love interests, or at his conniving to keep her away. Byron would then forward Caroline's reproaches to him back to Lady Melbourne with ironic commentary. In a dizzying escalation, these three-way epistolary exchanges were *themselves* the subject of extensive gossip in Whig society, with no less than the Prince Regent "telling the whole history of Caro" to a circle of people and remarking to Lady Bessborough, "I have never heard of such a thing in my life, taking Mothers for confidantes! What would you have thought of my going to talk to Lady Spencer [i.e., Lady Bessborough's mother] in former times!" To modern eyes especially, there remains something unrecognizable in the amoral intimacies of the Regency *ton*, starkly visible in the letters of Byron to Lady Melbourne. As Peter Cochran observes, "To carry on a long correspondence with a woman whose son you've been cuckolding may seem extreme; but neither Byron nor [Lady] Melbourne seems inhibited by the thought."

Byron was at the height of his early fame in London. The Duchess of Devonshire wrote to her son, "[*Childe Harold*] is on every table, and himself courted, visited, flattered, and praised whenever he appears. He has a pale, sickly, but handsome countenance, a bad figure, animated and amusing conversation, and in short, he is really the only topic almost of conversation – the men jealous of him, the women of each other." By September, he was in the midst of a slow-burning conversation with Annabella Milbanke, Lady Melbourne's niece, a strong-minded and fastidious young woman who, against her own better judgment, had become fascinated by Byron after speaking with him at a party at Lady Gosford's that spring. At one point, he had said to her with conspiratorial bitterness, "Do you think there is one person here who dares look into himself?" Recalling that evening later, Annabella would write, "I felt that he was the most attractive person.... but I was not *bound* to him by any strong feeling of sympathy till he uttered these words, not to me, but in my hearing – 'I have not a friend in the world!'" She added, "I vowed in secret to be a devoted friend to this lone being." Playing up the Childe Harold persona, Byron tempted Annabella to redeem him, a task she found almost irresistible.

Meanwhile, staying in the spa town of Cheltenham, Byron was toying with a "dark and lively" married opera singer, who spoke "nothing but Italian – a great point ... the very sound of that language is music to me, and she has black eyes, and *not* a very white skin, and reminds me of many in the Archipelago I wished to forget, and makes me forget what I ought to remember." The unspoken name is Nicolo Girard, Byron's lover, who taught him Italian in Athens: the opera singer's voice was leading him away from his supposed pursuit of marriage, back to Greece and the easy homosexuality of those days. Such dreams would have a great influence over the later stages of Byron's life, and, in some ways, this unnamed Italian songstress prefigures his most important lover, the Countess Teresa Guiccioli. However, there was one problem: the opera singer triggered Byron's lifelong phobia about watching women eat. No stranger to disordered eating, often starving himself on biscuits and water to lose weight, he wrote to Lady Melbourne, "I only wish she did not swallow so much supper, chicken wings – sweetbreads, – custards – peaches & *Port* wine," adding with a dandy's flourish, "a woman should never be seen eating or drinking, unless it be *lobster sallad & Champagne*, the only truly feminine & becoming viands."

By the autumn of 1813, Byron was requesting Lady Melbourne's "advice how to untie two or three 'Gordion knots' tied round me," punning on his last name and admitting that "some are rather closely twisted round my heart," even as Caroline Lamb was wondering to him plaintively "why a few conversations with the Queen Mothers always change you." The truth is that Byron was extremely adaptable to his audiences, playing roles in a kind of deadly serious method-acting that became, for an interval, his real state of mind. With Lady Melbourne, he was writing his way toward dismissing Caroline for good, even as he sent soothing missives to his "wild antelope." In so doing, he was developing his talent as a writer whose fame would depend on the personae he inhabited in language, producing so many refracted versions of himself. In his letters to Caroline and Lady Melbourne both, Byron was projecting his dangerous Childe Harold charm, a mixture of vulnerability, passion, and witty intimacy. Lord Melbourne observed ruefully that Byron had "bewitch'd the whole family Mothers & daughter & all" with his chaotic and seductive presence. As this chapter's letter from Aston Hall confirms, inviting Byron into your household – whether in person or via his writing – was a risky move.

Let's return to our October evening in Yorkshire and to Byron's intrigues among the Websters, and recall the scene in the billiard room. It centers on the delivery of a love letter, passed from Byron to Lady Frances under the very nose of her husband, who enters the room just after she has slipped the paper down the front of her dress "not very far from the heart," Byron writes, "which I wished it to reach." Written "in tender & tolerably turned *prose* periods," this letter is an agent of seduction, the intimate reception of which proves its success: "*she* kept her countenance & the paper," and, in those zeugmatic acts of concealment, betrays her husband. Keeping the paper, she loses her virtue – or at any rate, signals her openness to Byron's advances. "My billet prospered" and "produced an *answer*," he writes: the fevered exchange of letters continues, interrupted only by Webster himself who brings Byron "a political pamphlet in M.S. to decypher & applaud." Of the Aston Hall weeks, Byron later wrote, "the most amusing part was the interchange of notes – for we sat up all night scribbling to each other – & came down like Ghosts in the morning." Byron and Frances would then pass their notes in books or behind backs while Webster looked on unaware. There was much exchanging of paper, each document an index of the evolving relationships between Byron and both Websters, and all reported to Lady Melbourne in a letter that begins "I have volumes" and ends with a worry that Caroline will "repeat the last year's epistle & make it *circular* among my friends" – that is, go public with her letters of complaint against Byron. From this vantage, Byron's world seems made of paper, of the written and printed pages that constitute the record of his life.

Letters of love and gossip were not the only things Byron was writing during this period. In fact, by the time he was passing notes to Lady Frances, he already had another bestseller on his hands: *The Giaour*, a narrative poem of passion, betrayal, and murder set in Ottoman Greece, for which his publisher John Murray offered him the huge sum of 1,000 guineas (which Byron, as an aristocrat, declined to accept). This was the first of what would come to be known as Byron's Turkish Tales, which, like *Childe Harold's Pilgrimage*, drew upon Byron's travels in the Levant and offered further elaborations of the Byronic hero: a heedless, melancholy figure, haunted by loss and his own crimes of passion. *The Giaour* tells a story of doubled revenge, set against the backdrop of Turkish–Venetian conflict over the control of Greece. A nameless young Venetian nobleman has become the lover of Leila, the favorite wife of the Turkish emir, Hassan. Discovering her betrayal, Hassan has her sewn into a sack and drowned. Arriving too late to save her, the Giaour – that name, a Turkish slur for a non-believer in Islam – ambushes and murders Hassan. In the aftermath, he retreats to a monastery on Mount Athos, haunted by thoughts of Leila and his own guilty rage.

The Giaour had its origins in Byron's personal experience: while in Athens, so the story was told, he had rescued a young Turkish woman in similar circumstances. Encountering a procession of men carrying out just such an execution, Byron drew a pistol and demanded they all return to the Governor's house, where "partly by personal threats, and partly by bribery and entreaty," he had the girl transported safely to Thebes. Byron said this "was not very far from the truth," and that he was "nearly and deeply interested" in the event. Along these lines, some have suggested that Byron had been her lover and the cause of her condemnation in the first place. But the whole episode is shrouded in mystery, and the letter from Byron's friend Lord Sligo narrating the event has ten lines struck out in heavy ink, making them unreadable.

As Byron wrote darkly in his journal of "the Turkish girl's *aventure* at Athens," "to describe the *feelings* of *that situation* were impossible – it is *icy* even to recollect them." And yet such was his choice of subject for *The Giaour*.

Not only did *The Giaour* draw upon Byron's tumultuous experiences in Ottoman Athens (and anticipate his role as an honorary Venetian several years later), it was also fueled by thoughts of his relationship with Caroline Lamb. "Her treachery was truth to me," says the Giaour of Leila, who flees from husband to lover disguised "In the likeness of a Georgian page," just as Caroline had done when she came cross-dressed to Byron's rooms. And the Giaour says his blood "was like the lava flood / The boils in AEtna's breast of flame," an image borrowed from his "little volcano" letter. By the time *The Giaour* was written in the fall of 1812, their affair was mostly in its extended aftermath, having become a source of regret and guilt. In the poem's most famous image, Byron compares his mind to a "Scorpion girt by fire," driven in desperation to sting itself to death as the flames close in:

> The mind that broods o'er guilty woes
> Is like the Scorpion girt by fire
> ... So writhes the mind by conscience riven
> Unfit for earth, undoom'd for heaven,
> Darkness above, despair beneath,
> Around it flame, within it death!

Yet we should be wary of taking Byron's poetry as an unmixed confessional: he began writing *The Giaour* in the fashionable English spa town of Cheltenham, where he had already embarked on a new love affair with another married woman.

Jane Harley, Countess of Oxford (Figure 3.6) was fourteen years older than Byron and the mother of six children, all understood to be of various paternal origins (and thus waggishly referred to as the "Harleian Miscellany"). She was intelligent, warmhearted, and attractive, and politically engaged with the radical-reform wing of the Whig party, yet with a gentle temper that Byron welcomed as a contrast to Caroline Lamb's histrionics. Soon after the affair began, Byron left Cheltenham to join the Oxfords at their country seat, traveling in December 1812 through the Wye Valley to Eywood, a remote estate of luxury and quiet near the Welsh border. Deep in the wilds of Herefordshire, and with Caroline Lamb safely distant in Ireland, Byron could relax in what he called "the bowers of Armida," an allusion to the enchanted lovers' garden in Tasso's epic poem, *Jerusalem Delivered*. He spent the winter and most of the following spring there, writing *The Giaour* and indulging in the contentment of his situation, which included playing games with the Harley children. His favorite was Charlotte, then aged 12, to whom he dedicated the vaguely creepy lyric "To Ianthe," placed at the front of all future editions of *Childe Harold*: "Young Peri of the West! – 'tis well for me / My years already doubly number thine; / My loveless eye unmov'd may gaze on thee, / And safely view thy ripening beauties shine." As with his days at Harrow and his time among the schoolboys in the Athens convent, Byron had found a substitute family heavily laden with erotic possibilities. In fact, the whole Eywood scene appealed to the domestic longings that Byron cherished despite his fundamental restlessness. In January, with Lord Oxford away on business, Byron wrote to Lady Melbourne (who was by now jealous of Byron's new relationship), "It is snowing perfect Avalanches, & when we shall get away Jove knows." In this mood of pagan indulgence, Lady Oxford and Byron compared themselves to "the gods of Lucretius": deities happily distant from the struggles of the human world, living in blissful self-absorption. When a letter from Caroline arrived pleading for a lock of Byron's hair, the poet with casual cruelty sent a clipping from the head of his new mistress, enclosing it in an envelope fastened with Lady Oxford's wax seal: more social media, more epistolary damage. Especially as Lady Oxford had been Caroline's friend and confidante, the wound cut deep. Soon thereafter, Caroline started calling Byron himself "the Giaour" – the faithless one.

In keeping with the high theatricality of the affair with Byron, Caroline's immediate revenge was a symbolic ritual of her own. Back at Brocket Hall, she burnt an effigy of him, along with books, a ring, a chain, locks of hair, and *copies* of Byron's letters, while village girls in white dresses danced around the fire, intoning curses. She also ordered new buttons for the jackets of her pages' livery, having them (as well as a locket containing Byron's miniature portrait) inscribed with a negation of the Byron family motto: "*Ne* Crede Byron" ("*Don't* Trust Byron"). These antics were laughable at a distance, but when Byron returned to London in the late spring of 1813, he knew he would become entangled again with Caroline, who wrote to him in April with threats of revenge. Byron replied coldly, "You say you will '*ruin me*' – I thank you – but I have done that for myself already." Then, at an infamous party at Lady Heathcote's in July, "a scene occurred," as Byron put it, "which was in the mouth of everyone." As Caroline told the story,

> I clasped a knife, not intending anything. "Do, my dear," [Byron] said. "But ... mind which way you strike with your knife – be it at your own heart, not mine – you have struck there already." "Byron," I said, and ran away with the knife.

I never stabbed myself ... people pulled to get it away from me; I was terrified; my hand got cut, & the blood came over my gown. I know not what happened after.

Tragedy or farce, this was first-rate social theatre. Byron claimed to Lady Melbourne the next day that he was "totally ignorant of all that passed" regarding "this cursed scarification," but many assumed his ill treatment had caused it.

Byron would later relay this knife anecdote to his first biographer, Thomas Medwin (ensuring its circulation ever after), adding two sequels. First, Caroline promised Henry Grattan, a young Irish politician and (according to Byron) "a great villain & her particular protege," her "favours" if he would challenge Byron to a duel. When nothing came of that, she invaded Byron's apartments. As he told Medwin, "I was from home; but finding 'Vathek' on the table, she wrote in the first page, 'Remember me!'" In light of Caroline's promise to "ruin" and "destroy" Byron, her choice of *Vathek* may well have been a threat: the novel's author, William Beckford, was a wealthy, bisexual man who, in the face of scandal, had chosen self-exile. Byron wrote of him in a canceled stanza of *Childe Harold*, "thou wert smitten with unhallowed thirst / Of nameless crime." Caroline knew Byron's similar sexual tastes and experiences, and she seems to have been reminding him of the power this knowledge gave her. Enraged, Byron grabbed a pen and wrote under her inscription,

> "Remember thee," nay – doubt it not –
>   Thy Husband too may '*think*' of thee!
> By neither canst thou be forgot,
>   Thou false to him – thou fiend to me!

> "Remember thee"? Yes – yes – till Fate
> In Lethe quench the guilty dream.
> Yet then – e'en then – Remorse and *Hate*
> Shall vainly quaff the vanquished stream.

Byron's poem speaks with the voice of the damned, of a man tormented by the false fiend and cursed with eternal Remorse and Hate, unable to quench them in Lethe, the river of forgetfulness in Hades. This infernal lyric reply would become, in effect, Byron's last letter to Caroline, left unsent and unseen until Medwin published it after the poet's death, when his shade was already in the underworld. Reading Medwin in 1824, Caroline would call the poem "a bitter legacy" and "a dreadful legacy on me – [and] my memory." But for now, her work of revenge was just beginning. As Byron recognized, "she will never rest until she has destroyed me in some way or other." Self-destruction was also on the table: Caroline wrote to Murray in 1814, hearing rumors that Byron was looking for a wife, "I really believe that when that day comes, I shall buy myself a pistol at Mantons & stand before the Giaour and his legal wife & shoot myself, saying ... as I must not live for him, I will die."

The ongoing drama starring Byron as the faithless Giaour and Caro as the "false fiend" or "little Mania" (another of his nicknames for her) was prelude and partial background to Byron's seduction of Lady Frances Webster, which he pursued as a new distraction, a fresh effort to cleave that "Gordion" knot that Caroline had tied around him. But by October 1813, as Byron was stealing moments in the billiard room at Aston Hall, a deeper and more hazardous relationship had overtaken him. That summer, around the time of Caroline's "scarification" at Lady Heathcote's ball, he had begun a sexual affair with his half-sister, Augusta Leigh.

The wife of George Leigh (her cousin) and mother of three young children, Augusta reconnected with Byron after years of separation. They had first met when Byron was 15 and she 20, and they had corresponded at intervals since then. But now Byron found himself drawn to his father's daughter in a new way. He began spending time at Six Mile Bottom, the Leigh home near Newmarket, attracted to its atmosphere of domesticity and eroticism – just as he had been at Eywood with Lady Oxford and her children. The orphan was still seeking a substitute family, and Augusta *was* family, someone who united the roles of sister, mother, and wife in his imagination. They shared silly jokes and inside references, and Byron relished her easygoing and gentle manner with him, even as he savored the illicit, sinful aspect of their union. He would write in 1814, "As for my A – my feelings towards her – are a mixture of good & diabolical – I hardly know one passion which has not some share in them…. It is indeed a very trieste and extraordinary business – & what is to become of us I know not – and I won't think just now." Soon Augusta was accompanying Byron to balls and soirées in London, and it was obvious to others (including the sharp-eyed Caroline Lamb, as well as Byron's friends Hobhouse, Kinnaird, and Moore) that theirs was a romantic attachment. Byron also began dropping obvious hints in his letters to Lady Melbourne. Once again, he was steering directly, recklessly, into the storm – "the careful pilot," he would later write in a poem to Augusta, "of my proper woe."

As the affair progressed, Byron began making large additions to *The Giaour*, and the poem more than doubled in size from its first edition to its seventh, which was published in December. Byron referred to the work as his "snake of a poem – which has been lengthening its rattles every month."

Much of this expansion had to do with Augusta. As he wrote to Lady Melbourne in September, "Your opinion of ye. Giaour or rather ye. Additions honours me highly – you who know how my thoughts were occupied when these last were written – will perhaps perceive in parts a coincidence in my own state of mind with that of my hero…. I have tried & hardly too to vanquish my demon – but to very little purpose." *Childe Harold's Pilgrimage* may have inaugurated the idea of the Byronic hero, but here we see the raised-stakes elaboration of that avatar, drawn from Byron's "own state of mind" as it is animated by a "demon," in the midst of emotional chaos. "If ever evil angel bore / The form of mortal, such he wore," says one observer of the Giaour, who confesses,

> I grant *my* love imperfect—all
> That mortals by the name miscall—
> Then deem it evil—what thou wilt—
> But say, oh say, *hers* was not guilt!

In other lines added at this time, he calls his beloved Leila (now standing for Augusta), "My good, my guilt, my weal, my woe," and exclaims, "Tis all too late—thou wert—thou art / The cherished madness of my heart!" And so on, for many effusive lines that bring Augusta very close to the surface of the poem. This mode of writing, both confessional and encrypted, intimate and theatrical, dangerously revealing yet deeply duplicitous, was moving to the center of Byron's art, even as he recognized that self-betrayal and self-deception were basic to its procedures. Poems such as *The Giaour* and *The Bride of Abydos* (another Turkish tale written around this time, featuring an Augusta character at its center) are both "passionate" and "fake," with endless layers of quotation marks around both of those terms. It's unnerving, especially for those readers who know the biographical context and can perceive the emotional sources, personal costs, and fundamental iciness of this kind of writing. After reading another poem in this style (one that we will encounter in the next chapter), William Wordsworth wrote, "Let me say one word upon Lord B. The man is insane."

James Wedderburn Webster's invitation to Aston Hall had come as Byron was casting about for his next move and thinking seriously of going abroad to escape the chaos he had created. Webster was a cavalry officer and former boxing and drinking companion of Byron's from his Cambridge years, "a profligate fool" who earned the nickname "Bold Webster" both for his athleticism and for his narcissism; his biographer calls him "arguably the most offensive, despised, and ridiculed dandy of the Regency period." Byron counted Webster among his friends, and yet he frequently lost patience with him and also clearly enjoyed casting him in roles that amplified his foolishness. As he told Lady Melbourne, "all foolish fellows are alike – but [Webster] has a patent for his cap & bells." At first, Byron adopted the role of satiric observer of Webster and his new wife Frances, noting to Lady Melbourne that he "is passionately fond of having his wife admired – & at the same time jealous to jaundice of every thing & every body.... Every now & then he has a fit of fondness – & kisses her hand before his guests – which she receives with the most lifeless indifference – which struck me more than if she had appeared pleased or annoyed." Even just a few days before the billiard-room scene, Byron was claiming that

> never in word or deed – did I speculate upon his spouse –
> nor did I ever see much in her to encourage either hope
> or much fulfillment of hope – supposing I had any. – She

is pretty but not surpassing – too thin – & not very animated – but good tempered – & a something interesting
enough in her manner & figure – but … I have neither the
patience nor presumption to advance till met half-way.

You can hear Byron talking himself into a new attitude
toward Lady Frances as he writes; soon the game was afoot –
particularly after Augusta declined an invitation to join the
party.

Over the next two weeks, Byron and the Websters, along
with several other friends, moved back and forth from Aston
Hall to Newstead Abbey, about 30 miles distant. Byron was
angling to get Lady Frances onto his home turf, where he
felt he could manage their burgeoning affair more easily. Yet
behind the calculation and rakish irony of his letters, emotional tempests were shaking Byron apart. Lady Frances's
sister remembered observing him at Aston Hall one morning, unseen herself, as he stood "alone near the fire … perfectly *convulsed*" with sobbing tears. Meanwhile, Webster
was abetting his own betrayal, pursuing "a foolish nymph of
the Abbey" (one of Byron's serving girls) and boasting to the
men of his prowess *and* his wife's fidelity in ways that goaded
Byron on. Further, Webster had a vicious side that came out
at Newstead, when, at breakfast one morning, as Byron tells
it, "he attacked both the girls [Lady Frances and her sister] in
such a manner – no one knew why or wherefore – that on my
arrival I found one had left the room – & the other had half a
mind to leave the house – this too before servants & the other
guest!" Faced with these humiliations, Lady Frances began to
bend further toward Byron, and soon came the moment, in a
darkened room at Newstead, "the hour two in the morning –
[Webster] away," when she told Byron, "I am entirely at your

mercy – I own it – I give myself up to you … now act as you will." But Byron demurred: "was I wrong? – I spared her," in a strange moment of forbearance that he had trouble understanding himself. The following night, he drank an entire bottle of Claret "at *one draught*" from his monk's skull cup, "and nearly died the death of Alexander." Disturbed by the intense scenes he had been enacting, half in love with several women, struggling with his own mixed sexual preferences, Byron was "very feverish – restless – and silent," offering to run away with Lady Frances but also very clearly lost: "What a cursed situation I have thrust myself into," he wrote to Lady Melbourne.

Byron saw three paths of escape: poetry, travel, and marriage. During a single week in November, "stans pede in uno" ("standing on one foot"), he wrote *The Bride of Abydos*, a narrative poem of over a thousand lines, detailing the passionate and tragic romance of Selim and Zuleika. In his journal, he confided, "the composition of it kept me alive – for it was written to drive my thoughts from the recollection of – [quoting Alexander Pope] 'Dear sacred name, rest ever unreveal'd,'" adding a few days later, "It was written in four nights to distract my dreams from **.... had I not done something at the time, I must have gone mad, by eating my own heart, – bitter diet!" Lady Frances, now parted from Byron, wrote to him when she read it, "Zuleika, perhaps thy fate may ere long be mine – Dearest Byron, art thou still my Selim?" She had already written in a previous letter, quoting *The Giaour*, "Thou art the cherished madness of my heart," channeling her love for Byron through his heroes. But Byron's passion for her was already fading. Zuleika, who begins the poem thinking Selim is her half-brother, was modeled more closely on Augusta, even as the poem reflects the pain and hopelessness of both affairs. Byron planned to publish *The Bride of Abydos* in December and leave for Holland at the same moment, writing to Augusta in late November, "I must run down & bring you up next week to say a thousand farewells."

When his travel plans fell through, Byron settled down for the winter in London and rapidly wrote (in ten days) another quasi-confessional verse tale – *The Corsair* ("written *con amore*, and much from *existence*"), while casting about for a proper spouse. He wrote sardonically in his journal in January 1814, "A wife would be my salvation. I am sure the wives of my acquaintances have hitherto done me little good." Writing to Lady Melbourne that same month, he dismissed the Lady Frances affair, saying "I was the fool of her whimsical romance." He resumed his correspondence with Lady Melbourne's niece, the mathematically minded, well born, and highly eligible Annabella Milbanke, "the little demure Nonjuror" of this chapter's letter. Even as he deepened his connection with Augusta, snowed up together at Newstead for weeks as his twenty-sixth birthday passed, Byron began slowly turning toward a relationship he hoped would bring clarity and harmony to the troubled scenes of his personal life. Maybe the incipient tragedy could be headed off with a comic resolution. Maybe Annabella would be his redemption.

4

—— ◇ ——

Fare Thee Well!

[13 Piccadilly Terrace, London]

[To Lady Byron]   February 8th, 1816

All I ~~have~~ can say seems useless—and all I could say—
might be no less unavailing—yet I still cling to the wreck
of my hopes—before they sink forever.— —Were you then
never happy with me?—did you never at any time or times
express yourself so?—have no marks of affection—of the
warmest & most reciprocal attachment passed between
us?—or did in fact hardly a day go down without some
such on one side and generally on both?—do not mistake
me—[two lines crossed out] I have not denied my state of
mind—but you know its causes—& were those deviations
from calmness never followed by acknowledgement &
repentance?—was not the last which occurred more particularly so?—& had I not—had we not—the days before
& on the day when we parted—every reason to believe that
we loved each other—that we were to meet again—were not
your letters kind?—had I not acknowledged to you ~~the~~ all
my faults & follies—& assured you that some had not—&
would not be repeated?—I do not require these questions to
be answered to me—but to your own heart.— — — —

The day before I received your father's letter—I had fixed a day for rejoining you—if I did not write lately—Augusta did—and as you had been my proxy in correspondence with her—so did I imagine—she might be the same for me to you.—Upon your letter to me—this day—I surely may remark—that its expressions imply a treatment which I am incapable of inflicting—& you of imputing to me—if aware of their latitude—& the extent of the inferences to be drawn from them.—This is not just— —but I have no reproaches—nor the wish to find cause for them.— — — —

Will you see me?—when & where you please—in whose presence you please:—the interview shall pledge you to nothing—& I will ~~be~~ say & do nothing to agitate either— it is torture to correspond thus—& there are things to be settled & said which cannot be written.— — —

You say "it is my disposition to deem what I have worthless"—did I deem you so?—did I ever so express myself to you—or of you—to others?— —You are much changed within these twenty days or you would never have thus poisoned your own better feelings—and trampled upon mine.— —

ever yrs. most truly & affectionately

B

Picture a man on the edge of a cliff, unbalanced and about to fall. Each sentence and each quick dash of the pen is a flailing swipe of his hand, the action of someone now desperate for purchase on a life that he has been pushing away for months. In this letter, Byron asks a series of questions, demanding justice, cross-examining his primary witness, who is told to answer them to her "own heart": Weren't we ever happy? Weren't we often affectionate? When I hurt you, didn't I always say I was sorry? It's the letter of a baffled abuser – an attempt, at once frantic and cold, to turn up the gaslight and make Annabella return to him. But here, in the deserted rooms of their Piccadilly Terrace apartments, Byron's hands are grasping at empty air: his wife and infant daughter Ada (born less than two months ago) are gone, and they won't be coming back. He writes, "I still cling to the wreck of my hopes—before they sink forever." But he's the one sinking, falling off the edge with a precipitate momentum that his own cruelty has caused.

The day before, Annabella Milbanke – Lady Byron – had written to her husband from her father's house, "It is unhappily your disposition to consider what you have as worthless – what you have lost as invaluable." In this letter, Byron quotes those lines back to her, denying the charge, even as he admits that Annabella knows the causes of his recent state of mind. But does she? Does anyone, including Byron himself? On the surface, he may be alluding to his financial stresses (a bailiff was watching the Byron home at Piccadilly closely, attempting to collect debts), or to his heavy drinking, but the primary cause of Byron's increasingly alarming behavior was more obviously the presence of his half-sister Augusta, in his heart and in the lives of the married couple. For months, he had been flaunting his feelings for her, speaking of his love for her in lavish terms and darkly, persistently hinting at their sexual relationship. When Augusta was with them, Byron would stay up late with her, dismissing his wife with the words, "Now I have *her*, you will find I can do without *you* – in all ways." The Augusta problem was central and ongoing, yet ambiguous, and Byron's chaotic manipulations placed the two women in uneasy bondage that would last for decades. So there is something particularly ludicrous in Byron's defense here that Augusta had written to her in his stead: "as you had been my proxy in correspondence with her—so did I imagine—she might be the same for me to you." What a proposition, given their history, put forth either cynically or in a state of self-deception verging on the tragic, a compartmentalization that almost suggests a schizoid break.

A few weeks earlier, as Annabella had prepared to depart their home with the infant Ada, Byron had wryly quoted the witches in *Macbeth*, asking, "When shall *we* three meet again?" Annabella replied quietly, "In Heaven, I hope," and left the room. As she later recalled that last night in Piccadilly Terrace,

> I fell into a sound sleep ... as I believe is often surprisingly the case in such cases of deep sorrow. Next morning I woke exhausted. I went downstairs – the carriage was at the door. I passed his room. There was a large mat on which his Newfoundland dog used to lie. For a moment I was tempted to throw myself on it, and wait at all hazards, but it was only a moment – and I passed on.

In the cold morning air of a London January, Annabella pauses outside the door to Byron's bedroom. The carriage that will take her to Kirkby Hall, her parents' newly inherited home in Leicestershire, is already waiting in the street outside. Her luggage has been loaded, and little Ada is being bundled up by a lady's maid in preparation for the 100-mile journey north. But there's a moment of dolly-zoom vertigo as

Annabella gazes downward at the dog's mat, simultaneously drawn toward and repelled by that hard bed of refuge and surrender. Then, as she recalled, "I passed on."

When Byron wrote this anguished letter, he had only just realized that Annabella's departure some three weeks earlier was not merely a temporary parting. In early January, he had essentially ordered her to leave, expressing his intention of giving up the expensive Piccadilly apartments which they could no longer afford and possibly going abroad to avoid his creditors for a time, much like his father had done. But he had expected either to join her in Kirkby Mallory or to summon her when he had resettled elsewhere. Annabella had in fact encouraged this understanding, writing to him tenderly after her arrival at her parents' home, using their pet names for one another, "Dearest Duck – We got here quite well last night … Dad … and Mam long to have the family party completed…. If I were not always looking about for B, I should be a great deal better already for country air... Ever thy most loving, Pippin." But this mood of incipient welcome soon changed after Annabella conveyed the details of her treatment by Byron to her parents and advisors. The truth was that Annabella thought Byron had gone mad, and she was torn between treating him with love as a diseased invalid or fleeing from him as a cruel monster. Out of his reach and within the supportive circle of family and friends, she saw more clearly that this was a false distinction: "Disease or not," she wrote, Byron's "irritability is inseparably connected with me"; or, as she wrote to her plaintive husband, "remember that you believed yourself most miserable when I was yours." Under her parents' roof and encouraged by them to remain there, the morally upright Annabella decided that going back to Byron would be an indulgence of her own feelings at his expense: he did not want to be married to her, despite his protestations otherwise, and it was driving him to dangerous excesses. Augusta – writing from Piccadilly Terrace where she remained with Byron – pleaded with Annabella that "*your return* might be the *saving & reclaiming* of him." But the die was cast: on February 2, Sir Ralph Milbanke, Annabella's father, wrote to propose a permanent separation, citing concerns about his daughter's safety.

What had happened? How had it all gone so wrong? Whole books have been written on the Byron marriage, including, most notoriously, Harriet Beecher Stowe's 1870 bombshell, *Lady Byron Vindicated*, which revealed Byron's incest with Augusta to the shocked dismay of the Victorian reading public. Given the high profile of Lord and Lady Byron and the extensive paper trail left by them and their various friends, advisors, and family members, we have a great fund of anecdote and opinion to draw on. And yet the total narrative is elusive, perhaps as it would be for any relationship placed under such intense scrutiny by so many interested parties. The basic outline can be briefly told. Byron and Annabella met in April 1812 and courted almost exclusively through letters. After rejecting a first proposal, Annabella accepted a second, and the two were married on January 2, 1815. Almost immediately, Byron began tormenting his wife with threats and warnings regarding his past, alternating these, however, with episodes of tenderness and shared sexual enjoyment. Drinking heavily, continuing his intimacy with Augusta (who was often with the couple), sleeping with actresses at Drury Lane Theatre and performing a kind of manic, menacing paranoia at home, Byron seemed determined to ruin the marriage. He may have had a mental crisis or breakdown of some kind around this time. Soon after the birth of a daughter (Ada), Annabella left for good. But to understand how Byron's marriage and separation became the crucial double-jointed hinge of the poet's life, bending him at first toward domesticity and then to exile, we need to look more closely.

"I never saw a woman whom I *esteemed* so much": such was Byron's early confession to Lady Melbourne, not long after meeting her niece, Anne Isabella Milbanke (Annabella), in late March 1812 (Figure 4.1). It's not the most promising beginning. But Byron was looking for a proper wife, and aristocratic matches in Regency England were often based on far less – or rather, far more, in terms of cash. That too was part of Byron's calculation – despite claiming that he was unaware of Annabella's fortune, he knew she was the only child of wealthy, high-ranking, older parents: her father, Sir Ralph (the brother of Lady Melbourne) was in his mid-sixties. But she also tempted Byron as a young woman of intelligence, particularly in mathematics, and as someone with a strong moral center. Here was a romantic partner who had confidence in her own judgments and a fundamental stability, an appealing contrast to his own mercurial nature and the intense emotional chaos of Caroline Lamb. As Byron wrote to Lady Melbourne around this time,

> Miss M[ilbanke] I admire because she is a clever woman, an amiable woman & of high blood, for I have still a few Norman & Scotch prejudices on the last score, were I to marry. – As to Love, that is done in a week, (provided the Lady has a reasonable share) besides marriage goes on better with esteem & confidence than romance, & she is quite pretty enough to be loved by her husband, without being so glaringly beautiful as to attract many rivals ...

whomever I may marry, that is the woman I would wish
to have married.

It all sounds reasonable, complacent, and deeply self-
deceived. Perhaps not in the way he intended it, Byron would
get his wish.

For her own part, Annabella wrote to her mother after
her second meeting with Byron that she found him "very
handsome" and "certainly very interesting," but without
"that calm benevolence which could only touch my heart."
Yet she was already struggling to resist the allure of claiming
and reforming the notorious Childe Harold. The next letter
to her mother, dated April 16, 1812, is revealing on this score,
casting Byron as a fascinating "object of compassion":

> Lord B. is without exception of young or old more agreea-
> ble in conversation than any person I ever knew. Brilliant
> sense, in energetic & flowing language, softened at times
> by the more human feelings. He really is most truly an
> object of compassion. All his tender ties have been torn
> from his heart.... I think of him that he is a very bad, very
> good man. Impulses of sublime goodness burst through
> his malevolent *habits.*

That underscoring of "*habits*" tells us everything we need to
know: just weeks after meeting Byron, Annabella was determined to convince herself and others of his basic goodness,
of his capacity for redemption. A "very bad, very good man":
she wasn't exactly wrong. When the German phrenologist
Johann Spurzheim examined Byron's cranium in 1814, he
pronounced the poet's brain "very antithetical," an organ
in which "good & evil are at perpetual war." But Annabella
was also cautious. When Byron conveyed a hasty proposal of

marriage via Lady Melbourne in early October 1812, Annabella turned him down, determined "not to yield to any decided preference till my Judgment has been Strengthened by longer observation." She would spend the next year corresponding with Byron, taking her time and sounding him out.

With her rejection of the marriage proposal, Annabella also sent her aunt a sketch of Byron's character, which is both accurate in its own right and revealing of her way of seeing him. She observed,

> The passions have been his guide from childhood, and have exercised a tyrannical power over his very superior Intellect…. There is a chivalrous generosity in his ideas of love & friendship, and selfishness is totally absent from his character … but from the strangest perversion that pride ever created, he endeavours to disguise the best points of his character…. [H]is mind is continually making the most sudden transitions – from good to evil, from evil to good. A state of such perpetual tumult must be attended with the misery of restless inconsistency.

There is willed sympathy in Annabella's portrait, a desire to think the best of Byron, whose character certainly did have "selfishness" in fairly large admixture – as she would learn to her cost. But in this short sketch, taken from life after only a few meetings, we can see most of the main strands of Byron's personality: his self-damaging passions, his social deceptions, his proud perversities, and his fundamental changeability. Lost boy, cruel rake, selfless friend, evil angel, dearest Duck: Annabella had already glimpsed the many Byron versions to which she would have to minister and which, ultimately, would break her heart.

Byron received Annabella's rejection of the marriage idea with apparent good humor and equanimity, writing to Lady Melbourne, "I thank you again for your efforts with my Princess of Parallelograms, who has puzzled me more than the Hypothenuse…. Her proceedings are quite rectangular, or rather we are two parallel lines prolonged to infinity side by side but never to meet." Embarking immediately thereafter on his satisfying affair with Lady Oxford, he remarked, "I congratulate A[nnabella] & myself on our mutual escape. – That would have been but a *cold collation*, & I prefer hot suppers." As we saw in the previous chapter, Byron had his hands full, and Annabella receded into the background of his life for a time. Soon after his twenty-fifth birthday in January 1813, he began planning to go abroad, back to the Levant, and was trying to sell Newstead Abbey or his coalfields in Rochdale or both, in order to settle his massive debts. The affair with Lady Oxford lasted until June, and Byron was shuttling back and forth between the Oxfords' home at Eywood and his St. James apartments in London, fending off Caroline Lamb and writing *The Giaour*, the first of his "Turkish" verse-romances featuring a darkly passionate, emotionally wounded hero – poems (especially *The Corsair* and *The Bride of Abydos*) that would greatly amplify his popularity. As Byron describes the doomed outlaw hero of *The Corsair*, his name was "Linked with one virtue" – (love) – "and a thousand crimes." The Byronic hero was coming into his own.

Along with *Childe Harold's Pilgrimage*, Byron's Turkish Tales were commentaries upon the geopolitics of early nineteenth-century Europe: in the poems, tyranny defeats love, fathers betray sons, the old order collapses but drags the new one down with it. The pervading sense of gloom and failure reflects Byron's experiences on the political stage in

England. In June, he gave what would be his final speech in the House of Lords, abandoning any ideas of a traditional political career soon thereafter. From the start, Byron's allegiances had been shaped by his involvement with prominent statesmen and politicians of the Whig party in opposition, beginning with his Cambridge friends (including Hobhouse and Kinnaird) and continuing, during these years of fame in London, via his association with the Holland House circle of Whigs loyal to the legacy of Charles James Fox. Fox was the legendary liberal opponent of Pitt and George III in the generation just before Byron's. Animated by ideas of liberty, republicanism, and human rights, Fox had been a defender of the French Revolution, even after the Reign of Terror, and he had championed Napoleon and opposed Britain's war with France. These views came to seem increasingly radical as the war went on, and they essentially broke the Whig party in two. By the time Byron appeared on the political scene in 1812, the Foxites had become a more or less radical minority opposing the conservative government under Lord Liverpool. Byron, long a fan of Napoleon and disdainful of the monarchy, fell in naturally with Lord Holland (Fox's nephew) and the elite Whig society that he and Lady Holland gathered to them. As a result, Byron's political views were nurtured in this environment of heated and essentially hopeless liberal opposition to the hugely dominant conservative forces in British politics at that time.

As a hereditary member of the peerage, Byron was entitled to occupy a seat in the House of Lords, a privilege he had taken up in 1812. He gave only three speeches, all in support of Whiggish liberal and democratic causes. In his maiden address, on February 27, 1812, Byron led the debate over how the British government should respond to the Luddite rebellion in his home county of Nottinghamshire. Textile weavers had smashed new, more efficient machines that were replacing them in their jobs, and the government intended to make this a capital crime. Byron spoke passionately against this extreme penalty for the frame-breakers, pointing to "the most unparalleled distress" of "these miserable men" driven by "absolute want" to acts of destructive protest, and asking, "will you erect a gibbet in every field & hang up men like scarecrows?" To pass the bill, he argued, "would only be to add injustice to irritation & barbarity to neglect." Despite his rhetoric, judged intemperate by other members of the House of Lords, the bill passed. The following year, seventeen convicted Luddites who had been involved with raids and riots were executed at York, a sentence that the Tory Home Secretary Sidmouth said would have the "happiest effects in various parts of the kingdom." In April 1812, Byron gave his second speech, supporting Catholics being given equal protections and privileges under the law, and promoting the rights of Ireland within the United Kingdom. This bill failed to pass. Finally, in the midst of his affair with the liberal, politically engaged Lady Oxford, Byron spoke in 1813 in support of Major Cartwright, "whose long life has been spent in one unceasing struggle for the liberty of the people" – a man whom Andrew Nicholson calls "the politically embarrassing, indefatigable grand old father of reform," who was objecting to harassment by government officials. The house refused to accept or discuss the petition.

These failures in the House of Lords were to be expected, given the Tory dominance of the government at the time. They squelched Byron's interest in the business of British politics, increasing his natural cynicism and causing him to withdraw from an active career in the government of the nation. In addition, by 1813 the writing was on the wall for Napoleon. Byron observed despondently in his journal, after Napoleon's defeat at Leipzig in October which signaled the beginning of the end of the war, that he had hoped "all this … was a prelude to greater changes and mightier events. But Men never advance beyond a certain point: – and here we are, retrograding to the dull, stupid old system … posing straws upon kings' noses, instead of wringing them off!" Yet, as the most popular poet of the day, Byron was not without political resources. His short lyric, "Lines to a Lady Weeping," caused an uproar among the Tories, especially after it was reprinted in Byron's massive bestseller *The Corsair*, in early 1814. The poem addresses Princess Charlotte, whom Byron observed crying as she listened to her father, the Prince Regent, insult the Whigs, his former allies. It begins, "Weep, daughter of a royal line, / A Sire's disgrace, a realm's decay." Of the Tory reaction, Byron wrote, "You can have no conception of the ludicrous solemnity with which those two stanzas have been treated," "such a clash of paragraphs and a conflict of Newspapers … the Regent (as reported) wroth – Ld. Carlile in a fury – the Morning Post in hysterics and the Courier in convulsions of criticism and contention…. I really begin to think myself a most important personage."

Meanwhile, Byron and Annabella sent letters back and forth, slowly rebuilding their friendship in the wake of the marriage proposal. And it's worth noting that Annabella read *Pride and Prejudice* around this time, calling it "a very superior work … the interest is very strong, especially for Mr. Darcy," whose second marriage proposal to the heroine famously succeeds. Soon after receiving her denial, Byron wrote to Annabella, "You told me you declined me as a lover but wished to retain me as a friend," accepting his new role and encouraging her to write to him. In that same letter, he spoke of his "very useless & ill regulated life," praised the female sex over the male ("they are all better than us"), and assured her that he hoped to "derive some benefit from your observations," drawing her into the role of valued advisor. He also gave her a taste of seductive Byronism: "The great object of life is Sensation – to feel that we exist – even though in pain – it is this 'craving void' which drives us to Gaming – to Battle – to Travel – to intemperate but keenly felt pursuits of every description whose principal attraction is the agitation inseparable from their accomplishment." He doesn't mention sexual intimacy in this list of "keenly felt pursuits," but he slyly suggests it by quoting a phrase – "craving void" – from Alexander Pope's poem of illicit love, "Eloisa to Abelard," in which Eloisa pleads,

> make me mistress to the man I love;
> If there be yet another name more free,
> More fond than mistress, make me that to thee!
> . . .
> All then is full, possessing, and possess'd,
> No craving void left aching in the breast

Byron knew that his philosophy of Sensation would rouse Annabella, both in disapproval and in interest. She wrote back to say she did not like his "restless doctrines," to which Byron replied, "I should be very sorry if *you* did – but I can't *stagnate* nevertheless – if I must sail let it be on the ocean no matter how stormy." He then went silent for several weeks, wrapped up in his pursuit of Lady Frances Webster (as detailed in our previous chapter), while Annabella read *The Giaour* and wrote to Byron twice. As she confessed to Lady Melbourne, "The description of Love [in *The Giaour*] almost makes me in love. Certainly he excels in the language of Passion." She was already beginning to regret her rejection of this fascinating, annoying young man.

In his private journal around this time, Byron noted that he had received "a very pretty letter from Annabella," going on to reflect,

> What an odd situation and friendship is ours! – without one spark of love on either side, and produced by circumstances which in general lead to coldness on one side, and aversion on the other. She is a very superior woman, and very little spoiled, which is strange in an heiress – a girl of twenty – a peeress that is to be, in her own right – an only child, and a savante, who has always had her own way. She is a poetess – a mathematician – a metaphysician, and yet, withal, very kind, generous, and gentle, with very little pretension. Any other head would be turned with half her acquisitions, and a tenth of her advantages.

This accounting of Annabella's strengths brings us back to Byron's "*esteem*" for her: their connection is one "without one spark of love on either side," and yet nevertheless he senses their mutual entanglement. And so the exchange of letters continued, as Byron went about his regular rounds of leisure, lovers, and literary pursuits. His planned journey to the East was delayed indefinitely, in part due to an outbreak of the plague in Malta and consequent quarantines in the Mediterranean. And, in any case, he was enjoying his fame in London, *The Corsair* having sold 10,000 copies on the day of its publication, "a thing perfectly unprecedented" according to his publisher John Murray. Friends John Cam Hobhouse, Scrope Davies, and Thomas Moore were back in London as well, and, in their company, Byron was pursuing the city's pleasures: theatre (especially the performances of Edmund Kean, whom he adored), clubs such as the Cocoa Tree, dinners, routs, and balls (at Lady Jersey's, Lady Lansdowne's, Lady Rancliffe's, and more), and boxing with his trainer, John "Gentleman" Jackson. He also wrote *Lara*, the last of his Turkish Tales, which was composed, he later recalled, "while undressing after coming home from balls and masquerades in the year of revelry 1814." At one of these balls (Lady Sitwell's), Byron observed a woman – Mrs Anne Wilmot – wearing a black, spangled dress, and, after returning home and toasting her beauty with a large glass of brandy, wrote his most famous lyric, which begins "She walks in beauty like the night / Of cloudless climes and starry skies." Strangers sent him fan letters, some suggesting secret meetings and assignations. He was in many ways at the height of his fame, supported by his most extensive circle of friends.

Yet over and above all of this was Byron's secret affair with Augusta Leigh, which was taking its toll on his nerves (Figure 4.2). He wrote in his journal in February 1814 (quoting two of Shakespeare's errant sufferers, Macbeth and King Lear), "I am not well; and yet I look in good health. At times, I fear, 'I am not in my perfect mind;' … 'I 'gin to be a-weary of the sun.'" And in a letter to Annabella written around this same time, he hinted at the fact that he was seriously thinking of running off with Augusta: "I am at present a little feverish. – I mean mentally – and as usual – on the brink of something or other – which will probably crush me at last – & cut our correspondence short with every thing else." He was just 26 years old, but he told Annabella he was "six hundred in heart – and in head & pursuits about six." Part of this is bad-boy boasting – I live fully, recklessly, feverishly – but Byron was struggling, "as usual--on the brink," on the extreme edge of a different cliff. Publicly declaring his passion for Augusta and living that truth would mean ruin for them both: social ostracism, exile, loss of friends, of his publisher, his readers, all.

Writing to Moore in April, Byron floated the idea of an end to his career and celebrity: "No more rhyme for – or rather, from – me. I have taken my leave of that stage, and henceforth will mountebank it no longer. I have had my day, and there's an end." This may have been prompted by Augusta's giving birth to a baby girl, Elizabeth Medora, that seems to have been fathered by Byron. As he wrote cryptically to Lady Melbourne around this time, the infant "is not an *Ape* and if it is – that must be my fault." Anticipating the backlash, Byron began shaking the dust of England from his shoes as well: "Why should I remain or care? – I am not – never was – nor can be popular.... I never won the world.... I am sadly sick of my present sluggishness – and I hate civilization." Napoleon's abdication and banishment to Elba didn't help matters, as Byron sank into a state of enervated depression. He admitted to Moore in late May 1814 that "indifference has frozen over the 'Black Sea' of almost all my passions" – all, that is, except his passion for Augusta.

In this flat, fatalistic, and anxious mood, Byron extended another proposal of marriage to Annabella Milbanke. He had written in August, "I did – do – and always shall love you," but it took another month of carefully circumspect letters between them before he raised the question: "There is something I wish to say ... Are the 'objections' to which you alluded insuperable? Or is there any line or change of conduct which could possibly remove them?" Already he was promising to change, to become a better man for her, even as he wrote this letter from Newstead, where he was residing with Augusta as his companion. Annabella replied breath-lessly, "I am and have long been pledged to myself to make your happiness my first object in life," confessing, "This is a moment of joy which I have too much despaired of ever experiencing – I *dared* not believe it possible." Byron passed her letter – which arrived as Byron and Augusta sat down to dinner – to his sister, saying, "It never rains but it pours." In a miraculous coincidence, a servant had just entered to report that his mother's long-lost wedding ring had been found in the garden: an omen, but of what? With Augusta's encourage-ment, Byron wrote back to Annabella, "Your letter has given me new existence," telling her, "I have ever regarded you as one of the first of human beings." And so they were engaged. Byron wrote immediately with the news to Lady Melbourne and Thomas Moore, telling each of them that he would now "reform thoroughly," trying to convince himself that he was ready to walk the path of matrimony. The next day, in a part of the Newstead estate known as the Devil's Wood, he and Augusta carved their names together on a tree, a monument and an incipient farewell (Figure 4.3).

Byron soon began to make plans to visit his new fiancée, whom he had not seen for almost a year. He finally arrived in early November at her parents' home in the small village of Seaham, on the coast near Durham (Figure 4.4). He had been delayed partly by his own hesitation and partly by making arrangements with his lawyer to settle £60,000 on Annabella at marriage, a handsome figure predicated on the pending sale of Newstead Abbey (which soon fell through, causing further hesitations). Annabella later recalled the scene of his belated arrival in cinematic detail:

> He had been expected for the two preceding days…. I was sitting in my room reading, when I heard the Carriage. I

put out the Candles, deliberated what should be done, re-solved to meet him first alone. It was so arranged. He was in the drawing room standing by the side of the Chim-ney-piece. He did not move forwards as I approached to-wards him, but took my extended hand & kissed it. I stood on the opposite side of the fireplace. There was a silence. He broke it. "It is a long time since we have met" – in an undertone. My reply was hardly articulate.

There's a palpable chemistry in that scene, but also a lot of reticence and well-founded fearfulness. The couple would dance around each other for the remainder of a fortnight, alternating between intimate walks along the seaside cliffs, awkward dinners with her overbearing parents, irritated exchanges that sent Annabella to her room, stolen kisses and caresses, and dark hints from Byron about his sinful past, which included lavish praise of his sister. At one point, Anna-bella offered to break off the engagement, which sent Byron into a fainting fit. It was a peculiar and anguished visit, but with just enough promise and mutual attraction to keep the engagement glued together. Byron wrote to Lady Melbourne from Seaham that he found Annabella "quite *caressable* into kindness ... but very *self*-tormenting – and anxious – and romantic," observing "we are too much alike – & then again too unlike," but concluding, "if there is a break – it shall be her doing not mine." He left in mid-November, and Byron and Annabella went back to exchanging love letters, both of them in many ways more comfortable in that medium than in the same room.

However, by now the wedding preparations had devel-oped a momentum of their own. Lady Melbourne was urging her niece to proceed without delay, and Annabella began pressing Byron to return, writing in early December,

"I have learned that I cannot enjoy anything without you" and lamenting "these long blank days!" He replied with wry and equivocal encouragement, "I have great hopes that we shall love each other all our lives as much as if we had never married at all." Meanwhile, Byron was savoring his last weeks of bittersweet bachelor freedom in London, attending Kean's performance of *Macbeth* and carousing with friends. After a night of heavy drinking with Tom Moore, he awoke "with my head in a whirlwind and my fingers bitten by my abominable parrot." Around this time, the pending sale of Newstead collapsed, and Byron wrote to his fiancée to suggest postponing the wedding. Her response was unequivocal: "there shall not be any delay to our marriage on account of these circumstances." Strong-willed, generous, and truly committed to Byron, Annabella came to their union with an open heart. She must have had her doubts about his constancy and his past, but she firmly intended to crush them.

Byron chose Hobhouse as his best man, and the pair set out from London on Christmas Eve, 1814. Byron stopped at Six Mile Bottom to spend Christmas with Augusta and her family, sending Hobhouse off to Cambridge for a few days. "Never was lover less in haste," observed Hobhouse, "The bridegroom more and more *less* impatient" to complete the journey back to Seaham. The two friends finally arrived in late December, to the relief of Annabella and her family. The next day, documents were signed, and rehearsal for the ceremony took place, with Hobhouse in the role of the bride. As he sat up over late brandies with his old friend, Byron struck a wistful note, saying "Well, Hobhouse, this is our last night; to-morrow I shall be Annabella's." Recording this in his diary, Hobhouse added the notation, "*absit omen*": let this be no bad omen. Hobhouse, who knew Byron better than anyone and was well aware of his complex sexual and emotional history, had grave doubts about the match. In fact, he had already taken it upon himself to speak to Annabella's uncle, Reverend Thomas Noel, who would officiate at the wedding, trying to persuade him to call the whole thing off. But the clergyman refused to intervene.

The next morning, on January 2, 1815, the wedding took place in the upstairs drawing room of Seaham Hall, with views of the North Sea as backdrop. The 22-year-old bride, dressed simply in white muslin, spoke her vows firmly and clearly, keeping her eyes fixed on the groom. For his part, Byron was drifting – as he later recalled in a poem entitled "The Dream," imagining himself as "the Wanderer":

> I saw him stand
> Before an Altar – with a gentle bride;
> … in that hour – a moment o'er his face
> The tablet of unutterable thoughts
> Was traced, – and then it faded as it came,
> And he stood calm and quiet, and he spoke
> The fitting vows, but heard not his own words,
> And all things reel'd around him

To Byron, the whole scene seemed unreal, with "unutterable thoughts" struggling to surface amidst the uncanny calm. Outside, local colliers in fantastic costumes performed a celebratory sword-dance, an ancient New Year's folk ritual that culminated in the mock beheading of a fool. All in all, it was a strangely ominous day. As a gift, Hobhouse presented Annabella with a complete set of Byron's poems, bound in orange morocco leather. All made their farewells, and Hobhouse felt, he later confessed in his diary, like he "had buried a friend." And as the newly weds' carriage departed, Byron thrust his arm out of the window, holding on to his best man's hand for as long as he could, while civic bells pealed in celebration.

Panic set in almost immediately. Cornered in the small carriage, Byron dropped his mask of placid bridegroom – or, perhaps, put on his mask of cruelty – and transformed into a villain before her eyes: "his countenance changed to gloom and defiance," remembered Annabella. Soon he gave voice to some of those unutterable thoughts: that Annabella was a fool to have married him; that she ruined them both by turning down his first proposal, leading him to dark transgressions; that he would be revenged upon her; that he had inherited the Byron family madness; that he pitied her. She could only listen in shocked silence, the color draining from her face. Their honeymoon destination was Halnaby Hall, another of the Milbanke homes, about 40 miles south. They arrived in deep snow, and Byron immediately leapt from the carriage and stormed off, leaving the confused and by now despondent Annabella to greet the servants and tenants alone.

Most of what we know of the honeymoon comes from Annabella's recollections after the separation, when she had cause to emphasize Byron's dark side. But there's no reason to doubt the honesty of her reports, all of which have a kind of dreadful coherence. Byron wrote his own version of that first day at Halnaby in his now-lost memoirs, and those who read them before they were destroyed recalled two events. First, he "*had* Lady Byron on the sofa before dinner," which might indicate a particularly eager couple – we do know that both Byron and Annabella shared a strong sexual bond and appetite for one another – or might have been a rushed and anxious power play on Byron's part, with Annabella hoping to calm him and bring him closer to her. Probably it was both.

Second, later that night, waking suddenly next to her in bed, with the candlelight flickering through the crimson damask curtains, Byron exclaimed, "Good God, I am surely in hell." According to Annabella, he spent the rest of that first night pacing the hall's deserted gallery, carrying loaded pistols, hunted by an unseen adversary. When he finally returned to bed, exhausted, she laid her head on his chest to comfort him. Byron said, "You should have a softer pillow than my heart." Annabella replied, "I wonder which will break first, yours or mine."

During this period, Byron's gothic episodes of depression alternated, disorientingly, with days of calmness and real intimacy with Annabella. His rage would subside into child-like states of remorse, in which he would say to her, "You are a good kind Pip – a good-natured Pip – the best wife in the world" and speak piteously of himself in the third person, perhaps remembering the collier's beheaded fool at Seaham: "B's a fool – Yes, he *is* a fool ... poor B – *poor* B." In fact, the marriage would be easier to understand, and might have ended with less damage, if the couple had been consistently wretched. As Byron reminds Annabella in this chapter's let-ter, "marks of affection—of the warmest & most reciprocal attachment passed between" them almost daily, and there were episodes of playfulness and pleasure too. Annabella had discovered a "'ruling passion' for mischief in private" (as she reported to Augusta) with her husband, and, at least sexually, the honeymoon seems to have been a success. Byron con-veyed contentment in letters to both Lady Melbourne and Tom Moore, writing, "Bell and I go on extremely well so far" and "She don't bore me.... I have great hopes this match will turn out well." He was also writing poetry, continuing work on the *Hebrew Melodies* collection for Isaac Nathan, with Annabella making fair copies for him as the snow fell outside. One of the lyrics, "Herod's Lament for Mariamne," concludes with a flourish of Byronic anguish,

> And mine's the guilt, and mine the hell
> This bosom's desolation dooming;
> And I have earn'd those tortures well,
> Which unconsumed are still consuming!

As was often the case, the language and imagery of his personal pain – guilt, hell, psychic torture, the desolate heart – fed his work. Furthermore, displacing his emotions onto the personae of Herod, Saul, and other biblical sufferers helped him regain control over his mental state. As he had written to Annabella when they were courting, he saw poetry as "the lava of the imagination whose eruption prevents an earthquake."

The problem was Augusta – or rather, Byron's passion for her. As his sister, she offered unthreatening, secure affection, even as their affair fed Byron's addiction to self-destructive, taboo sex. Augusta herself was not good at drawing boundaries either, and soon she was enmeshed in the lives of the married couple. A letter from her arrived at Halnaby as the honeymoon began, addressed to her brother as "Dearest, first, and best of human beings," prompting Byron to tell his wife that "no one loved him as [Augusta] did" and "no one understood how to make him happy but her." He immediately encouraged a correspondence between the two women, and they became confidantes and frenemies, with Augusta giving the new bride advice on how to manage Byron's moods. Augusta sensibly refused Byron's invitation, conveyed through Annabella, to join them at Halnaby, but her presence loomed in the near distance. At the Municipal Art

Gallery in Messolonghi, one can view a tantalizing envelope addressed to Augusta in Byron's hand, dated January 13, 1815 from Halnaby Hall, but the letter itself is gone. It would be extremely interesting to know what he was privately urging on his sister in the midst of his uncertain honeymoon. Soon thereafter, following another sojourn at Seaham with the Milbankes, the bride and groom went to stay at the Leigh home, Six Mile Bottom – with Colonel Leigh away as usual. Annabella and Augusta met for the first time, shaking hands awkwardly as Byron watched. He later reproached his wife for not greeting Augusta with a kiss.

Soon Annabella found herself living in a kind of nightmare. While in Augusta's presence, Byron turned selfish and cruel. He seemed determined to humiliate his wife, exacting a kind of perverse revenge on her for delinquencies of his own. "We don't want *you*, my charmer," he would say, sending Annabella off to her room while brother and sister stayed up late, laughing and whispering. Byron would lie on the couch and order the two women to take turns embracing him, comparing their displays of affection. Drinking heavily, he became savage and sarcastic, alluding frequently to intimacies with Augusta, which Annabella tried to ignore. And he bade Augusta read aloud his own letters, expressing passion for his sister, giving details of his various affairs with other women, speaking lightly of Annabella, and conveying his desire to marry only for money. Annabella later wrote of their stay at Six Mile Bottom, "He never spent a moment with me that could be avoided, & even got up early in the morning … to leave me and go to her." Bewildered and scared, Annabella looked to Augusta herself for help: "I turned from his barbarity to her affectionate care," hoping that together they could manage Byron. But Augusta, for all of her advice and expressions of solicitude, was too deeply compromised, too pliable in the face of Byron's needs, and too weirdly involved with the couple's relationship. Byron and Annabella left after two exhausting weeks, but it wasn't long before they invited Augusta to join them at their new home in London. Annabella later defended this invitation as an attempt to establish some normalcy: "It was hopeless to keep them apart. It was not hopeless, in my opinion, to keep them innocent."

Around the time Augusta arrived at Piccadilly Terrace for a stay that would last over two months, Annabella discovered she was pregnant. Her parents were thrilled and, from the outside, it seemed that the marriage was thriving. The newly weds toured the London social scene, with Byron performing the role of – and fitfully trying to be – a fond, attentive husband. It seems clear that part of him wanted to be happy with Annabella; part of him even loved her. But he engaged in continual acts of sabotage, beyond the typical infidelities expected among the aristocracy. Byron began spending more time at the Drury Lane Theatre, helping to manage its operations while also drinking late into the night and sleeping with actresses and other ladies of the demi-monde. These dalliances themselves were one thing. But Byron would then boast of them to his wife, purposely upsetting her by flaunting "his adulteries and indecencies with loose women" and telling her that he enjoyed "toying with more than one at the same time naked." He was simultaneously giving jewelry to his mistresses (and superciliously providing his wife with a list of these gifts) and feeling increasingly anxious about money: he was £30,000 in debt, having taken extravagant loans on the expectation of the Newstead sale. As he wrote to Hobhouse, all of that money had already been "swallowed up by duns – necessities – luxuries – fooleries – jewelleries –

'whores and fiddlers,'" and still Newstead remained unsold. And yet, standing on his honor as a Lord, Byron would not accept money from his publisher: he rebuffed all of Murray's attempts at payment for his poetry, even as the bailiffs descended and his personal library was auctioned to pay his creditors.

Amidst all of this self-inflicted damage, Byron was mired in depression, expressed as ferocity and amplified by brandy and laudanum. As the time for Annabella to give birth approached, he experienced bouts of temporary madness, "paroxysms" in which he would smash furniture, scream and shout at Annabella, wish her and the unborn child dead, demand sex in ways that approached attempted rape, fire his pistols inside the house, and threaten suicide. Eventually the servants, with Augusta's help, kept Annabella locked in her room for her own safety, and would not let Byron see her alone. In this household terrorized by her husband's behavior, Annabella gave birth to a healthy girl, Augusta Ada (who would be known as Ada, or, in Byron's letters, "Da"), on December 10, 1815, as Byron sat in the drawing room below throwing empty soda water bottles loudly against the ceiling. Presented with his newborn daughter, Byron looked and said, "Oh, what an implement of torture I have acquired in you!" It's a remark usually read as sadistic – and Byron was passionately reading the works of Marquis de Sade at this time – but it also sounds like a lament, a recognition of his own vulnerability in the face of Ada, "The child of love – though born in bitterness / And nurtured in convulsion," as he would address her in the sequel to *Childe Harold* in the following year.

Byron only knew his daughter Ada for a month. Then, after continued cold and angry exchanges between the couple,

Annabella went back to her parents' home, taking their child with her. Hence the letter with which this chapter began, conveying Byron's belated sense of shock, of his life falling away. He wrote again to his wife the next week, "I know not what to say – every step taken appears to bear you further from me – and to widen 'the great Gulph between thee and me.' If it cannot be crossed I will at least perish in its depth." That "great Gulph" is from the Book of Luke, the uncrossable chasm between Heaven and Hell. Byron was beginning to realize that the marriage was ruined, not least because Annabella was now taking the advice of family, friends, and lawyers, all of whom, as they heard more details about Byron's recent behavior, grew more adamantly set against a reconciliation. Byron tried appealing to her directly: "I can only say in the truth of affliction – & without hope … that I love you: – bad or good – mad or rational – miserable or content – I love you – & shall do to the dregs of my memory & existence." But Annabella stood firm, heartbroken and resolved. Soon the tide of public opinion turned against Byron, as the stories of abuse, madness, incest, and (thanks to Caroline Lamb, who chose this moment to take revenge on Byron by telling Annabella what she knew of his time in Greece) homosexual sodomy spread. The latter was in fact the most dangerous charge against him, and the fear of prosecution and homophobic attacks haunted Byron until he left England for good, a few months later. When he and Augusta tried to brave a party at Lady Jersey's on April 8, they were both treated as pariahs: "Countesses and ladies of fashion" left the room "in crowds" upon their arrival, as Byron's years of fame in Regency society came to an end in public opprobrium. Only Miss Mercer Elphinstone, one of Byron's former flirtations, had the temerity to approach him as he stood alone, pale with defiant shame. "You had better have married me," she said; "I would have managed you better."

In the midst of the separation and the surrounding controversy, Byron wrote one of his most notorious poems, "Fare Thee Well!" Tellingly, it was the first poem he had ever written for Annabella. Ostensibly the lament of a forsaken husband, it reads as a highly equivocal expression of feeling (at once both theatrical and uncertain) and also as an effort to influence public opinion. Byron sent the poem to Annabella, who saw it for what it was: "and so he talks of me to Every one," she wrote to her mother. Sure enough, Byron was soon urging the poem into print, over the objections of his publisher, and it became a flashpoint in the public eye, resulting in parodic cartoons such as Isaac Cruikshank's "The Separation!" (Figure 4.5). Throughout, "Fare Thee Well!" oscillates between tenderness and veiled threats, between confessions and accusations, between sentiment and hypocrisy:

> Fare thee well! and if for ever –
>   Still for ever, fare *thee well* –
> Even though unforgiving, never
>   'Gainst thee shall my heart rebel
>   …
> Though my many faults defaced me,
>   Could no other arm be found
> Than the one which once embraced me,
>   To inflict a cureless wound!
>   …
> And when thou wouldst solace gather –
>   When our child's first accents flow –
> Wilt thou teach her to say – 'Father!'
>   Though her care she must forego?

...

> All my faults – perchance thou knowest–
> All my madness – none can know;
> All my hopes – where'er thou goest –
> Wither – yet with *thee* they go.

...

> Fare thee well! – thus disunited–
> Torn from every nearer tie –
> Seared in heart – and lone – and blighted –
> More than this, I scarce can die.

In these passages, Byron's self-pity is near the surface, along with apparent tenderness, but there are also embedded curses. "[W]here'er thou goest – / Wither": those disorienting lines remake the famous biblical passage from Ruth ("whither thou goest, I will go") and, in separating subject ("hopes") from verb so firmly, make "wither" sound like an imperative command. It's the same word ("Wither!") that concludes "The Incantation," a curse-poem Byron wrote around this time and eventually inserted into his gothic drama *Manfred*. Annabella wasn't fooled: she knew that "Fare Thee Well!" was based in Byron's "talent for equivocation ... of [which] I have had many proofs in his letters," including the insidious, plaintive letter with which we began this chapter. "All I can say seems useless," Byron wrote, and he was right: there would be no reconciliation. Nothing remained but aftermath and pastures new. He began making plans to leave England with all available speed.

5

— ◇ —

Haunted Summer

My dearest Augusta—

By two opportunities of private conveyance—I have sent answers to your letter delivered by Mr. H[obhouse].— —S[crope] is on his return to England—& may probably arrive before this.—He is charged with a few packets of seals—necklaces—balls &c.—& I know not what—formed of Chrystals—Agates—and other stones—<u>all of & from Mont Blanc</u> bought & brought by me on & from the spot—expressly for you to divide among yourself and the children—including also your niece Ada—for whom I selected a ball (of Granite—a <u>soft</u> substance by the way—but the only one there) wherewithal to roll & play—when she is old enough—& mischievous enough—and moreover a Chrystal necklace;—and anything else you may like to add for her—the Love!— —The rest are for you—& the Nursery—but particularly Georgiana—who has sent me a very nice letter.—I hope Scrope will carry them all safely—as he promised— —There are seals & all kinds of fooleries—

pray—like them—for they come from a very curious place (nothing like it hardly in all I ever saw)—to say nothing of the giver.— — — — — — — — —And so—Lady B[yron] has been "kind to you" you tell me—"very kind"— umph—it is as well she should be kind to some of us—and I am glad she had the heart & the discernment to be still your friend—you was ever so to her.—I heard the other day—that she was very unwell—I was shocked enough— and sorry enough—God knows—but never mind;—H[obhouse] tells me however she is not ill—that she had been indisposed—but is better & well to do.—this is a relief.— — As for me I am in good health—& fair—though very unequal—spirits—but for all that—she—or rather—the Separation—has broken my heart—I feel as if an Elephant had trodden on it—I am convinced I shall never get over it—but I try.— —I had enough before I ever knew her and more than enough—but time & agitation had done something for me; but this last wreck has affected me very differently,—if it were acutely—it would not signify—but it is not that,—I breathe lead.— While the storm lasted & you were all pressing & comforting me with condemnation in Piccadilly—it was bad enough—& violent enough—but it is worse now;—I have neither strength nor spirits—nor inclination to carry me through anything which will clear my brain or lighten my heart.—I mean to cross the Alps at the end of this month—and go—God knows where—by Dalmatia—up to the Arnauts [Albanians] again—if nothing better can be done;—I have still a world before me—this—or the next.— —H[obhouse] has told me all the strange stories in circulation of me & mine;—not true,—I have been in some danger on the lake—(near Meillerie) but nothing to speak of; and as to all these "mistresses"—Lord help me —I* have had but one.—Now—don't scold—but what could I do?—a foolish girl—in spite of all I could say or do—would come after me—or rather went before me—for I found her here— and I have had all the plague possible to persuade her to go back again—but at last she went.—Now—dearest—I do most truly tell thee—that I did all I could to prevent it—& have at last put an end to it—I was not in love—nor have any love left for any,—but I could not exactly play the Stoic with a ~~girl of eighteen~~ woman—who had scrambled eight hundred miles to unphilosophize me—besides I had been re- galed of late with so many "two courses and a _desert_" (Alas!) of aversion—that I was fain to take a little love (if pressed particularly) by way of novelty.— —And now you know all that I know of that matter—& it is over. Pray—write—I have heard nothing since your last—at least a month or five weeks ago.— —I go out very little—except into the _air_—and on journeys—and on the water—and to Coppet—where Me. de Stael has been particularly kind & friendly towards me—& (I hear) fought battles without number in my very indifferent cause.—It has (they say) made quite as much noise on this as the other side of "La Manche" [the English Channel] —Heaven knows why—but I seem destined to set people by the ears.— —Don't hate me—but believe me ever

yrs. most affectly.

B

---

* The manuscript ends here. The remainder of this letter is reproduced from a later typescript.

Set amidst vineyards and terraced gardens in the hills of Cologny, the Villa Diodati overlooks the blue expanse of Lake Geneva from its southern shore. Beyond the lake, viewed from the upper balcony of the elegant square mansion, the Jura range rises dramatically to snowy peaks in the distance (Figure 5.1). Byron described Diodati as "a very pretty villa in a vineyard – with the Alps behind – & Mt. Jura and the Lake before," and he conveyed the prospect in lines addressed to the lake itself:

> It is the hush of night, and all between
> Thy margin and the mountains, dusk, yet clear,
> Mellowed and mingling, yet distinctly seen,
> Save darken'd Jura, whose capt heights appear
> Precipitously steep

On the other side, behind the house and over the ridge, stands the Mont Blanc massif covered by Alpine glaciers, with the Mer de Glace ("the sea of ice") frozen across the northern slopes. The landscape is a dramatic study in contrasts: sublime and beautiful, white ice and green meadows, sparkling water and dark mountains – an ideal spot for Romantic creativity to flourish. Byron arrived there in June 1816, seeking refuge from his failed marriage and the surrounding public scandal, and he would reside there until his departure for Italy in October. The Villa Diodati has since become legendary for the events that took place within its walls during that "haunted summer," culminating in the conception of what would arguably become the most influential literary work of the era, *Frankenstein*. Even now, the villa quietly reverberates with the energy of that novel's origin and the productive, delirious tangle of personalities, relationships, conversations, and literary activity of those few months. If there are houses sacred to the Romantic movement, the Villa Diodati is surely one.

When Byron wrote this brotherly letter to Augusta, the haunted summer was already drawing to a close. Near the end of August, John Hobhouse and Scrope Davies had arrived in Switzerland and made their way to Diodati to check in on their old Trinity College friend, bringing with them letters, pistol brushes, condoms, books, and tooth powder, along with a new sword stick (Byron had accidentally dropped his in the lake). Their arrival constituted a kind of changing of the guard. Since late May, Byron had been living in close connection with an unconventional, highly charged trio: the poet Percy Bysshe Shelley, his partner Mary Godwin, and her step-sister Claire Clairmont (Figures 5.2, 5.3, and 5.4). The Shelley group had rented a smaller lakefront house, the Maison Chappuis, just a short walk down the slope from Diodati. The result had been three months of increasing intimacy – some of it exhilarating and some of it uneasy – with Byron and his household, which included John Polidori, a young doctor whom Byron had invited as his personal traveling physician (Figure 5.5). Now that period was coming to an end, and soon Scrope Davies, a committed gambler, was headed back alone to England for the Newmarket races, charged with bringing with him souvenirs for Augusta, her children, and Byron's daughter Ada – "all kinds of fooleries" purchased from the hawkers at the base of Mont Blanc, a site popular with tourists.

Although he doesn't mention it in this letter, Byron had also entrusted Davies with something more valuable: a notebook, bound in scarlet morocco leather, containing a copy of the powerful sequel to *Childe Harold's Pilgrimage*, which Byron had written over the past months of travel, reflection, and pain. He had begun this third canto of the poem almost immediately upon his departure from England, on-board the ship from Dover to Ostend. As with the first two cantos, travel propelled composition, as Byron reflected on the scenes around him, occasionally invoking the Childe Harold persona, but most often speaking in the first person. The third canto opens with an address to his daughter: "Is thy face like thy mother's, my fair child! / Ada! sole daughter of my house and heart? / When last I saw thy young blue eyes they smiled, / And then we parted." On the one hand, like "Fare Thee Well!," these lines were part of a public relations campaign, in which Byron cast himself as a loving father. On the other, he was genuinely agonized by the separation from his wife and child, not least because he knew it was in large part the result of his own behavior. He wrote in a lyric to Augusta around this time, "The fault was mine; nor do I seek to screen / My errors with defensive paradox; / I have been cunning in mine overthrow, / The careful pilot of my proper woe." An ironic perspective on his own self-destructive tendencies did little to mitigate the suffering he had brought down upon himself and others. As he writes in this letter, "the Separation—has broken my heart—I feel as if an Elephant had trodden on it." Even more evocative is his simple metaphor for living in a severe depressive state: "I breathe lead."

For Byron, the summer in the Alps was a time of transformation. Cast out by the Regency society that once adored him, estranged from the wife and daughter he had hoped would bring stability, separated from the close male friends and literary associates who had supported him, and parted from Augusta, "dearest & deepest in my hope & my memory," Byron was vulnerable and yet open to new connections, again casting himself as an Adam cast out of Eden: "I still have a world before me." In his poetry, Byron often presented himself as a solitary exile, "Proud though in desolation," "the most unfit / of Men to herd with Man." But despite all of his misanthropic rhetoric, he was intensely social. He thrived in the elaboration of intimacies within small groups, from his "Theban band" at Harrow, to his Cambridge set, to the Drury Lane crew of managers and actors, and beyond. Even the bizarre *ménage* with Annabella and Augusta partook of his tendency to form intimate cadres, and it had found an echo in the Shelley–Godwin trio (Percy, Mary, and Claire). Their arrival in Geneva had set the stage for a particularly intense experiment in communal living for Byron, a welcome change of domestic texture from the stressed madness and impulsive cruelty of those final months at Piccadilly with Annabella.

Percy Shelley was a radical, utopian poet, a baronet's son who envisioned a world without kings, or priests, or prisons, and who had been expelled from Oxford for circulating a pamphlet entitled "The Necessity of Atheism." Leaving behind his wife Harriet and their two small children, the 23-year-old poet had departed England in 1816 in the company of two step-sisters from the household of the political philosopher William Godwin: his daughter, Mary, and his stepdaughter, Claire Clairmont, both aged 18. Shelley was a passionate admirer of Godwin's ideas, which were centered in a rejection of state power and a defense of our natural morality: left unconstrained, humans will seek the good. Godwin had been a bright star of revolutionary political thought in England during the 1790s, a status amplified by his union with the equally formidable feminist pioneer Mary Wollstonecraft, author of *A Vindication of the Rights of Woman*. Their months-long marriage was happy but tragically brief: Wollstonecraft died soon after giving birth to Mary. When Godwin remarried a few years later, his new wife came with a young son and a 3-year-old daughter, Clara Mary Jane Clairmont (later shortened to Claire). Mary and Claire had been raised alongside another daughter, Fanny, from Wollstonecraft's earlier passionate, scandalous affair with an American, Gilbert Imlay. All three sisters were precocious and unconventional, and all would, to varying degrees, fall under the spell of the young Percy Shelley, who started visiting their London home to pay homage to Godwin when Mary and Claire were both 16. Mary and Percy declared their love at her mother's grave in St. Pancras Churchyard in June 1814, and soon, despite Percy's marriage to Harriet, the couple departed for Europe – taking Claire with them, as both a companion and, at various points, another lover for Percy. Fanny was left behind, and, increasingly isolated and feeling cast out from the warmth of Percy's regard, committed suicide two years later.

It was not a coincidence that Percy, Mary, and Claire were residing in the Hotel d'Angleterre in Sécheron, near Geneva, when Byron's coach pulled into the hotel's gravel drive in late May. William Godwin had cut contact with his rebellious daughters, but continued to request money from Shelley, who, like Byron, had serious financial troubles of his own. Feeling unwelcome and persecuted in England, Shelley had intended to take his irregular family (which, by 1816, included his and Mary's baby, William, and a nurse, Elise) to Italy. But Claire had other plans. In late March and April, as Byron was in the final throes of his separation from Annabella, Claire had written to him out of the blue. Jealous of Mary, who compelled Shelley's affections at that time, Claire was determined to land a poet of her own. All three of them were passionate fans of Byron's work, and the news of his break from Lady Byron gave Claire an opening. In the past, Byron had mostly ignored anonymous fan letters, but this one caught him at a vulnerable moment. As he explains to Augusta in this letter, "I had been regaled of late with so many 'two courses and a *desert*' (Alas!) of aversion—that I was fain to take a little love (if pressed particularly) by way of novelty." After exchanging a few letters with Byron, Claire proposed they travel to an inn outside of London, where "we shall be free & unknown," making her intentions clear: "we can return early the following morning." On April 21, the same day that Byron signed the deed of separation from Annabella, Claire wrote that she hoped to "be able to offer you *that* which it has long been the passionate wish of my heart to offer you." Byron was ambivalent, but pliable in the face of Claire's importunate desires. As he wrote later to his friend Douglas Kinnaird, "I never loved nor pretended to love her – but a man is a man – & if a girl of eighteen comes prancing to you at all hours – there is but one way." Almost immediately, she was pregnant. Byron left for Geneva mere days after their brief affair, and Claire was determined to follow.

Byron's departure from England had been a melancholy, almost desperate occasion, with the poet fleeing his creditors as they descended on Piccadilly Terrace to seize his possessions for debt. He traveled in a brand-new coach (never to be paid for) modeled on Napoleon's military carriage, which had been captured at Waterloo and displayed extensively in London. Outfitted with a writing desk, collapsible bed, a washbasin, china plates, and a liquor cabinet, the coach was something between a limousine and campervan, a small home on wheels. With loyal servants Fletcher and Rushton in tow, Byron met Hobhouse and Davies at Dover to say farewell. They dined, along with Polidori, at the Ship Inn, and, while waiting for the tide to turn the next day, wandered over to St. Martin's cemetery to offer tribute at the grave of the satiric poet Charles Churchill. Byron measured his length on the grave, and then paid the sexton to clean and re-turf the neglected spot. Soon thereafter, he wrote a poem which begins, "I stood beside the grave of him who blazed / The comet of a season." He was obliquely reflecting upon his own meteoric rise and fall, a public career that at best had brought him, as the poem concludes, "The Glory and the Nothing of a name."

The next morning, Byron boarded the ship bound for West Flanders just as the impatient captain was ready to sail without him. There were hurried and earnest goodbyes, with promises from Hobhouse and Davies to follow him in the coming months. As the ship departed, according to Hobhouse, "The dear fellow pulled off his cap & wav'd it to me – I gazed until I could not distinguish him any longer – God bless him for a gallant spirit – and a kind one." Soon the white cliffs of Dover slipped behind the horizon, and Byron lost sight of England for good, with a mixture of emotions, including a sense of relief and bewildered triumph. As he wrote on board, after the lines about Ada, "Once more upon the waters! yet once more / And the waves bound beneath me as a steed / That knows its rider, Welcome to their roar! / Swift be their guidance, whereso'er it lead!" Disembarking at Ostend, they checked into an inn, where, Polidori noted in his diary, Byron "fell like a thunderbolt upon the chambermaid."

Switzerland was Byron's destination, attractive not only for the dramatic wonders of the Alpine landscape but also as the birthplace of Jean-Jacques Rousseau, whose philosophical writings (such as *The Social Contract*) had helped prompt the French Revolution, and whose intimately autobiographical *Confessions* and wildly popular novel of sentiment, *Julie; or, The New Heloise*, had established Geneva and its environs as a spiritual center of the Romantic movement in Europe. Switzerland itself also had an admirable history of political liberty, in which fiercely independent cantons resisted both kings and Napoleon's recent attempts at federal control. The country would thus be a welcome contrast to France, which Byron now saw as debased back to monarchical rule. As he wrote to Hobhouse, "We have not French passports – and no desire to view a degraded country – & oppressed people." Outside of Brussels on May 4, Byron paid a memorable visit to the battlefield of Waterloo which he hailed sardonically in newly written *Childe Harold* stanzas – "Thou first and last of fields," "this place of skulls" – as "The grave of France" containing "an Empire's dust." England and much of Europe were still celebrating Napoleon's final defeat, but Byron was disgusted at both the waste of life ("in vain years / Of death, depopulation, bondage, fears, / Have all been borne") and the "reviving Thraldom" of monarchical rule, a "patched-up idol" that had no place in modern "enlightened days." As he had written to Moore in July 1815, "Every hope of a republic is over, and we must go on under the old system…. I am sick at heart of politics and slaughters." In a kind of mystic sympathy with the fallen emperor, Byron's Napoleonic carriage broke down three times in the vicinity of Waterloo.

A journey up the Rhine valley led Byron and his entourage through Bonn, Koblentz, Mannheim, and Karlsruhe, a route surrounded by romantic scenery, "streams and dells, / Fruit, foliage, crag, wood, cornfield, mountain, vine, / And chiefless castles breathing stern farewells." In fact, Byron's imagination was held only fitfully by natural beauty alone, being drawn instead to history and the works of man, especially violence and scenes of loss. "A thousand battles have assail'd thy banks," he wrote of the Rhine, linking centuries-old "baronial feuds" to recent scenes of fierce conflict between the French and the Austrians, visible at Koblentz and in the "shattered wall" of the once-great fortress Ehrenbreitstein. Everywhere he looked, it seemed, Byron saw evidence of war. After all, Europe was just emerging from two decades of almost continuous armed conflict, and the scars on the landscape were fresh. Yet it's also true that Byron found inspiration in martial scenes, even as he scorned idealized pretensions to heroism and deplored Napoleon's defeat.

Scenes of "Battle's magnificently stern array" and the clashing of armies provide key moments in a number of Byron's greatest works, including *Childe Harold's Pilgrimage*, *Sardanapalus*, and *Don Juan*. Byron was attracted to scenes of intensity and was naturally historically minded: he saw landscape as everywhere peopled by what he called "the great of old," and marked by their deeds. He also had an aristocrat's half-hidden pride in military leadership, and a dim but nagging sense of shame that he had written poetry rather than participated in the great European conflict of his lifetime. In addition, war came readily to hand as a metaphor for his own personal and emotional struggles, as if history were a mirror reflecting his inner condition. At the same time, he dimly knew that he was *writing* history in the moment, composing stanzas of *Childe Harold's Pilgrimage* that would become powerful representations of (for example) Waterloo in public memory thereafter. Byron was layering personal, national, and mythic histories onto the landscapes through which he traveled, pressurized by rage and regret. His new canto would provide an influential model for anyone creating post-traumatic political art in the modern world.

Arriving at the Hotel d'Angleterre in Secheron, worn from the journey and broadcasting his ennui, Byron entered his age as 100 in the guest register. Claire Clairmont, who had been waiting impatiently for his arrival, soon saw this entry and sent a teasing note: "I am sorry you are grown so old … I suppose your venerable age could not bear quicker travelling." The next day, Byron and Polidori had been rowing on the lake, and, as they disembarked, the Shelley party approached to greet them. It was a quietly momentous event. Byron and Mary Godwin had met briefly once before, in London, when Claire introduced them, but now the air shimmered with a different energy, as Byron and Percy Shelley shook hands for the first time. There was some awkwardness, given their shared poetic vocation and Byron's celebrity, their mutual unconventionality, and the complex sexual dynamics of the scene. As Polidori described him, Shelley was "bashful, shy, consumptive … separated from his wife; keeps the two daughters of Godwin, who practise his theories; one L.B.'s." Godwin's "theories" here means free love or polyamory, with Polidori signaling that Byron's relationship with Claire was common knowledge. It was almost certainly one of the things the men talked about at dinner when the three of them dined together, without the ladies, that first evening in late May. That day marked the beginning of a season that would change all of their lives profoundly and alter the course of English literary history: the summer of *Childe Harold* III, *The Prisoner of Chillon*, and "Darkness," of Percy Shelley's "Mont Blanc," of the modern vampire novel (thanks to Byron and Polidori between them), and, above all, of Mary Godwin Shelley's *Frankenstein*.

With Byron and Polidori settled at the Villa Diodati and the Shelley circle in their nearby cottage on the lakefront below, the regular intimacy of the group was soon established. Leaving little William with his nurse, Percy, Mary, and Claire would spend many evenings at Diodati, dining, drinking, and talking late into the night. There was also opium in the form of laudanum, and other drugs (such as ether) from Polidori's medical kit. For a time, Byron resumed his sexual relations with Claire, but he also was attempting to keep her at arm's length, of which she was well aware. She had written knowingly to him on her way to Switzerland, "I love you yet you do not feel even interest for me," maintaining that she would be in "agony" if Byron met with the "slightest accident," "but were I to float by your window drowned all you would say would be 'Ah voila!'" He couldn't convincingly deny it. She made efforts to see Byron alone, and spent hours that summer making fair copies of the poems he was writing, in order to be closer to him. But Byron was merely tolerant and fitfully receptive to her overtures, preferring to spend time with the well-read and enthusiastically idealistic Percy Shelley and the more quietly brilliant Mary Godwin. Claire increasingly felt herself sidelined. On Byron's part, the affair was soon effectively over, but for her, the after-effects would last a lifetime. As Claire wrote a decade later to a friend,

I am unhappily the victim of a happy passion; I had one like all things perfect in its kind, it was fleeting and mine only lasted ten minutes, but these ten minutes have discomposed the rest of my life. The passion … disappeared, leaving no trace whatever behind it except my heart wasted and ruined as if it had been scorched by a thousand lightnings.

Claire's "thousand lightnings" recall the tempestuous weather of that summer in Switzerland. Sometimes the group took evening excursions on the lake, but these were relatively rare because of the wet, cold, stormy weather. Mary wrote in early June, "An almost perpetual rain confines us principally to the house," and Byron complained in late July of the "stupid mists – fogs – rains – and perpetual density" of the clouds that characterized the summer of 1816. What they didn't know was that a massive eruption of the Tambora volcano in Indonesia the previous year was the cause of the extraordinarily bad meteorological conditions. According to Gillen Wood, "The sun-dimming stratospheric aerosols produced by Tambora's eruption in 1815 spawned the most devastating, sustained period of extreme weather seen on our planet in perhaps thousands of years." Crops failed across the globe, and famine stalked large portions of the population. Locally, it was "the coldest, wettest Geneva summer since records began in 1753," with "130 days of rain between April and September" in a year remembered in Switzerland as "L'Année de la misère" and "Das Hungerjahr." As wealthy, well-born British expatriates, Byron and the Shelley circle were shielded from the humanitarian crisis unfolding around them, but they were aware of it. Shelley wrote to his friend Thomas Peacock in July, "Affairs are here rather in a desperate condition. The magistrates of Geneva have prohibited the making of white bread.—all ranks of people are in the greatest distress.—I earnestly hope that England at least will escape." The pervasive atmosphere of dread that accompanied that supernaturally cold, dark summer pressed on their imaginations and soon invaded their dreams.

Confined to Diodati, the group discovered some volumes of gothic tales of terror entitled *Fantasmagoriana*, which they read aloud to one another, inspiring Byron to suggest a friendly competition: "We will each write a ghost story." Claire was left out of this game, but the literary-minded Polidori, whose special interest in medical school had been dreams and somnambulism, was included. His diary for June 18 records a late night at Diodati, several days after Byron's suggestion, when all were in the midst of their attempts to scare each other out of their wits:

> Twelve o'clock, really began to talk ghostly. [Byron] repeated some verses of Coleridge's *Christabel*, of the witch's breast; when silence ensued, Shelley suddenly shrieking and putting his hands to his head, ran out of the room with a candle. Threw water in his face, and after gave him ether. He was looking at [Mary], and suddenly thought of a woman he had heard of who had eyes instead of nipples, which, taking hold of his mind, horrified him.

In Shelley's terrifying vision of an anatomically disordered body, we can see a trace of the subject that was increasingly occupying Mary's mind. As she remembered later, she had during these weeks been listening to Percy and Byron speculating about whether "a corpse would be re-animated; galvanism had given token of such things; perhaps the component parts of a creature might be manufactured, brought together, and endued with vital warmth." Soon Mary had a waking nightmare of her own:

> Night waned upon this talk, and even the witching hour had gone by, before we retired to rest. When I placed my head on my pillow, I did not sleep, nor could I be said to think. My imagination, unbidden, possessed and guided me…. I saw the pale student of unhallowed arts kneeling

beside the thing he had put together. I saw the hideous phantasm of a man stretched out, and then, on the working of some powerful engine, show signs of life, and stir with an uneasy, half vital motion.

In her imagination of a reanimated corpse, Mary was also reaching back to a dream she had had the previous year, after the death of her 3-week-old daughter, who had been born prematurely. As she had recorded then in her journal, "Dream that my little baby came to life again – that it had only been cold & that we rubbed it by the fire & it lived – I awake & find no baby – I think about the little thing all day." Mary's midnight vision at Diodati combined modern science (galvanic batteries and a "powerful engine"), gothic imaginings, and the domestic tragedies of birth and death – including her own mother's death in giving birth to her. That vision would soon fuel her famous novel, *Frankenstein*, and give rise to a modern myth of Promethean overreach and its monstrous results.

For his part, Byron began writing a story about a vampire: a man named Augustus Darvell who dies in Greece and, according to the intended plot as remembered by Polidori, returns from the dead to make love to his friend's sister back in England. Byron had already written briefly about vampirism in *The Giaour*, where he depicts the vampire as a vile undead corpse, compulsively preying not on anonymous victims but on family and loved ones:

> But first, on earth as vampire sent,
> Thy corse shall from its tomb be rent:
> Then ghastly haunt thy native place,
> And suck the blood of all thy race;
> There from thy daughter, sister, wife,

At midnight drain the stream of life;
Yet loathe the banquet which perforce
Must feed thy livid living corse

Now Byron took the myth in a different direction: his vampire would be a deceiver, able to pass as human and seduce victims with his suave charms and then drink their blood. Byron completed only a few pages of this story; but Polidori was fascinated by the idea, and, abandoning his own tale of a skull-headed lady, turned Byron's concept into a short novella, *The Vampyre*. In part, Byron himself was Polidori's model for the arrogant predator Lord Ruthven, an aristocratic vampire "who had passed years amidst his friends, and dearest ties, forced every year, by feeding upon the life of a lovely female to prolong his existence for the ensuing months." In the novella, relying on his seductive arts, Ruthven bites the throats and drains the life of young Ianthe in Greece and of Miss Aubrey soon after their wedding. When *The Vampyre* was first published in 1819, it appeared mistakenly under Byron's name, and its notoriety became further bound up with his own. In part fueled by Byron's fame, this slight tale had an outsized influence on horror fiction and film: every dangerously attractive, aristocratic vampire from Bram Stoker's Dracula to Anne Rice's Lestat can be traced back to Byron and Polidori. Victor Frankenstein's creature wasn't the only iconic monster brought to life during the haunted summer at Diodati.

Other literary productions emerged from those rainsoaked weeks on Lake Geneva. Byron wrote his pitiless apocalyptic poem "Darkness" on "a celebrated dark day – that the fowls went to roost at noon and candles were lighted as at night." As with *Frankenstein*, the work had its origin in "a dream, which was not all a dream," while also drawing on the atmosphere of impending doom that accompanied the dramatic climate change of that year. In "Darkness," Byron describes a catastrophic future in which "The bright sun was extinguished … / Morn came, and went – and came and brought no day." Living in permanent night, humans all over the earth "looked up / With mad disquietude on the dull sky, / The pall of a past world." In a reflection of the crop failures and shortages of "Das Hungerjahr" in Switzerland, the poem continues, "The crowd was famish'd by degrees." Everything is burned to maintain light and heat for as long as possible, but the end is inevitable: "The world was void," "Seasonless, herbless, treeless, manless, lifeless – / A lump of death – a chaos of hard clay." The last two men on earth meet as enemies, and, beholding one another's faces, "saw – and shriek'd, and died – / Even of their mutual hideousness they died." Byron ends his poem by channeling his great eighteenth-century poetic master Alexander Pope, whose *Dunciad* terminates with an invocation of the "dread Empire" of Chaos: "Light dies before thy uncreating word: / Thy hand, great Anarch! lets the curtain fall; / And Universal Darkness buries All." Byron's conclusion is quieter but even more desolate in its vision of pure entropy: "the clouds perish'd; Darkness had no need / Of aid from them – She was the universe."

The dark days and nights at the Villa Diodati were punctuated by epic thunderstorms that produced their own imaginative effects, not least Mary's conception of the galvanic, electrical science powering Victor Frankenstein's creation. In early June, she wrote home to Fanny,

> The thunder storms that visit us are grander and more terrific than I have ever seen before.... One night we *enjoyed* a

finer storm than I had ever before beheld. The lake was lit up – the pines on the Jura made visible, and all the scene illuminated for an instant, when a pitchy blackness succeeded, and the thunder came in frightful bursts over our heads.

Byron watched this same storm or others very like it, inspiring stanzas that would find a culminating place in the new canto of *Childe Harold*. In them, you can hear the influence of Shelley's sensibility, especially his love for nature as an emblem of the mind's own powers. Byron writes as he observes the storm with a mixture of admiration and longing:

The sky is changed! – and such a change! Oh night,
And storm, and darkness, ye are wondrous strong,
Yet lovely in your strength, as is the light
Of a dark eye in woman! Far along,
From peak to peak, the rattling crags among
Leaps the live thunder! Not from one lone cloud,
But every mountain now hath found a tongue,
And Jura answers, through her misty shroud,
Back to the joyous Alps, who call to her aloud!

And this is in the night: – Most glorious night!
Thou wert not sent for slumber! let me be
A sharer in thy fierce and far delight, –
A portion of the tempest and of thee!
How the lit lake shines, a phosphoric sea,
And the big rain comes dancing to the earth!
And now again 'tis black, – and now, the glee
Of the loud hills shakes with its mountain-mirth,
As if they did rejoice o'er a young earthquake's birth.

The sequence concludes with Byron's famous expression of thwarted desire to speak with the force of the storm, to "embody and unbosom" his inner self into a single word of power:

> Could I embody and unbosom now
> That which is most within me, – could I wreak
> My thoughts upon expression, and thus throw
> Soul, heart, mind, passions, feelings, strong or weak,
> All that I would have sought, and all I seek,
> Bear, know, feel, and yet breathe – into *one* word,
> And that one word were Lightning, I would speak;
> But as it is, I live and die unheard,
> With a most voiceless thought, sheathing it as a sword.

In its search for "*one* word," the stanza offers breathless lists of them, as Byron infuses the rising energy and speed of the storm into his verse, concluding with an assertion of concealed, potential masculine power: a sheathed sword, a voiceless word.

Mary remembered the rain that summer as "incessant," but there were some days of sunshine, all the more welcome when they came. Byron and Shelley spent the last week of June touring Lake Geneva by sailboat; Polidori had sprained his ankle, and so the two poets took the journey alone. The result was a deepened bond between them, as they sailed, explored, dined, and talked about nature, poetry, politics, and their personal lives amidst the stunning Alpine scenery. They walked through deep chestnut forests and meadows full of wildflowers and thyme, past mountain streams and waterfalls, with the icy summits and ravines in the distance against the sky. They climbed a ruined Roman tower at Hermance, watched a group of children – many afflicted with hyperthyroid deformities (due to low iodine in the Alpine diet) – play games on a "serene and glowing evening" in Nernier, and tasted the mineral waters at Evian and mountain-flower honey at Meillerie. But the strange weather of 1816 was never calm for long: they were "in some danger on the lake," as Byron writes to Augusta, being "most nearly wrecked in a Squall" on their way to Saint Gingoux. As the storm raged, both men stripped off their coats and waited on the deck, expecting to be capsized at any moment, with Byron silently admiring the sangfroid of Shelley, who couldn't swim. When the boat finally made it to shore, where large trees had been blown down by the storm, men on the dock "exchanged looks of wonder and congratulation with our boatman" for piloting the frail craft through it all.

The next day, Byron and Shelley sailed to the island castle of Chillon (Figure 5.6) and toured its dungeon, which impressed them deeply as a site of what Shelley called "that cold and inhuman tyranny, which it has been the delight of man to exercise over man." Byron was particularly interested in the history of François Bonnivard, held at Chillon as a political prisoner by the Duke of Savoy in the sixteenth century. Over the next few days, Byron wrote a narrative poem from the perspective of Bonnivard, chained to one of the "seven pillars of gothic mould" with his two brothers, who waste away and die before his eyes. *The Prisoner of Chillon* attests to the psychological horror of imprisonment and isolation, "A sea of stagnant idleness / Blind, boundless, mute, and motionless!" in which Byron's Bonnivard is so immersed that he "learn[s] to love despair" and even laments his eventual release at the poem's end. In the poem's mixture of gothic details, political critique, and close attention to mental events, we can again see Shelley's influence on Byron, who likely shared portions of the poem-in-progress with his traveling companion as they made their way to Clarens. At this same time, Shelley was writing his "Hymn to Intellectual Beauty," in which he expresses a hope that "the spirit of Beauty" would "free / This world from its dark slavery." The contrast between the gorgeous, ever changing scenery of the lake and the gloom of the Chillon dungeon became for both men a haunting emblem of the human condition.

The villages and landscapes surrounding Lake Geneva appealed to Byron and Shelley not only for their natural beauty but also for their literary associations, especially with Rousseau and his novel *Julie*, which they both adored, and from which Shelley read aloud to Byron during this journey. Originally entitled, "Letters of Two Lovers Living in a Small Village at the foot of the Alps," Rousseau's novel tells the story of Julie d'Étange's doomed love for her tutor Saint-Preux, her dutiful marriage to another man, and the price both lovers pay for not living their authentic lives. Byron and Shelley eagerly retraced the events of the novel, pleased to be "Surrounded by the scenes which it has so wonderfully peopled." To Shelley, Rousseau was "the greatest man the world has produced since Milton," and Byron added his own rhapsody to the new canto of *Childe Harold*, praising "wild Rousseau, / The apostle of affliction, he who threw / Enchantment over passion," and evoked the "ideal beauty" that "breathed itself to life in Júlie" and "invested her with all that's wild and sweet." For Byron, Clarens seemed to be the "birth-place of deep Love!" and the surrounding area resonated with the transcendental passion of Rousseau's characters. So uncanny was this effect that Byron was convinced that the landscape was *inherently* full of love "in its most extended and sublime capacity," something that Rousseau had sensed and drew

1.1 Letter 1. Byron to Elizabeth Pigot, October 26, 1807, Trinity College, Cambridge.

1.2 Silhouette of Elizabeth Bridget Pigot, *c.*1801.

1.3 Catherine Gordon Byron, by Thomas Stewardson.

1.4 Newstead Abbey, from F. O. Morris, *A Series of Picturesque Views of Seats of the Noblemen and Gentlemen of Great Britain and Ireland* (1880).

1.5 Tomb of Byron's dog, Boatswain, at Newstead Abbey.

2.1 John Cam Hobhouse, by Charles Turner, after James
Lonsdale, 1826.

2.2 Portrait of George Gordon, 6th Baron Byron, in Albanian dress, by Thomas Phillips, 1813.

2.3 Teresa Macri, the "Maid of Athens," by F. Stone, after an 1812 sketch by L. Allason.

2.4a Franciscan Convent, Athens, the residence of Lord Byron, 1811,
by C. Stanfield from a sketch by W. Page.

2.4b Monument of Lysicrates, showing the library where Byron
wrote, engraved by Charles Heath from a drawing by S. Pomardi,
from Edward Dodwell, *A Classical and Topographical Tour Through
Greece* (London, 1819).

3.1 Letter 3. Byron to Lady Melbourne, October 8, 1813, Aston Hall, Rotherham, Yorkshire.

3.2 Lord Byron, by Augustino Aglio, c.1814.

3.3 Elizabeth Lamb, Lady Melbourne, by George Romney, *c.*1780s–1790s.

3.4 Lady Frances Wedderburn Webster, by A. W. Devis, 1812.

3.5 Lady Caroline Ponsonby Lamb, by John Hoppner, *c.*1805.

3.6 Jane Elizabeth, Countess of Oxford, by John Hoppner, 1797.

4.1 Anne Isabella Milbanke (Lady Byron), by Charles Hayter, 1812.

4.2 The Hon.
Augusta
Leigh, from
a drawing by
T. C. Wageman,
engraved by
Walker and
Boutall.

4.3 "Byron" and
"Augusta" carved
into a tree.

4.4 Seaham Hall, Durham.

4.5 "The Separation, a Sketch from the private life of Lord Iron," by
Isaac Cruikshank, 1816.

LORD BYRON AT THE VILLA DIODATI NEAR GENEVA 1816.

5.1 "Lord Byron at the Villa Diodati" (*c.*1820).

5.2 Percy Bysshe Shelley, by William Edward West.

5.3 Mary Shelley,
from a miniature
by Reginald Easton,
1857.

5.4 Claire
Clairmont,
by Amelia
Curran, 1819.

5.5 John Polidori, by F. G. Gainsford, *c.*1816.

5.6 "The Castle of Chillon," by James D. Harding, after a sketch by W. Page, 1832.

"Vacca tua — 'falenga" (i.e. Excellenza)
your Cow — please your Excellency. —
In short — she was — as I said before —
a very fine Animal — of considerable
beauty and energy — with many good
& several amusing qualities — but wild
as a witch — and fierce as a demon. —
She used to boast publicly of her amours — now one — now another — contrasting
it with that of other women — and assigning
for it sundry reasons physical and moral
which did more credit to her person than
her modesty. — — True it was that they
all tried to get her away — and no one
succeeded — till her own absurdity helped
them. — Whenever there was a competition, and
sometimes — one moral be that is one woman
and one or another — to prevent battle —
she had generally the preference. — — — —

P.S. The Countess ____ ____ yours very truly
I never [wrote?] her [.....] before leaving — and afterwards
Venice — a letter containing the real original
witch — which gave rise to the "Vampire &c" "did you get it!"

6.1 Letter 6. Letter from Lord Byron to John Murray, 1812.

6.2 Lord Byron in Venice, by "M. B." after an 1818 drawing by George Henry Harlow.

6.3 Margarita Cogni, engraving after a drawing
by George Henry Harlow, 1818.

6.4 Byron and Marianna [Segati], by N. Currier, c.1850.

6.5 Allegra Byron, by unknown artist, *c.*1821.

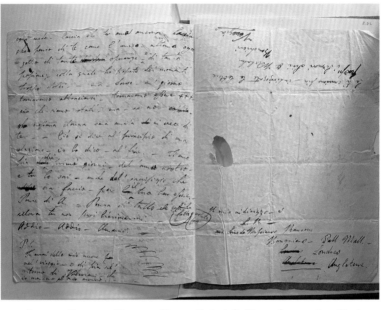

7.1. Letter 7. Byron to Countess Teresa Guiccioli, December 7, 1819, Venice.

7.2 Countess Teresa Guiccioli.

7.3 Palazzo Guiccioli, Ravenna. Reproduced from *The Works of Lord Byron: Letters and Journals*, ed. Rowland J. Prothero (1901).

7.4 Thomas Moore, engraving by John Barnet after a painting by
Martin Archer Shee, 1820.

upon in his novel. Again, Shelley's idealism was seeping into the poetry of the more characteristically pessimistic Byron, who could be productively swayed by listening to other voices. For a moment in *Childe Harold*, the skeptical pilgrim pays homage at the shrine of "Undying Love," enraptured amidst the crags and pines, the roaring torrents and sloping green meadows, "a populous solitude of bees and birds." After reading this new canto, Shelley pronounced it Byron's best work to date. Byron too called it "my favourite," writing sardonically to Moore that it was "a fine indistinct piece of poetical desolation.... I was half mad during the time of its composition, between metaphysics, mountains, lakes, love inextinguishable, thoughts unutterable, and the nightmare of my own delinquencies. I should, many a good day, have blown my brains out, but for the recollection that it would have given pleasure to my mother-in-law."

The two poets returned to their homes in Montalegre after visiting Ouchy, where they were delayed by rain for a few days, and Lausanne, where they visited the old summerhouse in which Edward Gibbon had finished writing *The Decline and Fall of the Roman Empire*. It had been a thoroughly Romantic trip, full of natural beauty, sublime thunderstorms, and affecting historical and literary associations. Byron lauded "Rousseau–Voltaire–our Gibbon–and de Stael – / Leman! These names are worthy of thy shore," noting that, thanks to these writers, "How much more, Lake of Beauty! do we feel, / In sweetly gliding o'er thy crystal sea." But Byron must have known that he was, even then, entering his own name into that authorial roll call, composing these *Childe Harold* stanzas and *The Prisoner of Chillon*, which would be firmly associated with Lake Geneva and its surroundings ever after. Shelley wrote later that his memories of that week sailing on the lake were surrounded by "the light of an enchantment which can never be dissolved," yet confiding to Peacock that he found Byron to be a rather disturbing companion, "an exceedingly interesting person ... and as mad as the winds." For his part, Byron wrote to Kinnaird that autumn, "Pray continue to like Shelley – he is a very good – very clever – but a very singular man – he was a great comfort to me here by his intelligence & good nature." Both poets registered the eccentricity of the other and noted their profound temperamental differences, even while recognizing the deeper affinities that would continue to draw them together.

Mary and Claire soon set to work making copies of the poems written during the tour, even as Byron continued to keep Claire at a distance. "It would make me happy to finish Chillon for you," she wrote to him a few days later: "you expressed yourself decisively last Evening that it is impossible to see you at Diodati; if you will trust it down here, I will take the *greatest* possible care of it." The manuscripts became a proxy for the man. Meanwhile, her pregnancy was advancing. She would sit by the windows of the Maison Chapuis through the long, rainy days, carefully copying Byron's new stanzas, even as their child was growing in her womb, with Mary somewhere nearby composing the novel she would call her "hideous progeny." In the end, both Mary and Claire produced neatly handwritten copies of the Chillon poem and *Childe Harold* III, but in both cases, it was Claire's copy that Byron sent via Shelley to England to be published by John Murray. She was hanging on, eager to remain useful to a man who had really only ever made use of her, and who yielded to her importunities for attention only when it suited his temper and his appetite.

As the summer wore on, Byron was drawn into the social circle of Madame de Staël, who hosted frequent dinners and salons at her chateau at Coppet, across the lake from Diodati. At age 50, de Staël was nearing the end of her fascinating and eventful life as a woman of letters and political influencer. The daughter of the legendary French finance minister Jacques Necker, de Staël had played a part in the French Revolution, made a personal enemy of Napoleon for her criticism of his regime, traveled widely, and collected many of the leading intellectuals of Europe around her, while publishing influential novels that combined sentiment and politics (*Delphine* and *Corinne; or, Italy*), and furthering the spread of Romantic ideas with her writings. Byron had met her in England in 1813 and was equally impressed by her brilliance and bowled over by her volubility, calling de Staël "the first female writer of this, perhaps of any, age" in a note to *The Bride of Abydos*, while privately describing her as "a very plain woman forcing one to listen & look at her," "obstinate, clever, odd, garrulous, and shrill." Compelled by her intensity, her intelligence, and her wide range of experience and acquaintance, Byron soon began accepting her frequent invitations to Coppet. As he writes here to Augusta, "Me. de Stael has been particularly kind & friendly towards me," and he told Murray that "she has made Coppet as agreeable as society and talent can make any place on earth" – a place where he met the German Romantic theorist August Wilhelm Schlegel and the Abbé de Brême, an Italian nationalist and man of letters, among other influential guests. Byron was expanding his European range of association, entering more fully into a cosmopolitan milieu that would increasingly become his own.

For several months, Byron had unevenly managed to distract himself from the painful emotions of his separation from Lady Byron and their child, as well as from his tortured desires for Augusta. Secure in his villa in the hills of Montalegre or sailing on the lake, and caught up in the local, summer-camp dramas of the Shelley circle and Polidori, he had felt a welcome distance from England and the difficulties of his personal life in Regency society. He wrote few letters, and avoided places where Englishmen would gather. But messages from that other world began to reach him. Caroline Lamb had published a novel, *Glenarvon*, featuring a thinly veiled Byron character who is an evil seducer, a coward and hypocrite who ruins the life of Calantha, Caro's avatar. Tellingly, Lady Byron admired the novel and recommended it to friends, including Lady Melbourne; and, as the novel sold widely, all of the old gossip about Byron and Caroline was revived. To "kiss and tell" was bad enough, Byron wrote to Murray, but this was a case of " – – and publish." After reading it, Byron offered a two-word review: "God damn!" But in the end, it was Caroline's reputation that suffered most from the novel's revelations and unkind depictions of family and friends. Around this time, Byron also heard that Lady Byron was "very unwell," inspiring complicated feelings that found expression in a poem of melancholy reproach addressed to "The moral Clytemnestra of thy lord," telling her, "Thou hast sown in my sorrow, and must reap / The bitter harvest." Mercifully, he kept this to himself for now. Madame de Staël had recently tried to broker a reconciliation between Byron and his wife, working through mutual acquaintances in England, but Annabella was unmoved by the appeal, relaying her determination to keep away from Byron, as much for his sake as for her own. Despite Byron's own mixed emotions, her firm rebuff came as a further press of the elephant's foot on his heart.

It was now late August. Leaving Mary at home, Shelley and Claire trudged up to Diodati to have the needful, difficult conversation with Byron about the coming baby. Together they determined that Claire would give birth in secret back in England, and Byron would adopt the child, allowing Claire visiting rights. This was better than Byron's first suggestion, which was that Augusta Leigh raise the child as one of her own. Claire reasoned that surrendering the child to Byron's custody would give it the advantage of a connection to an English peer, while also maintaining her own ties to him. She was still desperately committed to Byron, writing to him with surprising abandon on her way back to England, "There is nothing in the world I love or care about but yourself.... I make no account of Mary & Shelley's friendship so much more do I love you." Early the following year, sequestered in Bath, she would give birth to a healthy baby girl, initially called Alba (after Claire's nickname for Byron, Albé) and renamed Allegra at Byron's direction. Byron wrote to Kinnaird about Claire, calling her an "odd-headed girl" who

> returned to England to assist in peopling that desolate island.... – The next question is the brat mine? – I have reason to think so – for I know as much as one can know such a thing – that she had not lived with S[helley] during the time of our acquaintance – & that she had a good deal of that same with me. This comes of "putting it about" (as Jackson calls it) & be damned to it – and thus people come into the world. – – – – –

The fate of little Allegra would become a key point of contention in the ongoing relationship of Byron and the Shelley circle, and a source of lifelong pain for Claire. In the end, almost none of it worked out the way they had so carefully planned.

Hobhouse and Scrope Davies arrived at Diodati at just the right moment, a few days before the Shelley party departed, when Byron needed more than ever some nights of laughter with old friends. Shelley had been a compelling companion but a high-minded, serious one: he didn't approve of Byron's facetious attitude and his tendency toward seeing the ridiculous in everything. Claire was needy and Polidori was hot-tempered and self-regarding. But Hobhouse and Scrope couldn't go minutes without some witty jest or absurdity. Bidding hello and farewell to Percy, Mary, and Claire, they set off with Byron and Polidori on a tour of Chamonix and Mont Blanc, where Byron bought the "Chrystals— Agates— and other stones" to send home to Augusta. In the visitors' book at one of the hotels in Chamonix – the same one that the Shelley group had stayed in when they took the tour – Byron noticed that Shelley had inscribed the word "atheist" in Greek next to his name. Attempting to protect his heedlessly provocative friend, Byron scratched it out. Back at Diodati, the friends stayed up late each night to catch one another up on news and discuss Byron's affairs. For once, Byron was happy to connect his new life to his old. But his restlessness and depression were growing: "I have neither strength nor spirits," he writes to Augusta, telling her he intends "to cross the Alps at the end of this month—and go—God knows where—by Dalmatia—up to the Arnauts again—if nothing better can be done;—I have still a world before me—this—or the next."

In the short term, there was more touring to be done in Switzerland. When Scrope left for England, Byron and Hobhouse departed on a ten-day tour of the Bernese Oberland, on the road again together like the old traveling companions they were. By carriage, on horseback, and on foot, they moved through the German-speaking region of the country in all its Alpine gloom and glory, luckily hitting a spell of clear weather, with "only 4 hours rain ... in eight days." On their return, Byron wrote to Murray,

> Mr. H[obhouse] & myself are just returned from a jour-
> ney of lakes & mountains–we have been to the Grind-
> enwald–& the Jung-frau–& stood on the summit of the
> Wengeren Alp–and saw torrents of nine hundred feet in
> fall–& glaciers of all dimensions–we have heard Shep-
> herd's pipes–and Avalanches–and looked on the clouds
> foaming up from the valleys below us–like the spray of
> the ocean of hell.

Byron's hellish simile provides a precise contrast to Coler-idge's description of a similar misty Alpine vista in an 1801 poem, in which Mont Blanc seems to "Rise like a cloud of incense from the Earth," which "with her thousand voices, praises God." One might also think of Wordsworth's descrip-tion of looking from the top of Mount Snowdon down onto "a huge sea of mist" and comparing it to "a mighty mind ... exalted by an under-presence, / The sense of God." In their characteristically Romantic fashions, the poets project their mental states onto the landscape, with Byron's reaching instinctively toward the infernal.

On the tour, Byron had kept a journal in the form of an extended letter to Augusta, and there, similarly, he compared that 900-foot waterfall to "the tail of a white horse streaming in the wind," like "the '*pale* horse' on which *Death* is mounted in the Apocalypse." There is an almost hallucinatory quality to Byron's perception at this period. He sees "*whole woods of withered pines–all withered*–trunks stripped & barkless–branches lifeless–done by a single winter," and they morph into grotesque and accusatory human shapes in his mind's eye: "their appearance reminded me of me & my family." Byron's weird Alpine observations would soon become part of his gothic verse-drama *Manfred*, modeled in part on *Faust*, in which a proud, guilt-stricken conjurer, lamenting the death of his beloved Astarte and seeking forgetfulness or death, summons and struggles with demons. A running motif is the inability of nature to provide consolation or recompense. Standing on an extreme edge of the Jungfrau and intending a fatal leap, Manfred asks, "Ye Mountains, / Why are ye beautiful? I cannot love ye."

Throughout Byron's time in Switzerland, the natural beauty of the landscape had been in competition with his depressive mental state, occasionally lifting him out of himself and offering moments of enthusiasm and inspiration. But, much as the rare days of sunshine had been surrounded by weeks of tenacious gloom and rain that summer, the Alps were ultimately no match for Byron's darkness. In late September, he concluded his Alpine journal-letter to Augusta with the following lament:

> I was disposed to be pleased – I am a lover of Nature – and an Admirer of Beauty – I can bear fatigue – & welcome privation – and have seen some of the noblest views in the world. – But in all this – the recollection of bitterness – & more especially of recent & more home desolation – which must accompany me through life – have preyed upon me here – and neither the music of the Shepherd – the crashing of the Avalanche – nor the torrent – the mountain – the Glacier – the Forest – nor the Cloud – have for one moment – lightened the weight upon my heart – nor enabled me to lose my own wretched identity

in the majesty & the power and the Glory – around – above – & beneath me.

Not "for one moment" had he been happy: it seems an over-statement, in part calculated to win Augusta's sympathy, as she was drifting away from him under the influence of Annabella's monitory companionship. But there's an essential truth to Byron's admission of his failure to transcend his "home desolation" in Switzerland. It was time to move on. Soon he was passing through the doorway of the Villa Diodati for the last time, and, with Hobhouse at his side, heading for his next destination, the country that would become Byron's home for most of his remaining years and the site of his greatest poetic achievements, a place that Shelley would call the "paradise of exiles": Italy.

6

The Greenest Isle of My Imagination

[To John Murray]

Address yr. answer to Venice however

Dear Sir—Don't be alarmed.—You will see me defend myself gaily—that is—if I happen to be in Spirits—and by <u>Spirits</u> I don't mean your meaning of the word—but the spirit of a bull-dog when pinched—or a bull when pinned—it is then that they make best sport—and as my Sensations under an attack are probably a happy compound of the united energies of those amiable animals—you may perhaps see what Marrall calls "rare sport"*—and some good tossing and goring in the course of the controversy.—But I must be in the right cue first—and I doubt I am almost too far off to be in a sufficient fury for the purpose—and then I have effeminated and enervated myself with love and the summer in these last two months.—I wrote to Mr. Hobhouse the other day—and foretold that Juan would either fall entirely or succeed

---

* Massinger's *New Way to Pay Old Debts*, Act v, scene 1.

completely—there will be no medium—appearances are not favourable—but as you write the day after publication—it can hardly be decided what opinion will predominate.—You seem in a fright—and doubtless with cause.—Come what may—I never will flatter the Million's canting in any shape—circumstances may or may not have placed me at times in a situation to lead the public opinion—but the public opinion—never led nor ever shall lead me.—I will not sit on "a degraded throne" so pray put Messrs. Southey—or Sotheby—or Tom Moore—or Horace Twiss upon it—they will all of them be transported with their coronation.— — — — —

You have bought Harlow's drawings of Margarita and me rather dear methinks—but since you desire the story of Margarita Cogni—you shall be told it—though it may be lengthy.— —Her face is of the fine Venetian cast of the old Time—and her figure though perhaps too tall not less fine,—taken altogether in the national dress.— — — — — — — — — — —

In the summer of 1817, Hobhouse and myself were sauntering on horseback along the Brenta one evening—when amongst a group of peasants we remarked two girls as the prettiest we had seen for some time.—About this period there had been great distress in the country—and I had a little relieved some of the people.—Generosity makes a great figure at very little cost in Venetian livres—and mine had probably been exaggerated—as an Englishman's— — Whether they remarked us looking at them or no—I know not—but one of them called out to me in Venetian—"Why do not you who relieve others—think of us also?"—I turned round and answered her—"Cara—tu sei troppo bella e giovane per aver bisogno del' soccorso mio" [Darling - you are too beautiful and young to need my help]—she answered—if *you saw my hut and my food—you would not say so.—All this passed half jestingly—and I saw no more of her for some days—A few evenings after—we met with these two girls again—and they addressed us more seriously—assuring us of the truth of their statement.—They were cousins—Margarita married—the other single.—As I doubted still of the circumstances—I took the business up in a different light—and made an appointment with them for the next evening.— Hobhouse had taken a fancy to the single lady—who was much shorter—in stature—but a very pretty girl also.— — They came attended by a third woman—who was cursedly in the way—and Hobhouse's charmer took fright (I don't mean at Hobhouse but at not being married—for here no woman will do anything under adultery) and flew off—and mine made some bother—at the propositions—and wished to consider of them.—I told her—"if you really are in want I will relieve you without any conditions whatever—and you may make love with me or no just as you please—that shall make no difference—but if you are not in absolute necessity—this is naturally a rendezvous—and I presumed that you understood this—when you made the appointment".— — She said that she had no objection to make love with me—as she was married—and all married women did it—but that her husband (a baker) was somewhat ferocious—and would do her a mischief.—In short—in a few evenings we arranged our affairs—and for two years—in the course of which I had <almost two> more women than I can count or recount—she was the only one who preserved over me an ascendancy— which was often disputed & never impaired.—As she herself used to say publicly—"It don't matter—he may have five hundred—but he will always come back to me".— — — — The reasons of this were firstly—her person—very dark—*

tall—the Venetian face—very fine black eyes—and certain other qualities which need not be mentioned.—She was two & twenty years old—and never having had children—had not spoilt her figure—nor <u>anything else</u>—which is I assure you—a great desideratum in a hot climate where they grow relaxed and doughy and <u>flumpity</u> in a short time after breeding.— —She was besides a thorough Venetian in her dialect—in her thoughts—in her countenance—in every thing—with all their naïveté and Pantaloon humour.— Besides she could neither read nor write—and could not plague me with letters—except twice that she paid sixpence for a public scribe under the piazza—to make a letter for her—upon some occasion when I was ill and could not see her.— —In other respects she was somewhat fierce and "prepotente" that is—overbearing—and used to walk in whenever it suited her—with no very great regard to time, place, nor persons—and if she found any women in her way she knocked them down.—When I first knew her I was in "relazione" (liaison) with la Signora Segati—who was silly enough one evening at Dolo—accompanied by some of her female friends—to threaten her—for the Gossips of the Villeggiatura—had already found out by the neighing of my horse one evening—that I used to "ride late in the night" to meet the Fornarina.— —Margarita threw back her veil— (fazziolo) and replied in very explicit Venetian—"<u>You</u> are <u>not</u> his <u>wife</u>—<u>I</u> am <u>not</u> his <u>wife</u>—<u>you</u> are his Donna—and <u>I</u> am his <u>donna</u>—<u>your</u> husband is a cuckold—and mine is another;—for the rest, what <u>right</u> have you to reproach me?—if he prefers what is mine—to what is yours—is it my fault? if you wish to secure him—tie him to your petticoat-string— but do not think to speak to me without a reply because you happen to be richer than I am."— — — — —

Having delivered this pretty piece of eloquence (which I translate as it was related to me by a bystander) she went on her way—leaving a numerous audience with Madame Segati—to ponder at her leisure on the dialogue between them.—When I came to Venice for the Winter she followed.—I never had any regular <u>liaison</u> with her—but whenever she came I never allowed any other connection to interfere with her—and as she found herself out to be a favourite she came pretty often.—But She had inordinate Self-love—and was not tolerant of other women —except of the Segati—who was as she said my regular "Amica"—so that I being at that time somewhat promiscuous—there was great confusion— and demolition of head dresses and handkerchiefs—and sometimes my servants in "redding the fray"* between her and other feminine persons—received more knocks than acknowledgements for their peaceful endeavors. — —At the "Cavalchina" the masqued ball on the last night of the Carnival—where all the World goes—she snatched off the mask of Madame Contarini—a lady noble by birth—and decent in conduct—for no other reason but because she happened to be leaning on my arm.—You may suppose what a cursed noise this made,—but this is only one of her pranks.—At last she quarrelled with her husband—and one evening ran away to my house.—I told her this would not do—she said she would lie in the street but not go back to him—that he beat her (the gentle tigress) spent her money—and scandalously neglected his Oven. As it was Midnight—I let her stay—and next day there was no moving her at all.— —Her husband came roaring & crying—& entreating her to come back, not She!—He then applied to the Police—and they ap-

---

* Walter Scott, *Waverley,* chapter LIV.

plied to me—I told them and her husband to take her—I did not want her—she had come—and I could not fling her out of the window—but they might conduct her through that or the door if they chose it— —She went before the Commissary—but was obliged to return with that "becco Ettico" (consumptive cuckold), as she called the poor man who had a Ptisick.—In a few days she ran away again.—After a precious piece of work she fixed herself in my house—really & truly without my consent—but owing to my indolence— and not being able to keep my countenance—for if I began in a rage she always finished by making me laugh with some Venetian pantaloonery or other—and the Gipsy knew this well enough—as well as her other powers of persuasion— and exerted them with the usual tact and success of all She-things—high and low—they are all alike for that.— Madame Benzone also took her under her protection—and then her head turned.—She was always in extremes either crying or laughing—and so fierce when angered that she was the terror of men women and children—for she had the strength of an Amazon with the temper of Medea. She was a fine animal—but quite untameable. I was the only person that could at all keep her in any order—and when she saw me really angry—(which they tell me is rather a savage sight), she subsided.—But she had a thousand fooleries— in her fazziolo—the dress of the lower orders—she looked beautiful—but alas! she longed for a hat and feathers and all I could say or do—(and I said much) could not prevent this travestie.—I put the first into the fire—but I got tired of burning them before she did of buying them—so that she made herself a figure—for they did not at all become her.— Then she would have her gowns with a tail—like a lady forsooth—nothing would serve her—but "l'abito colla coua", or cua, (that is the Venetian for "la Coda" the tail or train) and as her cursed pronunciation of the word made me laugh—there was an end of all controversy—and she dragged this diabolical tail after her every where.— —In the mean time she beat the women—and stopped my letters.—I found her one day pondering over one—she used to try to find out by their shape whether they were feminine or no—and she used to lament her ignorance—and actually ~~learned~~ studied her Alphabet—on purpose (as she declared) to open all letters addressed to me and read their contents.— — — — — — —

I must not omit to do justice to her housekeeping qualities—after she came into my house as "donna di governo" the expences were reduced to less than half—and every body did their duty better—the apartments were kept in order—and every thing and every body else except herself.— —That she had a sufficient regard for me in her wild way I had many reasons to believe—I will mention one.— —In the autumn one day going to the Lido with my Gondoliers—we were overtaken by a heavy Squall and the Gondola put in peril—hats blown away—boat filling—oar lost—tumbling sea—thunder—rain in torrents—night coming—& wind increasing.—On our return—after a tight struggle, I found her on the open steps of the Mocenigo palace on the Grand Canal—with her great black eyes flashing through her tears and the long dark hair which was streaming drenched with rain over her brows & breast;—she was perfectly exposed to the storm—and the wind blowing her hair & dress about her tall thin figure—and the lightning flashing round her—with the waves rolling at her feet—made her look like Medea alighted from her chariot—or the Sibyl of the tempest that was rolling around her—the only living thing within hail at that moment except ourselves.—On seeing me safe—she did *not wait to greet me as might be expected—but calling out to me—"Ah! Can' della Madonna xe esto il tempo per andar' al' Lido?" (ah! Dog of the Virgin!—is this a time to go to the Lido?) ran into the house—and solaced herself with scolding the boatmen for not foreseeing the "temporale" [tempest].—I was told by the servants that she had only been prevented from coming in a boat to look after me—by the refusal of all the Gondoliers of the Canal to put out into the harbour in such a moment and that then she sate down on the steps in all the thickest of the Squall—and would neither be removed nor comforted.—Her joy at seeing me again— was moderately mixed with ferocity—and gave me the idea of a tigress over her recovered Cubs.— —But her reign drew near a close.—She became quite ungovernable some months after—and a concurrence of complaints some true and many false—"a favourite has no friend"*—determined me to part with her.—I told her quietly that she must return home—(she had acquired a sufficient provision for herself and mother, &c. in my service,) and She refused to quit the house.—I was firm—and she went—threatening knives and revenge.—I told her—that I had seen knives drawn before her time—and that if she chose to begin—there was a knife—and fork also at her service on the table and that intimidation would not do.—The next day while I was at dinner—she walked in, (having broke open a glass door that led from the hall below to the staircase by way of prologue) and advancing strait up to the table snatched the knife from my hand—cutting me slightly in the thumb in the operation.— Whether she meant to use this against herself or me I do know not—probably against neither— but Fletcher seized*

---

* Thomas Gray, "Ode on the Death of a Favourite Cat."

her by the arms—and disarmed her.—I then called my boatmen—and desired them to get the Gondola ready and conduct her to her own house again—seeing carefully that she did herself no mischief by the way.—She seemed quite quiet and walked down stairs.—I resumed my dinner.—We heard a great noise—I went out—and met them on the staircase— carrying her up stairs.—She had thrown herself into the Canal.—That she intended to destroy herself I do not believe—but when we consider the fear women and men who can't swim have of deep or even shallow water—(and the Venetians in particular though they live on the waves) and that it was also night—and dark—& very cold—it shows that she had a devilish spirit of some sort within her.—They had got her out without much difficulty or damage except the salt water she had swallowed and the wetting she had undergone.—I foresaw her intention to refix herself, and sent for a Surgeon—enquiring how many hours it would require to restore her from her agitation, and he named the time.—I then said—"I give you that time—and more if you require it—but at the expiration of the prescribed period—if <u>She</u> does not leave the house—<u>I</u> will".— — — — —

All my people were consternated—they had always been frightened at her—and were now paralyzed—they wanted me to apply to the police—to guard myself—&c. &c.—like a pack of sniveling servile boobies as they were— —I did nothing of the kind—thinking that I might as well end that way as another—besides—I had been used to savage women and knew their ways.—I had her sent home quietly after her recovery—and I never saw her since except twice at the opera—at a distance amongst the audience. She made many attempts to return—but no more violent ones.—And this is the story of Margarita Cogni—as far as it belongs to me.—I *forgot to mention that she was very devout— and would cross herself if she heard the prayer-time strike—sometimes— when that ceremony did not appear to be much in unison with what she was then about.—She was quick in reply—as for instance—one day when she had made me very angry with beating somebody or other—I called her a <u>Cow</u> (<u>Cow</u> in Italian is a sad affront and tantamount to the feminine of dog in English) I called her "Vacca" she turned round—curtsied —and answered "Vacca <u>tua</u>— 'Celenza" (ie. Eccellenza) <u>your</u> Cow—please your Excellency.—In short—she was—as I said before—a very fine Animal—of considerable beauty and energy—with many good & several amusing qualities—but wild as a witch—and fierce as a demon.—She used to boast publicly of her ascendancy over me—contrasting it with that of other women—and assigning for it sundry reasons physical and moral which did more credit to her person than her modesty.— —True it was that they all tried to get her away— and no one succeeded—till her own absurdity helped them.— Whenever there was a competition, and sometimes—one would be shut in one room and one in another—to prevent battle—she had generally the preference.— —*

yrs. very truly and affectly

B

P.S.—The Countess G is much better than she was.—I sent you before leaving Venice—a letter containing the real original sketch—which gave rise to the "Vampire" &c. did you get it?—

You have just read the longest letter Byron ever wrote: it runs to almost 3,000 words covering five sheets of blueish-white paper folded in half to make twenty pages front and back, sent at the height of the summer in 1819 as he was moving between Ravenna and Venice. Each page is filled entirely with writing, and one gets the sense that he could have kept going indefinitely with more juicy details, except he runs out of room (Figure 6.1). It is altogether a profligate record of a profligate period of Byron's life. Most of it looks backward to tell the history of his relationship with Margarita Cogni, his pre-eminent Venetian mistress of the previous two years. Margarita's story had been requested by John Murray, who wrote to Byron asking for "some little Account of Said Lady" after purchasing two portraits – one of Byron and one of Margarita – drawn from life by George Harlow in Venice the previous year (Figures 6.2 and 6.3). In sending this racy narrative, Byron was knowingly providing Murray with a story his publisher could read aloud to the literary men who gathered regularly at his Albemarle Street offices. The letter is thus a semi-public production, offered as an extensive gloss on the drawing of Margarita, which Murray would have shown to his visitors while sharing Byron's latest epistle. Yet Byron's descriptions of Margarita contrast sharply with Harlow's rendering of a demure young woman with a quiet expression, her hair covered modestly by a white headscarf. In Byron's memorable description, she becomes instead "the Sibyl of the tempest," "her great black eyes flashing through her tears," being "perfectly exposed to the storm," with "the wind blowing her hair & dress about her tall thin figure." Byron's Margarita is violent, funny, sexy, overbearing, and foolish, "wild as a witch – and fierce as a demon," the object of Byron's patronage and his appetite, and nevertheless a formidable presence in her own right. For Murray and the lads back in London, she is transformed into "a very fine animal," praised for her illiteracy, her youthful figure, her "great black eyes," her sexual enthusiasm, her "Pantaloon humour," and her operatic, possessive devotion to her English lover.

When Byron wrote this letter, three years had passed since the haunted summer in Geneva, a season of depression that had followed his separation from Lady Byron and their infant daughter. When we last saw him, Byron was suffering under the weight of his "wretched identity" despite the surrounding Alpine grandeur, and he had just written "the real original sketch—which gave rise to the 'Vampire'" that he mentions in the postscript. Now he seems light-hearted and ebullient, happily recalling Margarita and the Venetian scenes of their affair while also in the midst of a new romantic liaison with "the Countess G," seemingly untouched by the remorse and pain that had dogged him. We are hearing Byron the raconteur: the performer whose conversation charmed many, and whose confessional, improvisatory, and witty narrative style was the driving force behind his newly published poem, referred to here only as "Juan." We are also hearing the changes in Byron that three years of living in and around Venice had produced. In fact, the alteration had been almost immediate, a prime instance of the mobility of Byron's emotional life and of the deep influence a new social milieu often had on him. Switzerland had been a bridge, a summer of darkness only fitfully illuminated by the brilliant beauty of the landscape and the intellectual fireworks of the Shelley circle. But Italy, and Venice in particular, had done much to dispel the gloom.

As Byron would write of Venice in the fourth and final canto of *Childe Harold's Pilgrimage,*

I lov'd her from my boyhood – she to me
Was as a fairy city of the heart,
Rising like water-columns from the sea,
Of joy the sojourn, and of wealth the mart;
And Otway, Radcliffe, Schiller, Shakespeare's art,
Had stamp'd her image in me

Venice had long been, he said, "the greenest isle of my imagination," the home of Othello and Shylock and the setting of Otway's *Venice Preserved*, Radcliffe's *Mysteries of Udolpho*, and Schiller's *The Ghost-Seer*, a place that had "always haunted me most – after the East," and, experienced in person, it did not disappoint. "I like the gloomy gaiety of their gondolas – and the silence of their canals," he wrote to Murray shortly after his arrival in November 1816, praising the city's late-night society and the pervasive decadence of the place and its inhabitants. Fallen from its position as a major maritime power and commercial and artistic center, and occupied by the Austrians in the wake of Napoleon, Venice had dwindled to an impoverished provincial remnant of its former self. And yet, for Byron, it still retained the magic of its atmosphere and its literary and historical associations, enhanced by its desolation, "perhaps even dearer in her day of woe, / Than when she was a boast, a marvel, and a show." Feeling somewhat like a ghost himself, he slipped easily into the mysterious, lively decrepitude of Venice.

Almost immediately upon his arrival, Byron began organizing his life in Venice around sexual indulgence. He thus embarked on his last and greatest burst of promiscuity, one that would extend approximately until the time of this letter, the summer of 1819. He tells Murray here that he has had "more women than I can count or recount" in Venice, crossing out the "almost two [hundred]" that he began to write as an estimate. On the cusp of 30 years old, he was an international celebrity, an English peer of the realm, and a figure of glamour and scandal, known to be handsome and possessed of considerable wealth. His escapades in Venice were facilitated by all of these factors, most heavily the last, as it seems that most of his sexual experiences in Venice had a more or less transactional element to them. As he admits freely in this letter, "Generosity makes a great figure at very little cost in Venetian livres," especially given the "great distress in the country" caused by heavy Austrian taxation and the ongoing agricultural and humanitarian crisis that followed the Tambora volcanic eruption. While in Venice, Byron gave liberally to local subscription charities and offered money regularly to anyone who applied to him in need. We hear of the relationship with Margarita beginning essentially with a scene of charity, albeit a flirtatious one – "Why do not you who relieve others—think of us also?" – which launches an ongoing affair involving gifts and money, countenanced and even encouraged by her baker husband, Andrea Magnarotto, who would have been experiencing especially severe effects of the lost harvests of those post-Tambora years.

Looking back in another letter of 1819, Byron boasts that he has "run the Gauntlet" with Venetian women, offering a Leporello-like list of his sexual partners, "some of them ... Countesses – & some of them Cobblers wives":

> the Tarruscelli – the Da Mosti – the Spineda – the Lotti – the Rizzato – the Eleanora – the Carlotta – the Giulietta – the Alvisi – the Zambieri – The Eleanora da Bezzi – (who was the King of Naples' Gioacchino's mistress – at least one of them) the Theresina of Mazzurati – the Glettenheimer – & her Sister – the Luigia & her mother – the Fornaretta – the Santa – the Caligari – the Portiera – the Bolognese

figurante – the Tentora and her sister.... some noble –
some middling – some low – & all whores – I have had
them all & thrice as many to boot since 1817.

Calling these women "all whores" is distasteful – this letter
was written jointly to Hobhouse and Kinnaird, both of whom
Byron enjoyed shocking – but it is also revealing, especially as
Byron writes to request his friends' help in remitting money
from his publisher, adding, "what I get by my brains—I will
spend on my b[olloc]ks – as long as I have a tester or a testicle
remaining. – I shall not live long – & for that Reason – I must
live while I can." Having given up his lordly posture of refusing to accept payment for his works, Byron was now pushing
Murray for as much money as possible and using it to fund a
lifestyle of relentless hedonism and dissipation. Byron himself
estimated that he spent several thousand pounds on women
in his first two years in Italy. It may be too much to call Byron
a sex tourist in Venice, but he certainly took full advantage of
the mismatch between his own financial resources and those
of the Italians who variously implored, bargained for, abet-
ted, and tolerated his attentions. He had learned the pattern
as master of his female Newstead servants and had played
at it among the young actresses and courtesans of the London demi-monde during his years of fame. Now, wrapped in
his cloak and stepping from his gondola toward the private
casino he rented for the purpose, Byron would frequently be
headed for another elaborate assignation or sexual adventure arranged on the strength of his wealth and social status.
Speaking frankly, if a touch facetiously, Peter Cochran calls
Byron's life in Venice "a non-stop sex orgy."

When the Shelleys visited Byron in 1818, they were dismayed. Upon arrival, Percy at first was cheered by Byron's

appearance and mood. All his energy seemed to have brightened: "he is changed into the liveliest & happiest looking man I ever met." But after observing Byron's erotic activities among the Venetians, Percy wrote to his friend Peacock in a mood of panic and snobbish revulsion:

> the Italian women are perhaps the most contemptible of all who exist under the moon; the most ignorant, the most disgusting, the most bigotted, the most filthy. Countesses smell so of garlick that an ordinary Englishman cannot approach them. L[ord] B[yron] is familiar with the lowest sort of these women, the people his gondolieri pick up in the streets. He allows fathers & mothers to bargain with him for their daughters, & though this is common enough in Italy, yet for an Englishman to encourage such sickening vice is a melancholy thing.

To the high-minded and chauvinistic Percy Shelley, Byron's life in Venice seemed awash in a particularly Italian squalor, and Mary agreed: she wrote to friends that Byron was "lost ... among the worst inhabitants of Venise" and expressed fears that he would become "a lost man if he does not escape soon." Percy seems also to suggest that Byron's extravagances included sodomy and a return to the homosexual pleasures of his earlier years: "He associates with wretches who ... do not scruple to avow practices which are not only not named but I believe seldom even conceived in England." For all of their domestic unconventionality, the Shelleys had by this time settled into something closer to a typical English marriage, from which vantage point Byron's immersion in the murky sexual economy of Italy looked grotesque, exploitative, and dangerous. Honestly, it was almost certainly sometimes all of those things. But it was also a path of reinvention for a man who had failed at being a proper English husband, landowner, and member of the House of Lords. Taking the low road forward, Byron was undergoing a transformation that would enable his greatest and most ground-breaking poetic achievements.

Looking backward in 1819, soon after sending this chapter's letter to Murray, Byron would himself stress the connection between his extensive sexual experience and the style and content of *Don Juan*. As he wrote with defiant brio to Kinnaird that October,

> As to "Don Juan" – confess – confess – you dog – and be candid – that it is the sublime of *that there* sort of writing – it may be bawdy – but is it not good English? – It may be profligate but is it not *life*, is it not the *thing*? – Could any man have written it – who has not lived in the world? – and tooled in a post-chaise? – in – a hackney coach? – in a Gondola? against a wall? in a court carriage? – in a vis a vis? – on a table? – and under it?

Byron asserts that his bawdy and profligate poem could only have been written by a man of similar description – one able to turn his libertinage, with its wide-ranging, promiscuous experience of other humans, to creative account. Comic irony regarding erotic experience seems to have been the great lesson Byron learned from the Venetians and other Italians who entered his orbit and his bed (and coach and gondola, etc.) during these years of personal growth. The tortured Byronic hero of *Childe Harold*, the Eastern Tales, and *Manfred* gives way to a spirit of carnival, to the "Venetian pantaloonery" that Byron admires laughingly in Margarita Cogni, and that he carries over to the farcical scenes of *Don Juan*. He felt this mere months after arriving in Venice, sending his gothic closet drama *Manfred* to Murray but remarking that "It is too much in my old style…. I certainly am a devil of a mannerist – & must leave off." Already, the tragic coloring of experience was seeming to Byron like a vestige of a former way of seeing, an overly mannered style that was growing stale. "I began in a rage," he tells Murray, but Margarita "always finished by making me laugh." Venice took him in, and estranged him from himself, giving him fresh control over his emotions while also enhancing his ability to laugh at himself and others. Byron had always enjoyed humorous scenes between lovers: Lady Frances hiding love notes in the billiard room, Caroline Lamb doffing her page costume, even Augusta's goofy teasing. In the aftermath of his failed marriage and the nightmares of 1816, the Italians helped him to reconnect comedy to romance, indulgence to passion – perhaps even, on some far horizon, happiness to love. In addition, as he wrote to Murray, Italian women "*kiss* better than those of any other nation," a fact he attributed to the Catholic "worship of images and the early habit of osculation induced thereby."

Amidst his countless ephemeral rendezvous, Byron formed two longer-term attachments: one to Margarita Cogni (whose story is told in detail in this letter) and the other to Marianna, "la Signora Segati," as he calls her here. He met Marianna Segati, the young wife of his new landlord, within a week of arriving in Venice in the late fall of 1816. She was "pretty as an Antelope," "two & twenty years old" with "great black Eastern eyes," a "light and pretty" figure, "the Italian countenance – and dark glossy hair." Byron had taken up temporary residence in a set of rooms above a draper's shop in the Frezzeria, just off St. Mark's Square, and Marianna was conveniently available as part of this arrangement.

As the baker Magnarotto would later do, her husband seems to have turned a blind eye in the Italian manner of the time, which tacitly allowed for married women to have an *amoroso* or *cavalier servente* as an accepted companion. Byron became Marianna's "Caro Giorgio" and settled into a liaison with her that lasted more than a year, with Byron spending lavishly on her: when she sold an expensive set of diamonds he had given her, he repurchased them and gave them to her again.

Soon after the *relazione* with Marianna began, Byron wrote to his friends Moore, Kinnaird, and Murray that he was in love, expanding on this theme to Augusta:

> I have fallen in love with a very pretty Venetian.... we have found & sworn an eternal attachment.... and I verily believe we are one of the happiest – unlawful couples on this side of the Alps.... This adventure came very opportunely to console me ... at present – at least for a month past – I have been very tranquil – very loving – & have not so much embarrassed myself with the tortures of the last two years – and that virtuous monster Miss Milbanke, who had nearly driven me out of my senses ... at present I am better – thank Heaven above – & woman beneath.

In this letter, you can sense Byron's inclination to domesticity framed by sin, his tranquility as the lover of already-married women who could only make certain demands upon him, while also providing the thrill of transgression and danger. You can also perceive the acid that Byron was attempting to pour on the bond between Augusta and Annabella, whom he now rightly suspected were colluding to shut him out.

We catch only glimpses of Marianna through Byron's letters. In one written to Moore in March 1817, we can almost see her peering over the edge of the letter itself, as Byron conveys her immediate presence to his correspondent (Figure 6.4):

> here is the Signora Mariana just come in and seated at my elbow.... I really cannot go on. There is a pair of great black eyes looking over my shoulder, like the angel leaning over St. Matthew's, in the old frontispieces to the Evangelists – so that I must turn and answer them instead of you.

Letter-writing gives way to love-making in this little scene of intimacy: so far, so tranquil. But Marianna was not just a pliable, admiring doll. When Byron offered some sardonic remarks on the Italian mode of love affairs, Marianna replied, "If you loved me thoroughly, you would not make so many fine reflections, which are only good *forbirsi i scarpi*": to clean shoes. Around this same time, catching her sister-in-law in an attempt to seduce Byron while he was home alone, she marched in, and, as Byron tells it, "seize[d] her said sister-in-law by the hair, and bestow[ed] upon her sixteen slaps, which would have made your ear ache only to hear their echo. I need not describe the screaming which ensued. The luckless visitor took flight." Marianna then collapsed on the couch, and, as Byron tried to revive her, her husband walked in, demanding, "What is all this?" But Byron soothed him, and soon he left quietly with his wife: "how they settled it, I know not," Byron wrote, "but settle it they did," while the sister-in-law "told the affair to half Venice, and the servants ... to the other half." It was another scene in the improvisatory Venetian follies that Byron essentially managed and produced, playing his part in character and then relating it with comic relish in his letters.

In order to counterbalance the ongoing erotic farce starring Marianna and soon featuring numerous other lovers, Byron took it upon himself to learn the Armenian language from the Mechitarist monks who lived in community on the island of San Lazzaro, just off Venice. For a while, being "studious in the day & dissolute in the evening," he went every afternoon to learn from Father Harut'iwn Avgerian (a name frequently Anglicized to Pasquale Aucher), and soon was working with him to produce an Armenian–English dictionary, along with translations of certain Armenian texts including apocryphal epistles between St. Paul and the Corinthians. As he wrote to Moore in early December, "By way of divertisement, I am studying daily the Armenian language. I found that my mind wanted something craggy to break upon; and this – as the most difficult thing I could discover here for an amusement – I have chosen, to torture me into attention." But Byron's teacher recalled him later as a "tête brûlante" ("a hothead"), an indifferent student more interested in pleasure than scholarship, despite their collaborations. He also reported once finding Byron "bitterly sobbing and weeping" in front of a crucifix, which sounds both like a bit of invented propaganda and like a characteristically Byronic episode. For all of the satisfaction that Byron broadcast in his reports from Venice, privately and chronically, he was still struggling with his demons.

Byron and Hobhouse had visited the Armenian monastery on San Lazarro soon after arriving in Venice, and it appealed immediately, offering a reprise of the all-male camaraderie the poet had experienced in a monastery in Athens in 1810, when he was the lover of Nicolo Girard. Byron's imagination was enlivened by moving between realms of flesh and spirit, of sexual indulgence and religious study. It was an old habit that had been forced on him as a child by his nurse May Gray, who alternated catechisms with intimate caresses, and had been extended in his role as "the Abbot" of Newstead Abbey, where, dressed in robes, he would drink wine from the monk's skull amidst sex games with the servants. For Byron, Romantic longing after some ideal meets skeptical irony, and yet neither is cancelled by the other. Rather, they persist along the line of his writing, visible most clearly when he takes up carnal and spiritual matters simultaneously. Thinking of both his Armenian lessons and his Venetian lovers, Byron recalled later, "my master the Padre Pasquale Aucher ... assured me 'that the terrestrial Paradise had been certainly in Armenia' – I went seeking it – God knows where – did I find it? – Umph! – Now & then – for a minute or two."

The Carnival season quickly became central to Byron's experience of Venice, not least because it brought into focus his attraction to fleshly pleasures that came wrapped in the mantle of religious ritual. Although by Byron's era the Venetian Carnival had dwindled from its former wild glories that had been the wonder of Europe, the impoverished and occupied city still erupted in the weeks leading up to Lent. There were masked balls and parties, ballets and operas, gambling and drinking, prostitutes and street musicians, puppet shows and theatrical displays on trestle stages, all energized by a sense of increased licentiousness and indulgence that kept revelers up until sunrise. Byron dove into everything with relish. These experiences would shape his comic poem *Beppo: A Venetian Story*, written in the fall of 1817 in the early months of the Margarita Cogni affair. In *Beppo*, Byron's first experiment with *ottava rima*, he describes Carnival as a time when:

The people take their fill of recreation,
And buy repentance, ere they grow devout,
However high their rank, or low their station,
With fiddling, feasting, dancing, drinking, masquing,
And other things which may be had for asking.

He tells his readers that "there are songs and quavers, roaring, humming, / Guitars, and every other sort of strumming. / And there are dresses splendid, but fantastical," and "Masks of all times and nations," piling up his lists of sights, sounds, and experiences that comprised the delirium of those late Venetian nights.

Recovering from a fever as the 1817 season ended, Byron wrote to Moore:

> The Carnival – that is, the latter part of it – and sitting up late o' nights, had knocked me up a little. But it is over, – and it is now Lent, with all its abstinence and Sacred Music ... and, though I did not dissipate much upon the whole, yet I find "the sword wearing out the scabbard," though I have but just turned the corner of twenty-nine.

He followed this with one of his most famous short lyrics, a soft farewell to the farewell to flesh that was Carnival:

> So, we'll go no more a roving
>   So late into the night,
> Though the heart be still as loving,
>   And the moon be still as bright.
>
> For the sword outwears its sheath,
>   And the soul wears out the breast,
> And the heart must pause to breathe,
>   And love itself have rest.
>
> Though the night was made for loving,
>   And the day returns too soon,
> Yet we'll go no more a roving
>   By the light of the moon.

The apparent finality of Byron's "no more" strikes a note of melancholy, as if Carnival were over forever and the soul about to depart from the exhausted body, like a sword that has outworn its scabbard. But the poem suggests that, like the moon in its phases and the ecclesiastical calendar based upon them, the heart will continue in its cycles. Byron's lyric commemorates only a pause for breath, a hiatus or rest that is also a time of quiet awakening: the season of Lent, its name (from the Old English word *lencten*) referring to the lengthening of the days in springtime. Although he needed a break, Byron was not finished with the pleasures of the flesh: at age 29, he still had seasons of roving ahead of him.

Hobhouse had left Venice the previous December for Rome. In April 1817, Byron was on his way to join his old friend in the Eternal City, passing through Ferrara, Bologna, and Florence on the way. In Ferrara, he communed with the spirit of the sixteenth-century Italian poet Torquato Tasso, whom Byron believed had been unjustly imprisoned because of his love for Leonora d'Este. A few days later, Byron had written a poem of several hundred lines, "The Lament of Tasso," a brief reprise of *The Prisoner of Chillon*, again depicting a persecuted literary genius, another version of how he saw himself. In Florence, he visited Santa Croce, which he called "the Westminster abbey of Italy," and the Uffizi Gallery, where he was thrilled by the Venus de Medici among other paintings and sculptures: "We gaze and turn away, and know not where, / Dazzled and drunk with beauty," he wrote. But, ultimately, Byron was not much of an art connoisseur: he responded viscerally to images, especially those of beautiful women, but he scorned "the paltry jargon of the marble mart." In some ways, he told Hobhouse, more than anything in the galleries, he was struck by the sight of a crying, starving child outside Florence, eating bread made from grass: another sign of the humanitarian crisis of the post-Tambora years. Byron gave the child money and took the grass bread with him as a sad curiosity.

Rome had a far deeper appeal for Byron, primarily because of its layered historical grandeur and its moody desolation: it offered another version of the contrast between past glories and present decline that attracted him to both Greece and Venice. For a "broken dandy" (as he had called himself in *Beppo*), Rome was an ideal place "To meditate amongst decay, and stand / A ruin amidst ruins." Reunited with Hobhouse, Byron toured the standard sites of the city – the Palatine Hill, the Pantheon, the Colosseum, the Vatican and St. Peter's, the Grotto of Egeria – and began storing up material for the fourth canto of *Childe Harold's Pilgrimage*, which he would complete that summer and which remains the best record of his enthusiasms and reflections regarding Rome. He wrote to Murray soon after arriving, "As a *whole – ancient* & *modern* – it beats Greece – Constantinople – every thing – at least that I have ever seen." And in *Childe Harold*, he proclaimed, "Oh Rome! my country! city of the soul! / The orphans of the heart must turn to thee, / Lone mother of dead empires." Contrasting the past triumphs of Roman civilization with the sorry state of Italy in post-Napoleonic Europe, Byron laments "the hostile horde / Of many-nation'd spoilers," which has conquered and occupied the once-great land. Yet he also felt strongly the larger lesson of Rome, "the moral of all human tales," regarding the vanity and ephemerality of empire: "First Freedom, then Glory – when that fails, / Wealth, vice, corruption, – barbarism at last," as Time brings about the inevitable fall and eventual erasure. In Byron's imagination, it was a monitory prophecy of Britain's future as well.

With his reading in the classics at school as a basis, Byron relied on books as guides to what he was seeing in Rome: Joseph Forsyth's *Remarks on Antiquities, Arts, and Letters During an Excursion in Italy*, Gibbon's *Decline and Fall of the Roman Empire*, and Goethe's *Italian Journey*. This form of tourism was ideal for Byron's imaginative mode, allowing him to project and speculate, overlaying the monuments and ruins with literary associations and his own preoccupations. Of the grand tomb of Cecilia Metella on the Appian Way, "a stern round tower of other days," he asks a series of speculative questions about "the lady of the dead" – "Was she chaste and fair?" "How lived–how loved–how died she?" – evoking various possible Cecilias until the spell of haunting has taken effect:

> I know not why – but standing thus by thee
> It seems as if I had thine inmate known,
> Thou tomb! and other days come back on me
> With recollected music, though the tone
> Is changed and solemn, like the cloudy groan
> Of dying thunder on the distant wind;
> Yet I could seat me by this ivied stone
> Till I had bodied forth the heated mind
> Forms from the floating wreck which Ruin leaves behind;
>
> And from the planks, far shattered o'er the rocks,
> Built me a little bark of hope, once more
> To battle with the ocean and the shocks
> Of the loud breakers, and the ceaseless roar

> Which rushes on the solitary shore
> Where all lies foundered that was ever dear

Out of the fragments and ivy-covered monuments of Rome, Byron will build "a little bark of hope" powered by his sympathetic imagination of other lives. It amounts to a statement of Romantic poetic faith, a continuation of the claim with which he begins Canto IV: "The beings of the mind ... create / And multiply in us a brighter ray / And more beloved existence ... / Watering the heart whose early flowers have died." Or, as he had proclaimed in Canto III, "'Tis to create, and in creating live / A being more intense, that we endow / With form our fancy, gaining as we give / The life we image." Poetry may not save us, says Byron, but, strengthening the channels of sympathy, it can bring us to a life of greater brightness and intensity – perhaps our best hope for salvation after all.

Byron returned to Venice after three weeks and immediately moved to the Villa Foscarini on the Brenta Canal in the village of La Mira, about a dozen miles from Venice. He reunited eagerly with Marianna Segati and installed her for the summer out at La Mira, where his visitors included Matthew Gregory "Monk" Lewis, Hobhouse, and the young American writer George Ticknor. It was a relatively relaxing season for Byron, and a productive one: he completed the fourth canto of *Childe Harold* in July, working late into the night. Through these months of *villeggiatura*, he found himself settling into his Italian existence, with Marianna as a soothing and exciting companion. "I am just come out from an hour's swim in the Adriatic; and I write to you with a black-eyed Venetian girl before me, reading Boccacio," he told Moore in another one of his in-the-moment letters. But it was also during this period, while riding along the

Brenta, that Byron and Hobhouse met the beautiful, fierce, impoverished, 22-year-old Margarita Cogni, "la Fornarina," about whom Byron tells Murray so much in this chapter's letter. That meeting inaugurated Margarita's ascendancy, "which was often disputed & never impaired.—As she herself used to say publicly—'It don't matter—he may have five hundred—but he will always come back to me.'" Soon Byron was writing *Beppo*, his comic verse narrative of Venetian adultery that ends with the lady keeping both husband and lover, each of them complacent about the arrangement: it was the polar opposite of his vengeful and tragic poem *The Giaour*. Under the influence of Italy, he had evolved past the tortured gothic Byronism of his earlier years, and, as Leslie Marchand puts it, "something of the careless and relaxed realism of his letters invaded his verse." In the early fall, Hobhouse pronounced Byron "well, and merry and happy, more charming every day."

The sale of Newstead Abbey for £94,500, finally agreed upon in December, meant that Byron could clear most of his debts (though it took almost another year for the sale to close), even as it severed one of his earliest and strongest ties to England. As he wrote to Samuel Rogers of Venice, "here have I pitched my staff – & here I propose to reside for the remainder of my life," claiming he had "no desire to visit" England again. Byron was reinventing himself amongst the Italians, but the consequences of his activities in England still had power in his life. His natural daughter Allegra, conceived with Claire Clairmont in London in the spring of 1816 just before he departed the country, had been born and was growing into a toddler (Figure 6.5). Since the Geneva summer, Claire had been sending Byron pleading love letters, all of which remained unanswered. She wrote to him on Allegra's first birthday – January 12, 1818 – sending a lock of the child's hair and describing her "little darling" as having "eyes of a dazzling blue … rosy projecting lips & a little square chin dented in the middle exactly like your own."

Claire was preparing to deliver Allegra to Byron, as per their agreement, driven on her part by an overriding desire to maintain a connection with her distant quondam lover. Although Byron had clearly set his face against Claire, she dared to hope that their daughter would form an ongoing tether between them. In the birthday letter, she wrote,

> My dear friend, how I envy you. You will have a little darling to crawl to your knees and pull you till you take her up – then she will sit in crook of your arm & you will give her raisins out of your own plate & a little drop of wine from your own glass & she will think herself a little Queen in Creation. When she shall be older, she will run about your house like a lapwing; If you are miserable, her light and careless voice will make you happy, [and] you may delight yourself in contemplating a creature growing under your own hands as it were. You may look at her and think, "This is my work."

Here Claire offers a powerful vision of parental domesticity and authorship, not without a hint of Frankensteinian associations, as if Allegra might become both a magnum opus and a second self for a poet whose métier was the projection of avatars. Byron was susceptible to the idea, particularly as he was beginning to understand that contact with his daughter Ada was going to be minimal at best. On his return trip from Rome, he had written to Augusta:

> They tell me [Allegra] is very pretty – with blue eyes & dark hair – & although I never was attached nor pretend-

ed attachment to the mother – still in case of the eternal war & alienation which I foresee about my legitimate daughter – Ada – it may be well to have something to repose a hope on – I must love something in my old age.

In January 1818, Byron again entered the wild round of the Venetian Carnival, sending Hobhouse off to England with the manuscript of the new canto of *Childe Harold's Pilgrimage*. For Murray, he included a high-spirited, smutty letter in the form of a poem, extolling the connection between rhyme-making and love-making, the mutual dependence of writing and sexual hedonism. It begins,

> My dear Mr. Murray,
> You're in a damned hurry
> To set up this ultimate Canto,
> But (if they don't rob us)
> You'll see Mr. Hobhouse
> Will bring it safe in his portmanteau. –

And concludes,

> Now, I'll put out my taper
> (I've finished my paper
> For these stanzas you see on the *brink* stand)
> There's a whore on my right,
> For I rhyme best at night
> When a C—t is tied close to *my Inkstand*.
>
>   …
>
> For, in rhyme or in love
> (Which both come from above)
> I'll *stand* with our "*Tommy*" or "*Sammy*"   ("Moore"
>   and "Rogers")
> But the Sopha and lady

Are both of them ready
And so, here's "Good Night to you dammee!"

The jokey sexual frankness and double rhymes – "rob us / Hobhouse" and "brink stand / ink stand" – look forward to the *Don Juan* style which had emerged with *Beppo* (which Byron was also about to send to Murray) and would soon become Byron's primary poetic mode. And like parts of *Don Juan*, this lyric was deemed unfit for a wide audience: its final stanzas remained unpublished until 1970.

Somewhere in the midst of Carnival, Byron briefly met the woman who would soon become the love of his life without recognizing her (and about whom we will hear more in the coming chapters). Instead, he wound up with a venereal disease caught from a different Italian gentlewoman, "the first Gonorrhea I have not paid for." But none of it really dampened his spirits: he told Rogers soon thereafter that Venice "is a very good place for women … & the romance of the place is a mighty adjunct." The city itself seemed to conspire with him for pleasure: as he had written in *Childe Harold* IV, "Of the happiest moments which were wrought / Within the web of my existence, some / From thee, fair Venice! have their colours caught." By late spring, in addition to his liaison with Margarita Cogni and "a world of other harlotry," he had begun an affair with an opera singer, Arpalice Taruscelli, "the prettiest Bacchante in the world – & a piece to perish in," writing to Hobhouse in mid-May that he has "fucked her twice a day for the last six – today is the seventh – but no Sabbath day – for we meet at Midnight." Even allowing for some padding of accounts, the intensity of Byron's sexual activity during this period was off all normal charts. His own boasts are one thing, but the surviving letters from his Venetian lovers paint a similar picture, full as they are of requests for assignations, expressions of fervent attachment, pleas for attention, and laments over his other interests. Arpalice Taruscelli wrote to Byron while she was traveling with her opera company, "Tell me something, Baby! how many baker-girls, how many little seamstresses, how much mischief have you made in the last two days? Already I seem to read your black crimes on your handsome face. Poor Arpalice! but poor Giorgio, if I find out about them upon my return!" Her letters reveal an intelligent, humorous woman, full of charm, who called Byron "my Baby" and "my everything" while also registering his frustrating oddities: "You are the most bizarre man in the world, and I the wisest Woman in paying no attention to your eccentricities…. [but] I must forgive my Madcap everything on account of his mischievous little face."

In May 1818, Allegra arrived with her nurse from England. Byron was preparing to move again, this time to what became his signature Venetian residence, the Palazzo Mocenigo on the Grand Canal. To mark the occasion, driven by an almost demonic energy, he performed another one of his epic swims, this time from the Lido to the end of the Grand Canal, a distance of about 4 miles "without touching or resting," despite his "having had a *piece* in the forenoon – & taking another in the evening at ten of the Clock." He wrote to Moore in early June, "It is four, and the dawn gleams over the Grand Canal, and unshadows the Rialto. I must to bed; up all night – but … 'It's life, though, damme it's life!'" From the marble balcony of the *piano nobile*, Byron could look down on the gondolas passing or approaching his open steps which allowed visitors water access to the ground floor. There he kept a menagerie of animals: caged birds, monkeys, dogs, a fox, and a wolf, successors of his beloved canines at Newstead and his Trinity college bear. In addition, at Mocenigo he had more than a dozen servants, all relatively unmanaged: "my ragamuffins – Gondoliers, Nurses – cook – footmen &c.," along with his long-standing English valet, Fletcher, and the newly hired Venetian, Tita Falcieri, who would remain loyal to the last. Add to this the many mistresses coming and going more or less indiscreetly, with the "prepotente" Margarita Cogni doing her best to sustain some kind of order and keep Byron in her corner, and you have a household ill suited for the reception of a toddler. Allegra stayed with her father for the summer, and became "a great favourite with every body," as Byron wrote to Augusta, wondering if she resembled his legitimate daughter Ada and remarking on her "devil of a Spirit – but that is Papa's." Somewhere in the midst of all of this, late at night, when the summer heat had faded from the high-ceilinged rooms of the palazzo, he began writing what would become his finest and most important work, *Don Juan*.

In August, Percy Shelley came to Venice to visit Byron and to give Claire a chance to see Allegra again. The Shelleys, their two children (William, age 2, and Clara, age 1) and Claire had all traveled to Italy early that summer and were now perched in Tuscany. But Shelley was restless and eagerly volunteered to travel with Claire to Venice, leaving Mary behind with the children – another episode in this ongoing saga of careless fathers. And, perhaps predictably, it seems that Shelley and Claire recommenced their sexual connection during these weeks of shared travel. They found Allegra at the home of Byron's friend Richard Hoppner, the British consul at Venice. He and his wife Isabella had taken the little girl into their home when it had become clear that Byron's irregular mode of domesticity would not do. Seeing Allegra again that morning, Shelley wrote to Mary that she was "so grown you would hardly know her – she is pale & has lost a good deal of her liveliness, but is beautiful as ever, though more mild." While Claire lavished caresses on the daughter she had not seen for months, Shelley met with Byron, who was in a generous mood. He instantly agreed to let Claire spend time with Allegra in Italy and even offered to let her reclaim the girl altogether, promising financial support and telling Shelley, "after all I have no right to the child." Later that fall, he would alter his will to leave Allegra £5,000. And he also had a place for the Shelley *ménage* to stay; he was currently renting Hoppner's country villa, I Cappuccini, located at Este in the Euganean foothills just south of Padua, but had never stayed there: would Shelley like to take it for a season? The answer was yes.

As the evening came on, Shelley and Byron traveled by gondola over to the Lido to ride Byron's horses along the strand. Shelley was particularly struck by the stark beauty of the twilit landscape and the emotional intensity of the day, and would recreate the whole scene in his autobiographical poem, *Julian and Maddalo*:

> I rode one evening with Count Maddalo
> Upon the bank of land which breaks the flow
> Of Adria towards Venice: a bare strand
> Of hillocks, heaped from ever-shifting sand,
>
>   ...
>
> So, as we rode, we talked; and the swift thought,
> Winging itself with laughter, lingered not,
> But flew from brain to brain, – such glee was ours.
> Charged with light memories of remembered hours.

It was a day that further cemented the connection between the two men, even as it highlighted some basic differences between the idealist Shelley and the dark-minded Byron. In *Julian and Maddalo*, the Shelley character insists, "if we were not weak / Should we be less in deed than in desire?" to which Byron-as-Maddalo replies, "Ay, if we were not weak – and we aspire / How vainly to be strong! … You talk Utopia." In a letter, Shelley wrote that their "conversation consisted in histories of his wounded feelings, & questions as to my affairs, & great professions of friendship & regard for me." They also talked of "literary matters" and Byron recited "some stanzas of great energy" from the fourth canto of *Childe Harold*. Both poets were arguably at the height of their powers, feeding off each other's energy and the rapturous influence of Italy: soon, in addition to writing *Julian and Maddalo*, Shelley would begin composing his masterpiece *Prometheus Unbound* in the summerhouse at Este.

Mary was told to bring the children to the Hoppner villa, a six-day journey in the late summer heat that produced tragic results: little Clara developed dysentery on the way and died a few weeks later. While at I Cappuccini that autumn, a place now blanketed with grief, Shelley composed his haunting "Lines Written Among the Euganean Hills," a poem that covertly mourns his daughter and looks forward to a happier domicile, a sort of Este villa of the mind:

> for me, and those I love,
> May a windless bower be built,
> Far from passion, pain, and guilt,
> In a dell 'mid lawny hills,
> Which the wild sea-murmur fills,
> And soft sunshine, and the sound

Of old forests echoing round,
And the light and smell divine
Of all flowers that breathe and shine:
We may live so happy there ...

Amidst this period of loss, Allegra stayed a month with Claire and the Shelleys; she was then sent back to her father in Venice, and the Shelleys moved on. For his part, Byron was winding up the reign of Margarita Cogni, who had threatened him with a knife and thrown herself into the canal, eventually becoming too unmanageable even for him. And although he may not have known how fully he meant it, he was also beginning to close down the Venetian fun house: "I have quite given up Concubinage," he wrote in January 1819 as he turned 31, his last full-blown Carnival essentially behind him. Before him now were the two subjects of this chapter's letter other than Margherita, both of which, by August 1819, had come to dominate his attention and would change the course of his poetic and personal life: in the first paragraph, *Don Juan*; and, in the letter's postscript, the Countess G.

7

—◇—

Strictest Adultery

[To Countess Teresa Guiccioli]   <u>*Venice, 7 December 1819*</u>

Amor Mio,

    *Io parto per <u>salvarti</u>; e lascio un paese divenuto insop-
portabile senza di te. – – Le tue lettere alla Fanni – ed anche
a mi stesso – fanno torto ai miei motivi, ma col' tempo tu
vedrai la tua ingiustizia. – Tu parli del' dolor – io lo sento –
ma mi mancano le parole. – – Non posso scriverti – ma se
tu vedessi il mio cuore come tu lo vedevi quando eravamo
insieme – non mi diresti delle ingiurie cossi crudeli. – – –
Non basta – lasciarti per dei motivi dei quali tu eri persuasa
(non molto tempo fa) non basta partire dall'Italia – col' cuore lacerato – dopo aver' passato tutti i miei giorni dopo la
tua partenza – nella solitudine – ammalato di corpo – e di
anima – ma ho anche a sopportare i tuoi rimproveri – senza
replicarti – e senza meritarli. – –*
    *Addio – in quella parola – è compresa la ~~partenza di
tutta~~ morte di mia felicità – ma in ogni modo – lascia che
ti ama ancora – lascia che penso di te come l'unico – ultimo
oggetto di tante ~~desideri~~ speranze – e di tanta passione; –*

colla quale ho passato dei momenti troppo dolci – – ma –
forse – un' giorno tornaremo abbracciarci – tornaremo es-
serre + + + – cio che siamo stati – ma – se no – ~~sappia~~ –
nessuna donna sara amata in vece di te. – – Ció si dice al'
principio di una relazione – io lo dico – al' fine. – Ti amo piu
dei primi giorni – del' amor nostro – e tu lo sai – anche dal'
sacrifizio che ~~adesso~~ ora faccio – per la il' tuo ben essere. –
Pensa di A[lessandro] – Pensa di tutto che egli ha fatto o
voluto fare – allora tu non puoi biasimarmi. – – –
Addio – Addio – Amami –
P.S – Tu avrai delle mie nuove nel' viaggio – e di più al'
ritorno di Valeriani – che io mandero al mio arrivo. – – Il
mio indirizzo – è L.B. – aux Soins de Messieurs Ransom,
Banquiers – Pall Mall. – Londres Angleterre. Si ti conviene
più – indirezzate le lettere presso i Signori Siri & Willhalm
Banchieri Venezia

Translation

My Love,

I am leaving in order *to save you*; and I am leaving
a country that has become unbearable without you. – –
Your letters to Fanny – and also to myself – do wrong to
my motives, but in time you will see your injustice. — You
speak of pain – I feel it – but words fail me. – – I cannot
write to you – but if you could see my heart as you did
when we were together – you would not write such cruel
abuses to me. – – – It is not enough – to leave you for motives of which you were convinced (not very long ago) – it
is not enough to leave Italy – with a heart torn in pieces
– after having passed all my days since your departure –

in solitude – sick in body – and in spirit – but I must also suffer your reproaches – without answering you – and without deserving them – – – Farewell – in that word – is contained the death ~~departure of everything~~ of my happiness – but in any case – let me love you still – let me think of you as the single – last object of so much hope ~~you desire~~ – and of so much passion; – with which I passed some moments too sweet – – but – perhaps – one day we shall embrace again – we shall be again + + + – what we have been – but – if not ~~know~~ – – no woman will be loved in your stead. – – That is said at the beginning of a relationship – I say it – at the end. – I love you more than in the first days – of our love – and you know it – even more from the sacrifice I ~~now~~ am making now – for your well being. – Think of A[*lessandro*]. – Think of everything he has done or wanted to do then you cannot blame me. – – –

Farewell – Farewell – Love me. — —

P.S. You will have news of me during my trip – and more at Valeriano's return – whom I shall send on my arrival. – – – – My address is L.B. – aux Soins de Messieurs Ransom, Banquiers – Pall Mall. – Londres / Angleterre. If it is more convenient for you – address your letters to the care of Signori Siri & Willhalm / Bankers / *Venice.*

"Nothing so difficult as a beginning … unless perhaps the end": so Byron observed in the canto of *Don Juan* that he had completed just before sending this chapter's letter – written in imperfect Italian inflected by the Venetian dialect – to the

Countess Teresa Guiccioli in Ravenna (Figure 7.2). The letter was meant as a final farewell, not only to her but also to Italy, his adopted country of the past two years. He was leaving the next morning. He had already informed Douglas Kinnaird and John Murray to direct any future correspondence via Calais, whence he planned to depart for England after crossing the Alps with his daughter Allegra. He wrote to Richard Hoppner that same evening – December 7 – to apologize for not saying goodbye in person, enclosing a bank note to cover the Palazzo Mocenigo rent and staff wages and instructing Hoppner to "sell *my chattels*," including his "*Gondola* … books – bed – two Silver Coffee pots … and sugar basin – Chairs – tables – dog – monkeys – and fox." Packed crates and trunks were piling up in various corners of the cold, gloomy palazzo, and Byron's heart was heavy with a sense of failure. Teresa had gone back to her husband, and Italy had "become sad" and "unbearable." As he had written to Kinnaird, "I feel alone in it; and as I left England on account of my own wife, I now quit Italy for the wife of another." The next day, as reported by Fanny Silvestri (who served both Byron and Teresa), the poet appeared shortly after noon: "he was all dressed for travel, with gloves in his hands, with his bonnet, and even with his little Cane; nothing remained but for him to descend the stairs. All his chests were in the Boat, already all the Servants had set out – – his House was becoming a desert." As Byron stood at the top of the staircase, struck by the vacancy of the place and bewildered by a wave of loneliness, he hesitated. Italy had taken him in; Venice had sheltered him. But that was over. Where on earth was his home now?

Seven months before this moment, in early April, Byron had been at a *conversazione* held by the Countess Maria Querini Benzoni, chatting quietly with a friend, when his hostess approached with a request: may I introduce you to someone who has just arrived? It was midnight, and Byron initially demurred, saying, "I don't want new lady acquaintances; if they are ugly, because they are ugly – and if they are pretty, because they are pretty." But he soon allowed himself to be prevailed upon and was led across the drawing room and presented as "England's greatest poet" to the Countess Teresa Guiccioli, who was not yet 20 years old. Touching her hand, Byron smiled "one of those charming smiles which Coleridge admired so much, and called the 'Gate of Heaven,'" and the young woman was drawn in, later remembering "the surpassing melodiousness of his voice," and "his beauty." Soon the pair were sitting closely together, discussing Ravenna (the young woman's native city) and the poetry of Dante and Petrarch. But, as she tells it, the topics of their conversation rapidly became irrelevant: "the important thing was the fact of talking, the growth of that mysterious fellow feeling which increased on both sides with every word that was uttered." And when she was called away by her much older husband, who told her it was time to leave, "she arose as if emerging from a dream." In that short hour together, something vitally important had passed between Byron and Teresa. She would write later, sentimentally and accurately, "the effect of that meeting sealed the destiny of their hearts."

In fact, Byron and Teresa had already interacted once before, over a year earlier, at another Venetian gathering, where he had briefly given his arm to the young Countess. At that time, married to Count Guiccioli only three days earlier, Teresa had been, as she puts it, "too overwhelmed by her new position, too tired and too shy" to notice her escort. And Byron had been in the midst of his typical Carnival distractions while still juggling both Marianna Segati and Margarita

Cogni; that night had also been his thirtieth birthday. Only after the sparkling, promising midnight conversation at Casa Benzoni did Byron and Teresa compare memories and recall their previous missed encounter. This time, they barely hesitated: Byron sent a message requesting to meet her the next day, during her husband's afternoon siesta. As Teresa told it, in a later confession that her husband demanded she write,

> I felt attracted to him by an irresistible force.... At that time an old boatman appeared with a note, in an unknown gondola, and took me to Mylord's gondola, where he was waiting, and together we went to his *casino*. I was strong enough to resist at that first encounter, but was so imprudent as to repeat it the next day, when my strength gave way – for B. was not a man to confine himself to sentiment. And, the first step taken, there was no further obstacle in the following days.

She was soon sending passionate letters signed "your friend-lover forever [*tua Amica Amante in Eterno*]." For his part, just a few days after their meeting, Byron was writing to Hobhouse, "I have fallen in love with a Romagnuola Countess from Ravenna, who is nineteen years old, and has a Count of fifty – whom she seems disposed to qualify, the first year of marriage being over." He told Kinnaird soon thereafter, "She is fair as Sunrise, and warm as Noon; we had but ten days to manage all our little matters in beginning, middle and end; & we managed them; and I have done my duty with proper consummation."

This casual praise of a new romantic partner would have sounded familiar to Byron's male friends, but Teresa was not just another Italian mistress. Right away, Byron had recognized that this intelligent, attractive, and spirited Countess was going to be much more important and more troubling to his state of mind than his typical Venetian affairs. The second of six daughters of Count Ruggero Gamba and his wife Amalia, Teresa was part of a large aristocratic, liberal family whose sympathies were with the cause of Italian nationalism. She had been extraordinarily well educated at convent schools since the age of 5, particularly at Santa Chiara at Faenza, where the enlightened Mother Superior recognized Teresa's intelligence and supplied her with books of mathematics, art, science, rhetoric, and Italian poetry. During vacations, her brother's tutor gave her lessons in philosophy and literature. All of this cultivation (along with her youth and natural beauty) made Teresa an attractive partner, and at age 18, she had been married off to the powerful Count Alessandro Guiccioli, who was 57, twice a widower, and one of the richest men in the Romagna; as Byron remarked to Kinnaird, Teresa was a "sacrifice to Wealth – filial duty and all that." Part of this arrangement was the understanding, according to Italian custom at the time, that a woman of her class was permitted a *cavalier servente*: an accepted male companion of her choosing, who would accompany her to the opera, to *conversazioni*, and to parties. He would be an outward friend of the couple and, for the wife, an object of Platonic romance and (it was tacitly understood) of sexual attachment as well. When Teresa talked with Byron on the Benzoni's divan that April night, she was essentially interviewing him for this position.

Since her marriage to Count Guiccioli one year earlier, Teresa had been seasoned by grief: their son, born ten months after the wedding, had lived only a few days. This had been followed in short succession by the deaths of both her mother and her elder sister, with whom she had been very close. She had also experimented with love, having had a brief affair of the heart with the Italian poet Cristoforo Ferri while visiting her grandparents in Pesaro earlier that year. By April 1819, the sheen of novelty had worn from her marriage and she was ready to secure something for herself, something to match the romance of Petrarch and Laura, or Dante's Paolo and Francesca – even though she was by that time a few months pregnant again by her husband. For his part, Byron had arrived at another personal crossroads: burned out on promiscuity, his thoughts turning again to England, uncertain as to his next move. Yet, as an author, he had just turned a decisive corner. A few hours before he left for Casa Benzoni and the fateful meeting with Teresa, Byron had dispatched the manuscript of the second canto of *Don Juan* to England, after months of negotiation with Murray, Hobhouse, Kinnaird, and others who continued to warn him not to publish it, at least not without severe excisions. But Byron was adamant: "The poem will please if it is lively – if it is stupid it will fail – but I will have none of your damned cutting & slashing…. I will battle my way against them all – like a Porcupine."

The third point of this triangle – Teresa's husband, Count Alessandro Guiccioli – remains an enigma: he was intelligent and seductive, a devotee of the theatre, and a ruthless and calculating man of politics. While married to his first Countess (who was rich and older), he had six illegitimate children by his young housemaid Angelica Galliani, after which he banished and may have poisoned his wife – making sure first that she signed a will leaving him all of her money. He then married Galliani, who died not long thereafter. Guiccioli had also been briefly jailed for his part in a shady business deal, after which his accuser was killed by an unknown assailant.

So there were enough hints of violence in the Count's history for Byron to tell Hoppner soon after becoming Teresa's lover, "if I come away with a stiletto in my gizzard some fine afternoon, I shall not be astonished." Guiccioli seemed a man not to be trifled with, yet that's precisely what Byron was doing. Further, the Count maintained some kind of sexual hold over Teresa, despite their age difference. We might expect to see him as a laughable older cuckold from the start; but he was vigorous and sensual, and his relationship with Teresa included certain "eccentricities" and erotically charged cruelties that kept her bound to him, at least for a time. The resulting volatile interchange, as Byron moved into the lives of Teresa and Alessandro Guiccioli, would be marked by uncertainty, jealousy, and evolving debts and obligations on all sides.

When Byron and Teresa first began their affair in Venice, they only had about a week together, but it was enough. They would meet for trysts at Byron's casino in the afternoon and then cross paths later at the Benzona's *conversazione*, where at least once, Byron told Hobhouse, the indiscreet Teresa called out "Mio Byron" loudly "during a dead Silence of pause in the other prattlers, who stared & whispered to their respective Serventi"; "She has no tact – answers aloud – when she should whisper" and "talks of age to old ladies who want to pass for young." To Kinnaird, he described her as "a sort of Italian Caroline Lamb, except that she is much prettier, and not so savage. – But she has the same red-hot head – the same noble disdain of public opinion – with the superstructure of all that Italy can add to such natural dispositions." It was almost as if the sexual dramas and gossipy flirtations of Holland House during Byron's years of fame in London had been transposed to Venice, and Byron saw a chance to start again: to give up what he called "promiscuous concubinage" with prostitutes and the wives of bakers and drapers and reestablish himself within an aristocratic social milieu as the lover of a married Countess. But then, suddenly, Teresa was whispering to Byron as he sat watching Rossini's *Otello* at the San Benedetto theatre: her husband was taking her back to Romagna the next evening. The first chapter of their affair closed with Byron leading her to the Count's gondola and promising to join her in Ravenna soon. As Teresa remembered, she "sailed across the lagoon in body, but her spirit did not follow." The question then became, would Byron follow her?

Hobhouse was against the whole thing from the start:

> if you are making love to a Romagnuola and she only nineteen you will have some jobs upon your hands.... Don't you go after that terra firma lady: they are very vixens, in those parts especially.... take a fool's advice for once and be content with your Naiads – your amphibious fry – you make a very pretty splashing with them in the Lagune and I recommend constancy to the neighborhood.

Splashing with Venetian "Naiads" was one thing, but falling in passionate love with a Romagnola countess with a powerful husband was something else. To his male English friends, Byron seemed to be heading into dangerous territory. Richard Hoppner wrote to him a few months later, calling Teresa "an unworthy object" who has "entangled you in her nets merely from vanity," warning him, "when she thinks herself sure of you, [she] will leave you in the lurch, and make a boast of having betrayed you." Hoppner and Alexander Scott were both jealous and disapproving, and wanted Byron to stay in Venice with them; and Hobhouse was still hoping Byron would return to England to join the Reform movement in aid of the suffering manufacturing classes, who were starving in their thousands: "I wish to God you would be enrolled, as you say, in my corps – I am sure you have a geni for war, and if the Reformers had you they would be confident against the world in arms." By the summertime, he was imploring Byron, "Be my companion and a fig for everyone else… Leave the bitches to their bologna & come you away directly." By December and the writing of this chapter's letter, after a second departure of Teresa and her husband from Venice, it seemed as if Hobhouse was going to get his wish.

But back in April, in those early days of the relationship, Byron felt himself being pulled along in Teresa's wake. He wrote to her (in Italian) on 22 April, calling her

> my only joy, the delight of my life – you who are my only hope…. You sometimes tell me that I have been your *first* real love – and I assure you that you shall be my last Passion … Before I knew you – I felt an interest in many women, but never in one only. Now I love *you*, there is no other woman in the world for me…. without you where would Paradise be?

Reading Byron's letters to Teresa, you can watch him shift into a purely sentimental mode otherwise very rare in his correspondence. Part of this was the influence of writing in Italian, and part was Byron echoing Teresa's own elevated rhetoric of passion. But these letters are more than mere performances. They reveal Byron inhabiting new structures of feeling and their consequences, pushing past irony and self-protective coldness, past the calculated chaos of promiscuous sex toward something he had never really tried: monogamous commitment. As he confessed to Hoppner, he knew Teresa would be his last attachment:

> If any thing happens to my present *Amica*, I have done with the Passion for ever – it is my *last* Love. – And as to Libertinism, I have sickened myself of that, as was natural in the way I went on – and I have at least derived that advantage from Vice – to *Love* in the better sense of the word – *this* will be my last adventure.

Byron's feelings for Teresa had this sense of finality from the very beginning, and with it came feelings of gratitude and insecurity, erotic joy and quiet tragedy, and above all a kind of half-melancholy fatalism that so worried Hobhouse and Kinnaird. The Shelleys called Byron a "lost" man after seeing him in full dissipation mode in Venice; but now he was on the verge of being lost in a different way: that is, found – by the 19-year-old Teresa who became the love of his life, tying him to Italy. And here is perhaps the most striking fact: after the Teresa relationship began in earnest in Ravenna, Byron may never have had sex with anyone else again. There are a few hints dropped of possibilities – as we will see in the coming chapters – but as far as we know for certain, Teresa was his last lover.

But first, two accounts had to be closed: those of Augusta Leigh and the Venetian Naiads. First, as Byron lingered in Venice through April and May, wondering if he should pursue Teresa to Ravenna and exchanging clandestine, impassioned letters with her through various go-betweens, his thoughts turned to the half-sister whose image had so dominated his imagination during his years of fame and scandal. Writing to her in May, and admitting "we have now nothing in common but our affections & our relationship," he nevertheless asserted (in language seemingly borrowed from his Teresa file), "I have never ceased nor can cease to feel for a moment that perfect & boundless attachment which bound & binds me to you – which renders me utterly incapable of *real* love for any other human being – what could they be to me after you?" Even for Byron, it's a bizarre letter, given that he hadn't heard from Augusta for many months and that he was writing in similar terms to Teresa almost simultaneously, casting both women, in letters sent only days apart, as Francescas to his Paolo. Upon receiving it, Augusta immediately shared it with Lady Byron with the covering remark, "he is surely to be considered a *Maniac*." Annabella advised breaking off all communication. Second, almost out of habit, Byron pursued one more Venetian assignation, this time with a young nobleman's daughter named Angelina. On the same night that he sent his declaration of eternal love to Augusta, and wrote to Hobhouse that "the die is cast" and he was leaving Venice in pursuit of Teresa, he slipped and fell into the Grand Canal on the way to meet Angelina, and so, he told Murray, "in I flounced like a Carp – and went dripping like a Triton to my Sea-nymph – and had to scramble up to a Grated window" to her bed. It was perhaps a fitting, burlesque conclusion to Byron's career as a seductive playboy.

Meanwhile, Teresa was waiting for him in Ravenna. Already the wife of one of the most powerful men in the region, she was poised to become the beloved long-term mistress of one of the most attractively notorious cultural figures of the era. And it says much about her strength of character, her intelligence, and her personal attractions that she was able to manage these two difficult partners so successfully. But for now, she was in poor health, having suffered a miscarriage on the journey out of Venice. As Byron wrote to Kinnaird, "I can't tell whether I was the involuntary Cause of the miscarriage, but certes I was not the father of the foetus for She was three months advanced before our first Passade." Byron first wrote "abortion" for "miscarriage" in this letter, and there is some possibility that Teresa, having fallen in love with Byron and being unwilling to tie herself further to the Count, took matters into her own hands in terminating the pregnancy. In a later letter to Murray, Byron tells the story, in suggestive terms, of "a woman making herself miscarry – because she wanted to meet her lover." But, in any case, her illness was enough to tip the scales: Teresa needed him. And, after all, the inscrutable Count Guiccioli himself had invited Byron to visit whenever he liked. Once the final proof sheets of the first two cantos of *Don Juan* were on their way back to Murray in England, Byron's path was clear. On the first day of June, he left Venice for Ravenna (a journey of about 150 miles), intending to stay for a month. However, he was very uncertain about what reception he would receive. A stiletto in the gizzard remained a definite possibility.

Byron's route out of Venice took him through Padua and across the Po river to Ferrara, where he composed one of his greatest short poems, "To the Po," an address to the river as a mirror of his heart and a connecting force between himself and Teresa, another kind of letter "where she may read / The thousand thoughts" he has of her. It begins,

> River that rollest by the antient walls
>   Where dwells the Lady of my Love, when she
> Walks by thy brink – and there perchance recalls
>   A faint & fleeting memory of me –
> What if thy deep and ample stream should be
>   A mirror of my heart where she may read
> The thousand thoughts I now betray to thee
>   Wild as thy wave – and headlong as thy speed.

Byron's vision is an extravagant one: modern Ravenna is not located along the Po river. But in ancient times, the city fronted the Adriatic and was connected via a series of canals from a tributary, the Po di Primero. Viewing that branch of the river in Ferrara, Byron was remembering his Dante, again casting Teresa as Francesca, who says (in Byron's translation), "The Land where I was born sits by the Seas / Upon that shore to which the Po descends / With all of this followers in search of Peace." That search for peace resonates through the poem, which concludes,

> My blood is all meridian – were it not
>   I had not left my clime – I should not be
> 'Spite of old tortures ne'er to be forgot –
>   The Slave again, Oh Love! – at least of thee.
> 'Tis vain to struggle: let me perish young –
>   Live as I lived – and love as I have loved.
> To dust if I return – from dust I sprung –
>   And there at least my heart can not be moved.

As he wrote in the poem, the Po river "tendest wildly to the wilder main, / And I to loving one I should not love." Poised between onrush and retreat, anxious as to what he would find in Ravenna, struggling with the "wild … headlong" feelings of love for Teresa, Byron ends his poem in quasi-prayer, rededicating himself to a life of passion despite its costs, including his own early death which he knew – and perhaps even hoped – might be part of the bargain.

A longing for peace, for the cessation of the pain that he always carried with him and that had been amplified by his vulnerabilities in this new love affair, continued to haunt Byron as he moved closer to Ravenna. He found himself wandering through cemeteries. Settled in Bologna for several days, awaiting word from Teresa as to whether he should proceed, Byron wrote to Murray:

> Some of the epitaphs at Ferrara pleased me ... for instance
>
>> "Martini Luigi
>>
>> Implora pace"
>
>> "Lucrezia Picini
>>
>> Implora eterna quiete"
>
> Can any thing be more full of pathos! those few words say all that can be said or sought – the dead had had enough of life – all they wanted was rest – and this they "implore." There is all the helplessness – and humble hope and deathlike prayer that can arise from the Grave – "*implora pace.*"

He added that he hoped to be buried at the Venetian Lido under a stone with those last two words only, remarking, "I am sure my Bones would not rest in an English grave." Rest, peace, quiet, the unmoved heart, the silent grave: such are themes of Byron's writing during these weeks of transition, as he watches himself being impelled toward Teresa, emotionally and geographically, his heart again in turmoil, his life upended. Despite his reputation as a seducer, Byron had a streak of passivity or pliability with women, often finding himself swayed by their desires. He had mostly managed to stave this off with the casual dissipations and competing affairs of Venice, but now he was again in the grip of love: "'Tis vain to struggle," as he wrote in "To the Po." A bit later, refuting a rumor that he had abducted Teresa from her convent, he wrote to Kinnaird – disingenuously but tellingly, especially given the early sexual abuse he suffered at the hands of May Gray – "I should like to know *who* has been carried off – except poor dear *me*.

I have been more ravished myself than any body since the Trojan war."

Arriving in Ravenna on June 10, Byron installed himself at an inn and – awkwardly, and in a ferment of anxiety – awaited instructions. At the theatre the next evening, he saw Count Guiccioli, who welcomed him to Ravenna and told him Teresa's health was better but still seriously impaired. In the days that followed, Byron sat up late alone in his room, writing agonized, insecure letters to his beloved. On June 11: "It is impossible for me to live long in this state of torment – I am writing to you in tears – and I am not a man who cries easily. When I cry my tears come from the heart and are of blood." On June 15:

> I swear that these last few days have been among the most unhappy of my life. Love – doubt – uncertainty – the fear of compromising you when I see you in the presence of others – the impossibility of seeing you alone – the thought of losing you for ever – these combine to destroy the few hopes that inspired me until now. Society disturbs me – solitude terrifies me.

He seems to have been close to a nervous breakdown of some kind. Only able to visit Teresa's bedside as a guest of the family, and in the presence of others, he felt strongly the sense of his false position. But despite his anguished rhetoric, he does not appear to doubt that this is what he wants. His letters to Teresa of these weeks are essentially all variations of the same message: I am here; I love you; what should I do now?

Weeks passed and, under the care of Dr. Aglietti, a celebrated physician whom Byron summoned from Venice, Teresa's health improved. Eventually, she and her English *cavaliere servente* could start taking summer evening rides on horseback out to the Pineta, the famous coastal pine-tree forest of Ravenna. As Byron described the setting in the third canto of *Don Juan*,

> Sweet hour of twilight! – in the solitude
>   Of the pine forest, and the silent shore
> Which bounds Ravenna's immemorial wood,
>   Rooted where once the Adrian wave flow'd o'er,
> To where the last Cesarean fortress stood,
>   Evergreen forest! which Boccaccio's lore
> And Dryden's lay have made haunted ground to me,
> How I have loved the twilight hour and thee!

However, to Augusta, he confessed that riding with Teresa was not as serene as such descriptions indicate, "for she can't guide her horse – and he runs after mine – and tries to bite him – and then she begins screaming in a high hat and Sky-blue habit – making a most absurd figure – and embarrassing me and both our grooms." The double vision of these two passages takes us right to the heart of Byron's imagination as he was writing *Don Juan* under the influence of Italian culture: the simultaneous courting of the sublime and the ridiculous, the synthesis of romantic sentiment and comic absurdity in such a way that each supplements the other rather than canceling it out. As he wrote to Kinnaird of *Don Juan*, "is it not *life*, is it not the *thing*?"

As Byron and Teresa were advancing their affair, whether on evening rides in the Pineta or afternoon illicit meetings in the grand Saloon of the Palazzo Guiccioli (Figure 7.3), the first instalment of *Don Juan* (pronounced "Joo – un" in the poem) had been published in London. As Murray wrote to Byron, "there is a great outcry – but every body reads." Set in Spain and on a Greek island, the poem follows the young

Don Juan from an early adulterous affair to shipwreck to rescue by a beautiful Greek maiden, all relayed in the voice of a sly, flirtatious, digressive narrator whose provocative sidebar comments (on love, literature, morals, appetites, aging, fame, religion, politics – you name it) compel our attention at least as much as Juan's adventures. Hobhouse's reaction was fairly typical when he declared, "the immoral turn of the whole and the rakish air of the half real hero will really injure your reputation both as a man and a poet," while also declaring Byron at the same time "superior in the burlesque as in the heroic to all competitors." William Wordsworth was outraged by Byron's poem and encouraged the editor of the *Quarterly Review* to attack "the infamous publication," being persuaded that "*Don Juan* will do more harm to the English character, than anything of our time."

One reader called *Don Juan* "an extraordinary performance indeed. I am sorry that Lord B. has published it," noting its disturbing synthesis of "drollery" and "sublimity," the "grave and gay," and complaining that "they must not be mixed up together" since, in reality, "we are never drenched & scorched in the same instant." Drawing on his own exploits as a man of the world, Byron's response via Murray was a legendary piece of raillery:

> Blessings on his experience! … did he never spill a dish of tea over his testicles in handing the cup to his charmer to the great shame of his nankeen breeches? – did he never swim in the sea at Noonday, with the Sun in his eyes and on his head? … did he never draw his foot out of a tub of too hot water damning his eyes & his valet's? Did he never inject for a Gonorrhea? – or make water through an ulcerated Urethra? – was he ever in a Turkish bath – that marble paradise of sherbet and sodomy?

In this simultaneous "scorching and drenching," Byron had found his mature style, a mode of writing that could oscillate between comedy and tragedy, irony and sentiment, with alarming, thrilling speed. For his part, Murray was very pleased, despite his nervousness about certain offensive stanzas. He praised his star author, "you have infinitely surpassed all your former efforts … this poem isolates you compleatly from any thing that the age has produced…. you need attempt nothing further for immortality." He called the second Canto "the very Soul of Poetry," and assured Byron, "Depend upon this – the Public are astonished – & the Wonderful powers displayed in this poem – they are yet unable sufficiently to estimate – but you never did any thing greater."

As the initial reception of *Don Juan* was unfolding, Byron and Teresa resumed their sexual relationship, involving "such perils – and escapes" that "Juan's are a child's play in comparison." As he wrote to Murray in early August, "The fools think that my *Poeshie* is always allusive to my *own* adventures," but in his case, reality outstripped fiction: "I have had at one time or another better – and more extraordinary – and perilous – and pleasant than those any day of the week – if I might tell them – but that must never be." In Ravenna, a whole network of servants and aides was needed to ensure that the couple could meet away from the eyes of the Count, so that Byron must have felt that he was living in an Italian opera. As he described the situation, "By aid of a Priest – a Chambermaid – a young Negro-boy, and a female friend – we are enabled to carry on our unlawful loves." Characteristically, Byron enjoyed and even amplified the risky, forbidden nature of their meetings, taking Teresa in the large, open rooms of her husband's palazzo in which none of the doors had bolts. To Teresa, he wrote with relish, "*Think*, my love, of *those* moments – delicious – dangerous…. The hall! Those rooms! The open doors! The servants so curious and so near – Ferdinando – the visitors! how many obstacles! But all overcome – it has been the real triumph of Love – a hundred times Victor."

When the Guicciolis temporarily relocated to Bologna, Byron followed close behind. He was still ostensibly the welcome guest of the Count, who obligingly invited Byron to move into a set of rooms in their Bologna residence, the Palazzo Savioli. Count Guiccioli simultaneously asked for a loan of £1,000 to cover a debt, and requested Byron use his influence in England to have him appointed as a consul to Ravenna. Layers of theatricality had by now accumulated, with Byron playing multiple roles at once: the English peer abroad, the noble friend of the Count, the *cavaliere servente* of Teresa. But was he acting in a comedy or a tragedy, or both at once? His own perspective varied with the day, and the strain left his emotions unsettled. Attending a performance of Vittorio Alfieri's tragic play, *Mirra*, he was overcome by the events of the last two acts, in which the heroine confesses her incestuous passion for her own father and kills herself with his sword. Byron wrote to Murray that the play "threw me into convulsions," "the agony of reluctant tears – and the choking shudder which I do not often undergo for fiction." Weeks later he was still shaken by that evening, confessing in another letter, "I have never been quite well since the night of the representation of Alfieri's Mirra." We have heard reports of Byron's tearful outbursts before, in moments of emotional stress: at Aston Hall "alone near the fire … perfectly *convulsed*" with competing feelings for Augusta, Lady Frances, and Caroline Lamb; or in the Armenian Convent in

Venice, "bitterly sobbing and weeping," according to Father Avgerian. Now he was writing to Hobhouse, "I am so bilious that I nearly lose my head, and so nervous that I cry for nothing; at least to-day I burst into tears, all alone by myself, over a cistern of Gold fishes, which are not pathetic animals." Hobhouse's reply was that of a true friend: "I am distressed beyond measure at your account of yourself. Pray come home…. if you are sick I will nurse you."

The same late-August day that Byron wept unaccountably over that bowl of goldfish, he was wandering sadly through the empty garden of the Palazzo Savioli, awaiting Teresa's return from a trip to the countryside. Finding there her copy of the romantic novel *Corinne* by Madame de Staël, he inscribed it with a message in English, a language that his Italian mistress (and her husband) could not yet read. It is arguably the most romantic letter he ever wrote:

My dearest Teresa – I have read this book in your garden; – my Love – you were absent – or I could not have read it. – It is a favourite book of yours – and the writer was a friend of mine. – You will not understand these English words – and others will not understand them – which is the reason I have not scribbled them in Italian – but you will recognize the hand-writing of him who passionately loved you – and you will divine that over a book which was yours – he could only think of love. In *that word* beautiful in all languages – but most so in yours – *Amor* mio – is comprized my existence here and hereafter. – – I feel that I exist here – and I fear that I shall exist hereafter – to what purpose – your will decide – my destiny rests with you – & you are a woman nineteen years of age – and two years out of a Convent. – – I wish that you had staid there with all my heart – or at least that I had never met you in your married state. – but all this is too late – I love you – and you love me – at least you say so – and act as if you did so – which last is a great consolation in all events. – But I more than love you – and cannot cease to love you. – Think of me sometimes when the Alps and the Ocean divide us – but they never will – unless you wish it.

As a very private communication, essentially illegible to its addressee, the note has a shot at authenticity beyond Byron's typical epistolary performances. Significantly, when Teresa found the inscription on her return to Bologna, she asked Byron to translate it for her, and he refused. One of only a few messages he ever wrote to Teresa in his native language, the *Corinne* inscription allows us to hear Byron describing his feelings in his own untranslated voice. There is a pervading sense of fatalism – "my destiny rests with you," "all this is too late" – that resonates with the sense of passivity Byron had felt since the affair began. But, ultimately, the tenor of the letter is commitment, whatever the costs. As he confirmed to Hoppner later that autumn, "I am all for morality now – and shall confine myself henceforward to the strictest adultery."

And yet, as always, Byron had his doubts: how long could he stand to be a mere *cavaliere servente*, "a flatterer of fiddlers – and a fan carrier of a woman?" He knew it was an untenable situation for the long term. Around this time, remembering other allegiances, he requested that his daughter Allegra be brought from Venice. In his absence, she had been passed from family to family, moving from the Hoppners to the house of their servant Antonio and his wife, to the care of

Mrs. Martens, the wife of the Danish Consul. But by early September, Byron could tell Augusta with fatherly pride,

> Allegra is here with me – in good health – & very amiable and pretty … She is English – but speaks nothing but Venetian – 'Bon *di* papa' &c. &c. she is very droll – and has a good deal of the Byron – can't articulate the letter *r* at all – frowns and pouts quite in our way – blue eyes – light hair growing *darker* daily – and a dimple in the chin – a scowl on the brow – white skin – sweet voice – and a particular liking of Music – and of her own way in everything – is not that B. all over?

Byron was charmed in tracing similarities between his daughter and himself – the pout, the scowl, the dimpled chin, the blue eyes, the willful manner, even the Venetian accent that surely resembled his own. He was beginning to think of new domestic configurations, perhaps running away with Teresa and Allegra to build a new family elsewhere. One possibility that occupied him at this period was emigrating to South America. He imagined writing to his contemporary Simón Bolívar – who had just established the Third Republic in Venezuela – and becoming a wealthy landowner: "I should go there with my natural daughter, Allegra, – now nearly three years old, and with me here, – and pitch my tent for good and all." As he wrote to Hobhouse, "I want a country – and a home…. I might still be a decent citizen and found a *house* and family, – as good – or better than the former." England was out of the question, he observed, and "There is no freedom in Europe," which is "a worn out portion of the globe." Maybe the New World was his proper destination. Hearing this, Hobhouse wrote privately to Murray, "It is the wildest of all his meditations"; aside from fever and tropical disease, Byron would have "No tooth-brushes, no corn-rubbers, no *Quarterly Reviews*. In short, plenty of all he abominates and nothing of all he loves."

Soon after Allegra arrived in Bologna, it was time to relocate again: Teresa was still having health problems (or, perhaps, claiming them as an excuse), and received permission from her husband to consult Dr. Aglietti in Venice, with Byron as her traveling companion. The Count himself returned to Ravenna, while this strange modern family – Byron, Teresa, and Allegra – set out with their servants for the Villa Foscarini at La Mira, the summer estate on the Brenta where Byron had once read Boccaccio with Marianna Segati. Ahead lay weeks of togetherness, away from the prying eyes and tensions of Ravenna. On the journey, the couple stopped in Arqua, in the heart of the Euganean Hills, to visit the tomb of Petrarch, Teresa's favorite poet. It was a gorgeous Italian afternoon of blue skies and soft air, the late-summer landscape full of heavily laden grape trellises and groves of willow and cypress trees. As Teresa remembered, the pair walked arm in arm and "The sensations of the present, the uncertainty of the future, and the strangeness of the current situation, all combined to add to the solemnity of their pilgrimage." They visited Petrarch's home and examined the guest book. Byron's autograph was already there, from his visit in 1817, but now they signed it together, and Byron said he hoped that those two names would never be parted. It approached a ritual of union. Teresa recited one of Petrarch's love sonnets written for the unattainable Laura, while Byron, observing the poet's embalmed cat displayed in a nook, joked that the love between that pet and his master likely put Laura's coolness to shame. They drank together from the fountain on the property and descended slowly into the garden. It was harvest time, and children offered them golden moscato grapes, which Byron proclaimed the most delicious fruit he had ever eaten. For both lovers, it was a hyper-real, superlative day: a sojourn in paradise. Teresa remembered it as "one of the happiest hours of our life."

Once the couple arrived in Venice, the official story was that Byron would move back into the Palazzo Mocenigo with Allegra, while Teresa stayed in the Villa Foscarini at La Mira, as Dr. Aglietti pronounced the countryside location better for her health. In actuality, the whole entourage established themselves at La Mira, where Allegra played in the English garden and Byron worked on the new canto of *Don Juan*. According to Teresa, while he wrote, "he would tell her to stay and recount to him what she had been looking at, or thinking, or doing, and would add that ... he wrote better when he saw her and heard her talking." Thus, Teresa's voice blended with the *ottava rima* of Byron's poem, which took some of its Italian rhythms from her pleasant chat in the background. There was a domestic sweetness to these days, in part enhanced by the sense that they were temporary. Byron sent only a few letters during the weeks at La Mira, but the *Don Juan* stanzas he was writing at the time offer a window onto his thinking. On the one hand, he was lovingly describing the union of Juan with his Greek maiden Haidee: "They were alone once more; for them to be / Thus was another Eden; they were never / Weary, unless when separate." On the other, he was observing wryly, "There's doubtless something in domestic doings, / Which forms, in fact, true love's antithesis," and making this disparaging analogy: "Marriage from love, like vinegar from wine – / A sad, sour, sober beverage – by time / Is sharpen'd from its high celestial flavour / Down to a very homely household savour." The "delicious –

dangerous" perils and escapes of their liaison in Ravenna had yielded to peaceful "domestic doings," at least for a time. And the congenital Byron restlessness was never long subdued. He wrote to Hobhouse that he felt a man "should not consume his life at the side and on the bosom – of a woman – and a stranger." And, over Hobhouse's objections, he continued to plan his "South American project," which might or might not include Teresa.

In October, Thomas Moore arrived in Venice to visit his friend and fellow poet, whom he had not seen since the height of Byron's fame in London, five years ago (Figure 7.4). To Moore, Byron looked older and more decadent: he had put on weight; his hair, now worn long over his collar, was streaked with grey; and he was dressed in a gaudy, European fashion, wearing several large gold chains and "a curious foreign cap." But, Moore observed, he was still "eminently handsome" and "in high spirits and full of his usual frolicksome gaiety." Reminiscing and laughing about their "joint adventures" and "joyous nights" in the London social scene, Byron and Moore toured Venice each afternoon for several days, with Byron sleeping out at La Mira with Teresa, and Moore lodging in the Palazzo Mocenigo. Moore disliked Venice, calling it "a sad place" that did not live up to the romantic visions that Byron had been creating in his poems and letters. He noted in his journal, for example, that Angelina, the nobleman's daughter that Byron seduced by climbing her balcony after falling into the canal was in reality "an ugly, ill-made girl & the balcony is a portal window at the side of a hall door." Nevertheless, the two old friends "were very merry and tipsy," delighting in one another's wit, talking seriously about Byron's marriage and his reputation, dining at the Pellegrino with Alexander Scott, drinking hot punch at a public house until the early hours, and viewing Venice by night in Byron's gondola. One evening before dinner, Byron read aloud from the newly written canto of *Don Juan*, which Byron called "damned modest" due to the "outcry" from the British public. As he joked, "the *Cant* is so much stronger than *Cunt* – now a days: – that the benefit of experience in a man who had well weighed the worth of both monosyllables – must be lost to despairing posterity." And thinking of posterity, when Moore took his leave, Byron handed him a white leather bag containing his memoirs, "my Life in M.S. in 78 folio sheets brought down to 1816," meant as a gift to Moore's children, to be published after the poet's death. The two men would never meet again.

Around the time of Moore's visit, forces were beginning to gather to disrupt the illicit household of Byron and Teresa. The summer was over, and they had moved back to the Palazzo Mocenigo in Venice, where Byron was immediately overcome by a serious fever, accompanied by delirium. Teresa never left his side, and her constant presence fueled local gossip: why was Count Guiccioli's wife living with the scandalous English lord? Teresa's father, Count Ruggero Gamba, and her brother Pietro were both worried, given Byron's notoriety and the bad optics of the current separation of husband and wife. Count Gamba wrote to her, "The world at large will not be satisfied" with the cover story of her illness, and he privately urged Count Guiccioli to reclaim her. Pietro also wrote to Teresa from Rome, warning her of gothic rumors that Byron had married a young wife in England and then imprisoned her in a castle, "and tales fraught with dark secrets are told of the goings-on in that castle." Bowing slightly to the pressure, Teresa agreed not to accompany Byron on a projected trip to Switzerland (planned, again, for her health). Then Count Guiccioli arrived in Venice, his patience at last running thin. Attempting to coerce Teresa back into obedience, he presented her with a list of demands regarding her conduct as a wife, which included a stark choice: Byron or me. As Byron wrote to Murray on November 8, the Count "has presented his Spouse … with a paper of conditions – regulations – of hours and conduct and morals – &c. &c. which he insists on her accepting – and She persists in refusing. – I am expressly … excluded by this treaty – as an indispensable preliminary; so that they are in high discussion." The strong-willed Teresa quickly rebutted the list of conditions point by point, including a counter-demand of her own: "*To receive, without discrimination, any visitor who may come.*" She was determined to have her rights as an Italian Countess, which included Byron as her chosen *cavaliere servente*. They were at an impasse. Byron told Murray, "the Guiccioli business is on the eve of exploding in one way or another," and if she leaves her husband, "I shall retire with her to France or America – change my name and lead a quiet provincial life…. I am in honour bound to support her through – besides she is a very pretty woman."

Yet, in the end, the demands of honor prevailed on the opposite side of the question: Count Guiccioli appealed to Byron as a gentleman to persuade Teresa to return to her marriage, and Byron yielded. The great Byron biographer Iris Origo says that, in sending Teresa back to Ravenna, Byron "gave the name of duty to what was chiefly weariness," but I think that goes too far. Byron believed that the Count was morally in the right; he understood that Teresa's reputation would be ruined if she deserted the Count; he saw the pain that an elopement abroad would cause to her family, and to her as well; he felt the force of the Count's direct appeal to his honor; he was fearful of taking on the responsibility for Teresa's happiness thereafter; and finally, yes, he was uncertain about settling down with one woman to lead "a quiet provincial life," whether in Venezuela or Valenciennes or anywhere else. Arguments and tears followed, and it was only through the combined influence of all of the men in Teresa's life – her father and brother, her husband, and most of all her beloved Byron – that she was persuaded to leave Venice with Count Guiccioli, and only then because she believed Byron would soon follow her. But that was not his intention. He saw that Teresa was inextricably involved with the Count, her family, and her life in Ravenna, and he was weary of serving the mistress of another's man house; as he had written to Hobhouse, "I can't say I don't feel the degradation." However, as soon as she had departed with her husband, he was bereft. To Kinnaird, he called the relationship with Teresa "my pleasure, my pride and my passion," declaring, "I had every reason to be satisfied with my lot in all respects – but that is all over now."

With Teresa gone, Byron was determined to leave for England as soon as possible: Venice had lost its lustre and Ravenna seemed closed to him. But little Allegra had caught the same fever that had recently debilitated her father, and so the trip was postponed for some weeks. Byron wrote to Hobhouse in late November, "Alas! Here I am in a gloomy Venetian palace ... unhappy in the retrospect – & at least as much so in the prospect." Hobhouse was, of course, buoyed by the news, and began making plans for a reunion with his old friend, promising himself "such delight & so much to hear & to tell" once Byron returned to London. Meanwhile, as Allegra rested, Byron sat up late to complete what would become cantos 3 and 4 of *Don Juan*, which conclude with the death of Juan's greatest love, Haidee, and with Juan himself being sold in the slave market of Constantinople, his future destination (like Byron's) unknown. "Chain'd and lotted out per couple" in the market, Juan gets paired with a beautiful Romagnola girl (like Teresa), "But all that power was wasted upon him, / For sorrow o'er each sense held stern command." The canto thus ends with an emblem of Byron's doubled, opposing fears as he wrote: that he had lost Teresa forever, or that he would be chained unwillingly to her in a posture of servitude. He completed these cantos on November 30 and, the next day, wrote a bitterly careless lyric about the way love always fades: "Let's love a Season / But let that Season be only *Spring*." He gave the travel orders to his staff: it was time to pack up the palazzo. And thus we return to this chapter's letter, Byron's farewell message to Teresa, telling her, "I am leaving a country that has become unbearable without you."

Fanny Silvestrini consoled Teresa that Byron's impending journey was, in its way, a sign of her final triumph: "Mylord is leaving Venice, is abandoning Italy, is crossing the mountains and the sea in such a bitter season, is going to England for you, only for you." He was within an ace of departing. But as Byron stood at the top of that staircase, he wavered. He looked at his pocket watch, and then gave an order: if everything was not packed and ready to go by 1:00 p.m., they would delay until the following day. The hour came and went, and inertia prevailed. The next day, Byron received news that Teresa's illness had returned in earnest. She had a tendency toward consumption, and the stress of the previous weeks had apparently caused a flare-up so serious that, in a surprising reversal, both Count Gamba and Count Guiccioli requested that Byron come to her side. At that, Byron surrendered. He wrote to Teresa on December 9, "Your last letter caused me to give up my journey. – I love you – I shall love you, alas, – forever. Command me – you can arrange my future life." The next day, he wrote again: "Fanny will have told you, with her *usual sublimity*, that Love has won. I have not been able to find enough resolution to leave the country where you are, without seeing you at least once more…. I shall return – and do – and be – what you wish. I cannot say more."

Teresa was triumphant. In retrospect, it seems clear that everyone, including her husband, had essentially accepted the idea of Byron as her *cavaliere servente*, and that problems had arisen only when the couple overstepped the bounds of that arrangement. As he explained to Murray, "Their system has its rules – and its fitnesses – and decorums – so as to be reduced to a kind of discipline – or game at hearts – which admits few deviations unless you wish to lose." He returned to Ravenna with Allegra and his servants and slipped back into harness. Nothing had really been solved. Teresa's health cleared up almost immediately, but within a week the lovers were mired in suspicions and jealousies. Forced by the terms of servitude to watch as Teresa played the role of attentive, caressing wife, Byron began to imagine something sinister at work: had he been played for a mark all along? In early January, he wrote Teresa a bitter letter, one that she tore in anger:

> You would have done better to let me go away from you before I came here … I have suffered very much in seeing you, in my opinion, either degraded or weak. There is a mystery about these things that I cannot understand; – a morality without principle – a love without faith – and a friendship without esteem or trust … I have left

everything … for a woman who not only does not love me, – but never … [page torn and a line missing] … loved. – I cannot deny your gifts and your beauty; you write eloquent notes; in your physical attributes you are all that one can desire … [The page is torn and the rest of the letter is missing].

Yet, at some level, Byron liked this sort of drama: his love for Teresa had always been bound up with danger and uncertainty, and she knew Byron well enough to realize that boredom was the greatest enemy to their relationship. She managed him, and her husband too: soon, at the unexpected urging of the Count himself, Byron moved into the unused upper floor of the Palazzo Guiccioli, bringing with him Allegra, his servants, and "two Cats, six dogs, a badger, a falcon, a tame Crow, and a Monkey."

Byron would remain in the Guiccioli house for over a year, through being caught "quasi in the fact" with Teresa by her husband in May, the ensuing separation granted by the Pope and its fallout, and Teresa's decampment to her father's house, all of which she blamed on "the ill conduct of the Count, which will be proved *one day or other!*" Byron even stayed after the Gamba family was sent into political exile from Romagna and Teresa followed her father and brother to Florence. All of this no doubt greatly annoyed and puzzled Count Guiccioli, who could not seem to rid himself of the troublesome English lord. By this time, Byron had, through experience and force of habit, made Italy his adopted country. The process had begun in Venice and was cemented in Ravenna, where he joined the Carbonari, the secret revolutionary society of Italian nationalists, and where he created something like a family, however odd it may have been.

After all, what family isn't? As he wrote to Thomas Moore in August, "Now, I have lived in the heart of their houses, in parts of Italy freshest and least influenced by strangers, – have seen and become (pars magna fui [I was a great part]) a portion of their hopes, and fears, and passions, and am almost inoculated into a family. This is to see men and things as they are." England, the "land far beyond the mountains," seemed more distant than ever, as Byron would ride through the pine forest at twilight, hearing the cicadas and the vesper bells, and feel – almost – that he was home.

8

———— ◇ ————

A Funeral Pile

[To Thomas Moore]   <u>*Pisa, August 27th, 1822*</u>

It is boring to trouble you with "such small gear;" but it must be owned that I should be glad if you would inquire whether my Irish subscription ever reached the committee in Paris from Leghorn. My reasons, like Vellum's, "are three-fold:" *—First, I doubt the accuracy of all almoners, or re-mitters of benevolent cash; second, I do suspect that the said Committee, having in part served its time to time-serving, may have kept back the acknowledgment of an obnoxious politician's name in their lists; and third, I feel pretty sure that I shall one day be twitted by the government scribes for having been a professor of love for Ireland, and not coming forward with the others in her distresses. It is not, as you may opine, that I am ambitious of having my name in the papers, as I can have that any day in the week gratis. All I want is to know if the Reverend Thomas Hall did or did not remit my subscription (200 scudi of Tuscany, or about a thousand francs, more or less,) to the Committee at Paris.

---

* Vellum in Addison's *The Drummer* (1765) frequently enumerates his reasons.

The other day at Viareggio, I thought proper to swim off to my schooner (the Bolivar) in the offing, and thence to shore again—about three miles, or better, in all. As it was at midday, under a broiling sun, the consequence has been a feverish attack, and my whole skin's coming off, after going through the process of one large continuous blister, raised by the sun and sea together. I have suffered much pain; not being able to lie on my back, or even side; for my shoulders and arms were equally St. Bartholomewed.* But it is over,—and I have got a new skin, and am as glossy as a snake in a new suit.

We have been burning the bodies of Shelley and Williams on the sea-shore, to render them fit for removal and regular interment. You can have no idea what an extraordinary effect such a funeral pile has, on a desolate shore, with mountains in the back-ground and the sea before, and the singular appearance the salt and frankincense gave to the flame. All of Shelley was consumed, except his heart, which would not take the flame, and is now preserved in spirits of wine.

Your old acquaintance Londonderry has quietly died at North Cray!† and the virtuous De Witt‡ was torn to pieces by the populace! What a lucky * * * the Irishman has been in his life and end. In him your Irish Franklin est mort [is dead]!

Leigh Hunt is sweating articles for his new Journal; and both he and I think it somewhat shabby in you not to contribute. Will you become one of the <u>properrioters</u>? "Do,

---

* In Christian iconography, St. Bartholomew was flayed alive for his beliefs.
† Robert Stewart, Viscount Castlereagh, a political enemy of both Byron and Moore.
‡ Johan De Witt (1625–1672), Dutch statesman who was murdered by a royalist mob.

and we go snacks."* *I recommend you to think twice before you respond in the negative.*

I have nearly (<u>quite three</u>) four new cantos of <u>Don Juan</u> ready. I obtained permission from the female Censor Morum [moral guardian] of <u>my</u> morals to continue it, provided it were immaculate; so I have been as decent as need be. There is a deal of war—a siege, and all that, in the style, graphical and technical, of the shipwreck in Canto Second, which "took" as they say in the Row.

Yours, etc.

P.S. That ✶ ✶ ✶ *Galignani† has about ten lies in one paragraph. It was not a Bible that was found in Shelley's pocket, but John Keats's poems. However, it would not have been strange, for he was a great admirer of Scripture as a composition. <u>I</u> did not send my bust to the academy of New York; but I sat for my picture to young West, an American artist, at the request of some members of that Academy to <u>him</u> that he would take my portrait,—for the Academy, I believe.*

I had, and still have, thought of South America, but am fluctuating between it and Greece. I should have gone, long ago, to one of them, but for my liaison with the Countess G[uicciol]i; for love, in these days, is little compatible with glory. <u>She</u> would be delighted to go too; but I do not choose to expose her to a long voyage, and a residence in an unsettled country, where I shall probably take a part of some sort.

---

* Alexander Pope, "Epistle to Dr. Arbuthnot" (1735).
† The Galignani family published the daily newspaper *Galignani's Messenger* in Paris.

"We have been burning the bodies of Shelley and Williams on the sea-shore": Byron's flat declarative sentence almost leaps off the page of this chatty late-August letter sent to Thomas Moore from Pisa in 1822. Percy Shelley was dead at the age of 29, drowned in the Ligurian Sea, along with his friend Edward Williams (and an English boat boy, Charles Vivian), after their boat went down in a squall. They had been traveling north along the Italian coast from Livorno to Lerici in a fast, undecked boat carrying far too much sail and not enough ballast, attempting to run before the storm. But the weather had worsened with terrifying speed, and the boat foundered amidst huge waves that tore off both masts and the rudder. The shore was still 15 miles away, and none of the men made it there alive. Hauntingly, a reed-and-canvas dinghy, which could have been used as a lifeboat, washed ashore, empty. In mid-July, after a week of anxious waiting, the bodies of all three men were found on the beach near Viareggio, badly decomposed and identifiable only by their clothing and, in Shelley's case, by a copy of John Keats's poetry, hastily doubled over and shoved into his jacket-pocket. He had probably been reading it when the storm overtook them.

Byron was now in Pisa, where he had been living since early November of the previous year. Shelley's unexpected death had just brought to an end an experimental community of expatriate English writers – what Mary Shelley had called (using a phrase of Samuel Johnson's) "a little nest of singing birds" – along the 50 miles of coast that faces the Ligurian sea between La Spezia and Montenero. The idea had taken shape on a hot August night in Ravenna in 1821, when Percy Shelley visited Byron and the two men sat up through the small hours in the Palazzo Guiccioli, drinking gin and water, trading news and memories, and discussing one another's lives and poetry. They had not spent any time together for three years, not since their twilight ride on the Venice Lido that had inspired Shelley's *Julian and Maddalo*. Italy had in the meantime become familiar to them both, in very different ways – Byron immersed in Italian life and manners, in love with his Romagnola Countess, involved with the Italian nationalist movement, and surrounded by Italian associates, friends, and servants; and Shelley skating more upon the surface of the culture, associating primarily with a small circle of English expatriates while moving his family from Rome to Livorno to Florence to Pisa in search of that "windless bower ... Far from passion, pain, and guilt" that he had envisioned in "Lines Written Among the Euganean Hills." Reunited in Ravenna, Byron and Shelley glimpsed the possibility of a longer-term sojourn in one another's company, a reprise of the Diodati summer in Switzerland that had been such a generative experience for their younger selves, and plans had been quickly set in motion.

Given events preceding Shelley's visit to Ravenna, Byron was by August 1821 ready for a change of scene. Most immediately, Teresa Guiccioli had left the city for good. Two arcs of circumstance had played out simultaneously across the previous year, and they had converged to put an end to Byron's established if irregular domestic arrangements. First, the uneasy *ménage à trois* involving Teresa, her husband, and Byron had finally broken down completely. When Byron had returned to Ravenna from Venice, he had moved into the upper floor of the Palazzo Guiccioli, becoming a resident in the house of the man he was cuckolding. Soon he resumed his risky, clandestine trysts with Teresa. But just how clandestine were they, really? The whole situation suggests some sort of complex power play on the part of Count Guiccioli, who was eccentric but no blind dupe. He made sure that the jealous Byron saw him caressing Teresa, he paid domestic servants to spy on the lovers, he broke into his wife's writing desk to look for incriminating letters, and he extracted rent and loans from Byron throughout it all. Discovering Teresa and her *cavaliere* "quasi in the fact" (as Byron wrote to Murray) in the palazzo one afternoon in May, the Count ordered Byron to stay away from his wife. Byron spent the week or so thereafter expecting retribution, going to his daily rides always with a "stiletto and pair of pistols" in his pocket, "thinking that I can pepper his ragamuffins – if they don't come unawares." Perhaps the Count had finally reached the end of his patience; he may also have been pushing an agenda for political and financial ends; and, like Byron, he seems to have darkly enjoyed the heightened passions of the affair, which included his own ongoing sexual liaison with a housemaid (whom Byron distrusted and despised). Eventually, something had to give. Following a candid conversation during which Teresa accused her husband of cruel mistreatment, her father Count Ruggero Gamba wrote to the Pope via his Legate to request a decree of separation.

Byron told friends in England that public opinion in Ravenna was entirely on the side of the lovers and against the older husband, whom Byron called both a "clown" and a "bully": "they say he is either a fool or a rogue – fool, if he did not discover the liaison till now; and rogue, if he did know it, and waited, for some bad end, to divulge it." Teresa's father, who informed the Pope that the Count had "heaped ... many insults upon his unhappy bride," went so far as to challenge Count Guiccioli to a duel, suggesting some baleful revelation regarding the husband's behavior. Regarding this challenge, Teresa herself noted years later in the margin of her copy of

Byron's life and letters, "he would not have done so if Count G was not in the wrong and had not offended and ill treated her!" Yet while the separation decision hung in the balance, Byron fought jealously with Teresa over her continued compliance with her husband, warning her, "If … you go back to yielding to his false blandishments and dotardly caresses, it is you who will be to blame, and your weakness of character will be more confirmed than ever." He was ready to depart for good if the Pope denied the Gambas' request, with plans for England, Switzerland, or South America in his mind.

But in July 1820, word had arrived that the separation had been granted, its terms stipulating that Teresa had to move back into her father's house. If she attempted to live openly with Byron (or anyone else) as a partner, she lost her alimony, which Byron estimated equal to 1,000 pounds per year in England. Worse, she risked forcible confinement in a convent. Byron wrote to Murray, "I can only see her under great restrictions – such is the custom of the country," although he told Teresa that he was ready when she was "to live together and send A[lessandro] and his alimony" to the devil. Their relationship had suddenly become more serious, with the Count now in the background and Byron promoted beyond the limited range of the *cavaliere servente* to something more spousal: he began calling Teresa "Duck" in their letters, the pet name he once used for Annabella Milbanke. Before Count Guiccioli had received the news, the Gamba family relocated to their large country house at Filetto, about 12 miles outside of the city, to get Teresa away from the gossip and the men whose actions fueled it. Meanwhile, Byron stayed on at the Palazzo Guiccioli with his retinue of servants and large menagerie of pets, immovable and surprisingly insouciant about continuing to live in the same house as the aggrieved and potentially vengeful Count, who immediately appealed the Pope's decision.

While all of this was unfolding, so was a second, larger chain of events associated with the Risorgimento, the unification of Italy as a modern nation. After the end of the Napoleonic wars, Italy was a patchwork of city-states and republics ruled by the Austrian Empire, which also essentially controlled the Papacy. But the spirit of revolution was stirring, and, in Ravenna, Byron was drawn into what would become a prolonged struggle for a liberated and unified Italy. As he wrote to Murray, "I have lived long enough among them to feel more for them as a nation than for any other people in existence." Anticipating his similar commitment to the cause of the Greeks, Byron announced, "Whatever I can do by money, means, or person, I will venture freely for their freedom." Ravenna was simmering in the late spring of 1820, the city walls covered with graffiti reading "up with the Republic" and "death to popes & priests," and Byron wrote to Murray in late April, "the police is all on the alert, and the Cardinal glares pale through all his purple." Encouraged by Teresa and the Gamba family, who were friends of Italian liberty and supporters of the insurrectionists, and based on his own natural political inclinations, Byron embraced the cause. In August, in a ceremony of mystic rituals not unlike those of the Freemasons, Byron was initiated into the Carbonari, a clandestine political society devoted to shaking off the Austrians and establishing a free republic. The famous English lord was soon made the leader of one of the local bands, the *Cacciatori Americani* (or American Hunters), numbering several thousand men; and he attended secret meetings with other Carbonari leaders in the pine forest of Ravenna and at the Gamba house in Filetto. Police spies reported that Byron "gives orders right and left on the strength of the money that he freely distributes to the bad characters who form his society. He is the protector of the Cacciatori Americani and the leading revolutionary in Ravenna." The cause of Italy was rapidly becoming his own.

These two intersecting chains of events – the Guiccioli separation and Byron's involvement with the Carbonari via the Gambas – exerted a combined pressure that would push Byron out of Ravenna. His wealth, rank, and celebrity, along with his well-known liberal sympathies, rendered him obnoxious to the local authorities and made him the object of an indirect harassment campaign. Byron's servants were fined for carrying arms in the streets and for wearing livery that resembled that of the Ravenna guards, and his own movements were watched and reported on. One blustery December evening around eight o'clock, the military commandant of Ravenna, Luigi Dal Pinto, was shot by an unknown assailant mere steps from the entrance to the Palazzo Guiccioli. Although Dal Pinto was theoretically the enemy of the Carbonari, Byron ordered the man brought up to his apartments while sending word to the city guard and the cardinal and summoning a surgeon. But Dal Pinto was dead, "Kill'd by five bullets from an old gun-barrel," as Byron would write in rendering the incident in *Don Juan*. Byron helped conduct the post-mortem, and spent long moments pondering the man's body,

> To try if I could wrench aught out of death
> Which should confirm, or shake, or make a faith;
> But it was all a mystery. Here we are,
> And there we go:—but *where*? five bits of lead,
> Or three, or two, or one, send very far!

It was an unsettling incident, especially as Dal Pinto was a rumored double agent for the Carbonari, suggesting that forces of reaction were ready to shed blood; Byron himself might be the next target.

The situation in Ravenna remained hot for months, with Byron investing further in the cause, both figuratively and literally. By early 1821, he was writing of his "Carbonari cronies," who were storing arms and ammunition (that Byron paid for) in the basement of the Palazzo Guiccioli:

> my lower apartments are full of their bayonets, fusils, cartridges, and what not. I suppose they consider me as a depot, to be sacrificed, in case of accidents. It is no great matter, supposing that Italy could be liberated, who or what is sacrificed. It is a grand object – the very poetry of politics. Only think – a free Italy!!

In February, Byron had recorded that he believed there could be "a resurrection for Italy, and a hope for the world" and expected "a general and immediate rise of the whole nation," even as he suspected that the Carbonari tended toward passionate speechifying rather than practical action. By the time Shelley arrived for that late-night conversation that would bring Byron to Pisa to join the "nest of singing birds," the Italian liberation movement had fallen into disarray. The Neapolitan revolutionaries, who had temporarily deposed King Ferdinand I, had surrendered to the Austrians, and Byron's hope to take part in the liberation of Italy faded. "Thus the world goes," he wrote, "and thus the Italians are always lost for lack of union among themselves." He remarked in an April letter to Murray (most likely speaking of Teresa), "a very pretty woman said to me a few nights ago, with tears in her eyes, as she sat at the harpsichord, 'Alas! The Italians must now return to making operas.' I fear that and macaroni are their forte, and 'motley their only wear.'" That same week, he wrote to Shelley of his disappointment and issued an invitation: "Could not you and I contrive to meet this summer? Could not you take a run *alone*?"

Meanwhile, reflecting the increasingly political turn of his experiences and imagination, Byron had begun writing a series of blank verse dramas exploring heroic and tragic aspects of leadership. He completed *Marino Faliero, Doge of Venice* as he was becoming involved with the Carbonari in the summer of 1820, and its plot reflects the clandestine insurrectionist atmosphere of those months, combined with an anxiety over Teresa's reputation as she broke with Count Guiccioli. It tells the story of a fourteenth-century Venetian Doge, who joins a conspiracy to overthrow his own republic after the Council of Forty gives a mere slap-on-the-wrist punishment to a man who had insulted the honor of Faliero's wife by writing graffiti that read "others kiss [or enjoy] her, but he keeps her." The plot is discovered, and the unrepentant Faliero is executed. The following summer, Byron would write another Venetian tragedy, *The Two Foscari*, in which a reluctant fifteenth-century Doge must preside over the torture and banishment of his own son, who has betrayed the republic. Begun as Austria and its forces clamped down in the wake of the Neapolitan surrender, the play was completed as Teresa's father and her brother Pietro were both being exiled from Ravenna for their involvement in the Carbonari movement. The passions and the poetry of Italian politics were powering his imagination, just as his Carnival masquerading and dissolution in Venice had done to produce *Beppo* and *Don Juan*.

But it was Byron's play on the last monarch of the Assyrian Empire, *Sardanapalus*, written in early 1821, that was the most autobiographically revealing of his works from this period. Its tragic hero is an indolent and hedonistic monarch, "femininely garb'd" and "nurs'd in effeminate arts from youth to manhood," who lives (and urges his subjects to live) by the motto, "Eat, drink, and love; the rest's not worth a fillip." He is roused to action and martial bravery by a *coup d'état*, and his friends and enemies alike realize that

> In his effeminate heart
> There is a careless courage which corruption
> Has not all quench'd, and latent energies,
> Repress'd by circumstance, but not destroy'd—
> Steep'd, but not drown'd, in deep voluptuousness.

Much of the play reads like a self-diagnosis written as Byron wavered between the life of an indolent *cavaliere servente* and his dreams of becoming a military or political leader. In meditating on this choice, Byron daringly suggests Sardanapalus's fluid gender identity, yet ultimately the play presents a character arc that restores the monarch's traditional masculine virtues. Teresa had read an early draft and told Byron to "put more love" into the play, and he obeyed, pairing Sardanapalus with a proud yet adoring Greek slave girl as his beloved consort. As Byron developed the drama, Sardanapalus became less the convener of indiscriminate sensual orgies and more a heterosexual man divided between a lawful wife and a passionate soulmate from another nation. That change tracked with Byron's own transition from Venetian concubinage to "strictest adultery" with Teresa in Ravenna, with Lady Byron in a role as Zarina, the forgiving, neglected spouse. If you listen closely, throughout the play you can hear Byron's own self-analysis in the dialogue, at times approaching the intimacy of his Ravenna journal which he was keeping at the time: "I am the very slave of circumstance / And impulse—borne away with every breath! ... / I know not what I could have been, but feel / I am not what I should be." Even as he produced some of his greatest literary work, he was plagued by ennui and longing for a defining purpose. As he had written in his journal on his birthday that same year, "What have these years left to me? / Nothing – except thirty three."

Byron's daughter Allegra was still in his keeping through this period, but, given the erotic tensions and potential violence of the Palazzo Guiccioli, she had been placed with a nurse in a country house, the Villa Bacinetti, some few miles from the Villa Gamba in Filetto. This had also given Byron a pretext for visiting Teresa after the separation when she was with her family, and so their relationship could continue and deepen, away from the prying eyes of Ravenna. Used as a summer residence and a hunting lodge, the Villa Gamba was a spacious, informal country house built in the seventeenth century, set amidst a wide lawn surrounded by olive trees. There Byron spent time with and grew fond of Teresa's extended clan, playing with her little sisters, talking politics in the shade of the trees with her brother Pietro, whose head was "hot for revolutions," and shooting with Count Gamba, all in an atmosphere of great informality. One day in early September 1820, they all watched a solar eclipse, "armed with optical instruments and with smoked glasses" as the earth was enveloped in shadow. After it was over, they all played bowls on the lawn. Byron was once again drawn into a familial circle: he told Teresa that "he liked *le beau sang* of the family; he felt as if he had become part of it."

Allegra no doubt accompanied Byron on some of these visits to the Villa Gamba and was petted by Teresa and her sisters. But when the child turned 4 the following year,

Byron decided it was time for a change of scene. Allegra was becoming willful and "obstreperous," "obstinate as a Mule," with a disposition her father called "perverse": "she thinks herself handsome – and will do as she pleases." The alternately spoiled and neglected child needed socializing and more structure than Byron could provide, particularly given his decidedly casual attitude toward parenting. The Capuchin convent of S. Giovanni Battista at nearby Bagnacavallo had established a school for girls, and it was drawing children from the noble families of the region. In March 1821, Allegra was enrolled as its youngest resident pupil.

Part of Shelley's purpose in visiting Byron in Ravenna that August was to check on Allegra. From Pisa, Claire had been pleading for her daughter and was horrified by the idea of a convent education, as was Shelley, the passionate atheist, who ranted at "the idea of bringing up so sweet a creature in the midst of such trash till sixteen." But on his side, Byron was equally dismissive of the Shelley clan as caretakers of children; as he wrote to Hoppner,

> About Allegra – I can only say to Claire – that I so totally disapprove of their mode of Children's treatment in their family – that I should look upon the Child as going into a hospital. – Is it not so? Have they *reared* one? ... the child shall not quit me again – to perish of Starvation, and green fruit – or be taught to believe that there is no Deity.

Byron digs cruelly at the deaths of the Shelley children in Italy – Clara of dysentery in 1818 and William of cholera in 1819 – to bolster his claim to custody over Allegra. When Hoppner's wife showed this letter to Claire, she called it a "strange Jumble" and noted in her journal, "I spend the day in cogitation, and I write to *my damn'd Brute*." We don't have that letter, which Byron ignored, but we do have Claire's satiric venting from this same era, in which she imagines Byron's recipe for becoming a "great pathetic poet": "have as many & as dirty mistresses as can be found; from their embraces ... catch horrible diseases [;] thus a tolerable quantity of discontent & remorse being prepared ... give it vent on paper, & to remember particularly to rail against learned women." And so their war continued from afar, with Percy Shelley caught in the middle as arbitrator: as he wrote to Mary of Byron and Claire, "Gunpowder & fire ought to be kept at a respectable distance from each other."

On August 6, 1821, Shelley arrived in Ravenna, to find Byron "in every respect an altered man" from the libertine he had known, "in excellent cue of both health and spirits" and "rid of all those melancholy and degrading habits which he indulged at Venice." The Gamba family was in exile in Florence, following the July banishment of Pietro for his activities with the Carbonari, and of Count Gamba for his revolutionary sympathies. It seems clear that the real goal of the local Romagnole authorities was to get rid of Byron: they dared not menace the powerful English lord directly, but they harassed those close to him, and they expected he would follow his mistress when she was forced to relocate. For now, Byron was alone with his servants (including Tita the Venetian gondolier and Fletcher, Byron's English valet) and his many animals, which Shelley describes in a letter as the menagerie of a Circean enchanter hidden away in a "barbarous & wild" part of Italy:

> Lord B's establishment consists, besides servants, of ten horses, eight enormous dogs, three monkeys, five cats, an eagle, a crow, and a falcon; and all these, except the

horses, walk about the house, which every now and then resounds with their unarbitrated quarrels, as if they were the masters of it … P.S. I find that my enumeration of the animals in this Circean Palace was defective … I have just met on the grand staircase five peacocks, two guinea hens, and an Egyptian crane. I wonder who all these animals were before they were changed into these shapes.

One can only imagine what Count Guiccioli thought about the noise and mess of this startling collection of pets that his wife's *amica* had carelessly installed in his house. But in Shelley's eyes, the animals were a welcome improvement from the collection of lovers and concubines – Shelley had called them disgusting wretches – that had populated the Palazzo Mocenigo in Venice. To Mary, Shelley wrote, "He is becoming what he should be, a virtuous man."

One thing that remained unchanged was Byron's regular habit of rising late and staying up until dawn: his favorite times were twilight and the darkest hours of the night. As Shelley reported, it wasn't easy to keep up with this schedule:

Lord Byron gets up at two. I get up, quite contrary to my usual custom … at 12. After breakfast we sit talking till six. From six to eight we gallop through the pine forests which divide Ravenna from the sea; we then come home and dine, and sit up gossiping till six in the morning. I don't suppose this will kill me in a week or fortnight, but I shall not try it longer.

Other than riding horses in the Pineta at sunset and shooting pistols at pumpkins, talk was their primary activity, with Byron particularly starved for English conversation with a fellow poet, a man whom, despite their differences, Byron deeply respected. To convince Shelley to prolong his stay, Byron hinted darkly with a half-hidden smirk that he would likely "fall into his old habits" – i.e., harlotry and orgies – if left alone, knowing how much Shelley deplored "the terrible & degrading consequences of his former mode of life" in Venice.

In any case, the two men had so much to discuss: not only literary and political news from England, the progress of the Greek revolution and the failure of the Italian cause, and memories of the *Frankenstein* summer and their *Julian and Maddalo* days in Venice, but also immediate things like the problem of Claire and Allegra, rumors (likely, but not definitely, false) that Shelley and Claire had had a secret love child in Naples, and Byron's impending move to follow the Gambas. Shelley urged him to abandon the idea of returning to Switzerland and postpone going to Greece with Pietro Gamba to support the Revolution, and instead join Teresa and her family in Tuscany, where they could all live in proximity in the environs of Pisa. The relative convenience and the blend of English and Italian friends appealed to Byron, provided Claire could be kept at a distance, and soon it became a settled plan. Reviving an old conversation, Shelley proposed that the radical writer Leigh Hunt (Figure 8.1) could join them to co-edit a new literary journal espousing liberal principles and offering a venue for politically charged work that mainstream publishers such as John Murray were afraid to touch. And so they talked on – Shelley, enthusiastic and urbane, and Byron, sardonic, mercurial, and self-mocking – through the early morning hours, energized and enervated by draughts of gin and soda water, as light began to appear through the windows of the palazzo, rousing the peacocks and the guinea hens.

8.1 Leigh Hunt, engraved by Samuel Freeman after a painting by John Jackson.

8.2 Edward John Trelawny, from a sketch by Seymour Kirkup.

8.3 The Bay of Lerici, with Casa Magni (right) and the *Don Juan* in the foreground. Watercolor by Captain Roberts, 1822.

8.4 Byron, by William Edward West, painted in Pisa, 1822.

8.5 Countess Teresa Guiccioli, by William Edward West, 1822.

9.1 John Fitzgibbon,
Earl of Clare.

9.2 Lord Byron as
Don Juan, hand-
colored mezzotint
by Welby Sherman
after Alexandre
Marie Colin, c.1830.

9.3 Marguerite Power, Countess of Blessington (after Sir Thomas Lawrence) by James Godsell Middleton, 1822.

9.4 Lord Byron in Genoa, March 1823, by Alfred D'Orsay.

9.5 Lord Byron's helmet.

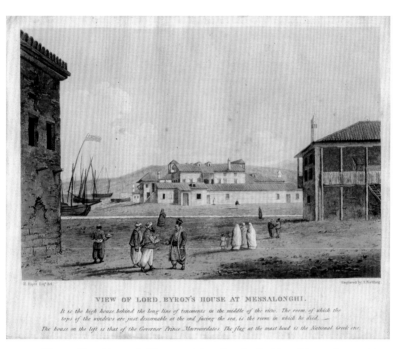

VIEW OF LORD BYRON'S HOUSE AT MESSALONGHI.

It is the high house behind the long line of tenements in the middle of the view. The room, of which the
tops of the windows are just descernable at the end facing the sea, is the room in which he died. —

The house on the left is that of the Governor Prince Mavrocordato. The flag at the mast head is the National Greek one.

10.1 View of Lord Byron's House at Messalonghi, by T. Fielding after an H.
Raper drawing from 1824.

10.2 Letter 7. Letter from Lord Byron to John Murray, 1812.

PRINCE ALEXANDER MAVROCORDATO,
President of the Executive Body of the Greek Government in 1822;
At present President of the Legislative Body & Governor General of Western Greece.

Drawn from Life, & Published in London, September 1824, by A. Friedel.

10.3 Alexandros Mavrocordatos, by A. Friedel, 1824.

10.4 *The Reception of Lord Byron at Messolonghi*, by Theodoros Vryzakis, 1861.

10.5 Byron with his dog Lyon in Messolonghi, by Robert Seymour.

10.6 *Lord Byron on his Deathbed*, by Josef Odavaere, 1826.

Byron also shared the latest canto of *Don Juan* with Shelley during one of their nightly sessions. Shelley listened with dawning admiration and wrote to Mary the next day, calling it "astonishingly fine," a work that "sets him ... far above all poets of the day: every word has the stamp of immortality." It's a judgment Shelley would confirm when he read the published version a month later, telling Byron, "Nothing has ever been written like it in English – nor if I may venture to prophesy, will there be." Shelley was captivated by the "splendour and energy" of the story of Haidee and Juan, but he was even more awed by "the language in which the whole is clothed – a sort of chameleon under the changing sky of the spirit that kindles it." Surveying the latest evidence of Byron's prolific genius, Shelley was both thrilled and dejected: "I despair of rivalling Lord Byron," he wrote, "and there is no other with whom it is worth contending."

Ironically, Shelley had just concluded a miraculous period of poetic creativity, publishing his *Prometheus Unbound* (about which Byron "was loud in his praise," as Shelley told Hunt) and writing "The Witch of Atlas," *Epipsychidion*, "A Defence of Poetry," and *Adonais*, his elegy for John Keats, all in the previous twelve-month period. But Byron seemed to soar above him, with unabated powers of invention and an international audience that brought him wealth, fame, and cultural influence. Not only was there *Don Juan*, but Byron had recently completed *The Two Foscari* and *Sardanapalus*, and was in the midst of writing one of his most powerful works, a radical metaphysical drama called *Cain, A Mystery*. Byron's Cain appears as an intellectual rebel, to whom Lucifer reveals the essential carelessness of the universe and its God, inspiring Cain's "rage and fury against the inadequacy of his state to his Conceptions – which discharges itself rather against Life – and the author of Life." In Byron's drama, the murder of Abel becomes a protest against the broken world, an attitude that may well have been fed by conversations with Shelley at this time. Shelley called *Cain* "apocalyptic ... a revelation not before communicated to man"; it was just the kind of thing that appealed to him, with some resemblance to his own *Queen Mab*. And he may have been thinking of *Cain* when he wrote of Byron's creative powers to a friend early in the following year, "Space wondered less at the swift and fair creations of God, when he grew weary of vacancy, than I at the late works of this spirit of an angel in the mortal paradise of a decaying body." Faced with Byron's leaping from strength to strength, Shelley struggled with jealousy and blamed his ugly feelings on Byron's lordly manner: "Byron and I are excellent friends," he wrote, but "the demon of mistrust & of pride lurks between two persons in our situation, poisoning the freedom of their intercourse." Nevertheless, both men continued to be drawn to one another, each judging the other – sometimes quite harshly – while also recognizing a strong core of fellow feeling as artists and nonconformists.

Meanwhile, Claire stood between the two poets as both a bond and an ongoing source of tension, particularly with regard to Allegra. One afternoon during his visit to Ravenna, Shelley went alone – Byron could not be bothered – to the convent at Bagnacavallo to visit the little girl for several hours. Allegra wouldn't have remembered rolling billiard balls across the marble-and-tile floors of the Palazzo Mocenigo with this tall, odd-looking man three years earlier, and she was initially shy. But after Shelley presented her with a gold chain and a basket of candy, she grew happy and led him all over the grounds (as Shelley told Mary) "skipping so fast that I could hardly keep up with her," eager to show him her little bed and chair, and loudly ringing the convent bell, to the confusion of the nuns. Shelley admired "the beauty of her deep blue eyes," "her light & airy figure & graceful motions," and the "contemplative seriousness" that the discipline of the convent had added to her natural "excessive vivacity." Somewhat ruefully, he observed that the school was devoted almost entirely to Catholic indoctrination, and so Allegra "talks & *dreams* of Paradise & angels & all sorts of things … and is always talking of the Bambino." Via Shelley, she had two requests to convey to her parents: that her mother bring her a kiss and dress of silk and gold, and that her father come visit and bring *la mammina* with him. But she was most likely thinking of Teresa rather than Claire.

Shelley left Ravenna in late August, and soon, on his advice, Teresa and the Gamba family had relocated to Pisa. Byron claimed he was in "all the agonies of packing" to join them, but he dawdled and delayed, and meanwhile wrote a brilliant satire on Robert Southey and George III, *The Vision of Judgment*, as well as another metaphysical drama called *Heaven and Earth*, and kept a nightly journal full of memories of England. He was arranging the records of the past, telling Murray to collect his letters from various English correspondents to give to Moore, as part of the eventual memoir project. Facing another transition, one that would put him back in the orbit of his countrymen, he became nostalgic and philosophical. He noted as the autumn rains came on, "I have found increasing upon me … the depression of Spirits (with few intervals) which I have some reason to believe constitutional or inherited." One evening in early October, he walked in the Ravenna moonlight with "a new woman" who "expected to be made love to," but Byron was not in the mood and "merely made a few common-place speeches," feeling (as he told Moore), "'a mountain of lead upon my heart,' which I believe to be constitutional, and that nothing will remove ... but the same remedy." When Byron was anxious or melancholy, he sought escape in new erotic adventures; but when he was truly depressed, even those seemed useless. He also knew that Teresa was his fate, writing to Augusta, "This is a finisher ... I have not the least wish – nor prospect of separation from her." In the same letter, he referred only half in jest to Teresa as "the *future* Lady B."

Finally, Byron roused himself and left the Palazzo Guiccioli for good, taking most of his menagerie with him (except for the crane, one dog, a goat with a broken leg, and two ugly monkeys). He had been, by any measure, an extraordinary tenant in that house: there was the long-standing affair with his landlord's wife; the murder of the military commandant; the storage of Carbonari weapons in the basement; and the squabbling of Byron's many animals, some now casually left behind in the care of his banker, Pellegrino Ghigi. In Byron's time in Ravenna, we can see how the privileged attitude of an English lord abroad combined with a natural self-centered attitude (which had been rewarded by immense poetic fame) to produce in Byron a carelessness that often overtook his generous impulses, even regarding those that he loved. In late September, Allegra wrote a small note to Byron, sent via the Mother Superior, begging him to come see her: "My dear Papa – It being fair time, I should so much like a visit ... will you not please your Allegrina who loves you so?" Byron annotated the letter: "sincere enough but not very flattering – for she wants to see me because 'it is the fair' to get some paternal Gingerbread – I suppose." And when his carriages rolled out of Ravenna, she remained at Bagnacavallo with the nuns, over the urgent protests of Claire and despite Shelley's suggestion that in Pisa "respectable private families might be found who would undertake the care of her." She never got that visit from her Papa.

Byron arrived in Pisa in early November, reuniting with Teresa and, with her, joining a close-knit community of unconventional British men and women, among whom they would spend the better part of a year. This Pisan circle included not only the Shelleys but Edward Williams and his partner Jane, the wife of a fellow naval officer from whom she was separated; Lady Mount Cashell, also separated from her husband and now living as "Mrs. Mason" with George William Tighe; Captain Thomas Medwin, Shelley's cousin and eventual biographer of Byron; John Taaffe, an Irish writer and translator who had fled Edinburgh in 1812 after a scandalous liaison; and Edward John Trelawny, the dashing adventurer, sailor, and possible pirate who styled himself after Byron's "Corsair" and would accompany Byron to Greece to fight in their war of independence (Figure 8.2). Of these, Byron grew to prefer Edward Williams, who was good-humored and witty, and possessed of a physical courage that Byron shared. Williams admired Byron in return, praising his "unaffected and gentlemanly ease," his "sunshine and good humour," and the brilliance of his conversation. By Christmastime, Williams was writing to Trelawny (who was on the verge of arriving in Pisa) that Byron had become "the very spirit of the place." Shelley told his friend Peacock that "Lord Byron ... and I are constant companions," even as Shelley registered a growing unease with Byron's unpredictable and domineering personality. Meanwhile, Byron began calling Shelley "the Snake," a pun on the Italian word for garden snake (*la biscia*, similar to Bysshe) and a sly reference to his Satanic reputation.

Assured that Claire Clairmont would remain at a distance in Florence, Byron had moved into the Palazzo Lanfranchi, which he called "a famous old feudal palazzo on the Arno – large enough for a garrison – with dungeons below – and cells in the walls … full of *Ghosts*." Medwin remembered it as "large, gloomy, and uncomfortable," but it soon became the site of regular all-male dinners that Byron hosted, "full of social hilarity" with Byron "keeping up the spirit of liveliness throughout the evening" as the drink and talk flowed freely. Laying aside his typically abstemious diet of biscuits or greens drenched in vinegar, Byron ordered good red wine, English mustard, and other "English household comforts" from Livorno, and once served a wild boar that his friend Captain John Hay had shot and sent from Maremma. Shelley wrote to Horace Smith, "Lord Byron unites us at a weekly dinner where my nerves are generally shaken to pieces by sitting up, contemplating the rest making themselves vats of claret &c. till 3 o'Clock in the morning," with Medwin taking notes unobtrusively for his memoir of Byron. Sometimes Count Gamba and Pietro, who were now living in the nearby Casa Parrà with Teresa, would also be included, along with other English visitors drawn into the gravitational field of this extraordinary congregation.

Of these regular gatherings of the men, Mary Shelley wrote with irony, "Our good cavaliers flock together, and … they do not like *fetching a walk with the absurd womankind*." As Byron was increasingly occupied with his male compatriots, or else writing poetry, Teresa was left to manage, in her halting English, with the ladies. In Ravenna, Byron had been a lone Englishman adapting to Italian customs and language, but now he was back among a circle of admiring countrymen who appreciated his verbal wit and manners, whereas

Teresa was separated from her extensive social circle, and she seems to have made few contacts with the local Italians in Pisa. Instead, she exchanged frequent visits with Jane Williams and took daily rides with Mary, who thought her "a nice pretty girl, without pretensions, good hearted and amiable." Percy had taken a similar view, with an added touch of condescension: "La Guiccioli … is a very pretty, sentimental, innocent, superficial Italian, who has sacrificed an immense fortune to live for Lord Byron; and who, if I know anything of my friend … will hereafter have plenty of leisure & opportunity to repent of her rashness." But Shelley was kind to her, and she in turn admired him immensely, seeing in him "an unequalled combination of contrasts and harmonies" that made him seem more spirit than man.

Byron, Shelley, Trelawny, and Williams were all passionate about boating, and the sea surrounding the Italian riviera offered a beautifully tempting waterway. Only Trelawny was particularly skilled at sailing, but the others were enthusiasts, and so, by early 1822, orders had been placed at Genoa for two boats. For Shelley and Williams, there would be a two-masted schooner of about 30 feet in length, and for Byron, a luxury yacht. Trelawny gave instructions to an old comrade, the English naval officer Captain Daniel Roberts, who would oversee the construction: Byron's boat should have an "*Iron Keel*, copper *fastenings* and *bottom* – the cabin to be as *high* and *roomy* as possible, no *expence* to be *spared* to make her a complete BEAUTY!" with two mounted cannons "to make a devil of a noise!" As a gesture of defiance on behalf of revolutionary principles, Byron would christen his boat the *Bolivar*, after the admired Latin American liberator. But the Tuscan authorities had their revenge: noting the boat's name and the presence of those cannons, and well aware of the Carbonari activities of Byron and the Gambas, they forbade the *Bolivar* within sight of the port. As a result, Byron's expensive plaything ended up getting much less use, and Trelawny was fatally prevented from sailing her in pursuit of Shelley and Williams when they piloted their own craft toward Lerici and into the storm.

While the boats were under construction, the men continued their round of leisure activities that centered on billiards, riding, and shooting. As the spring weather came on, they would ride out several miles beyond the city walls to an old farmhouse among orchards and vineyards to shoot pistols at targets, with Teresa and Mary sometimes directing their horses so they might join or meet them along the way. One visitor to the group, the poet Samuel Rogers, suggested that Byron had interests beyond mere target-shooting: "The farm-keeper's daughter was very pretty, and had her arms covered with bracelets, the gift of Byron, who did not fail to let me know that she was one of his many loves." But Rogers was a gossip and Byron enjoyed feeding him shocking confessions, so the anecdote rings true and false at the same time. Byron seems to have been content during these early months in Pisa, happy to be back at the heart of a social circle and feeling himself on the far side of the storms of passion that had shaken him since his marriage. Now 34 years old, he was slipping into middle age. Both he and Shelley had traces of grey in their hair.

Everything started to go wrong in late March. Returning at twilight from one of their shooting expeditions, Byron, Shelley, Trelawny, Pietro Gamba, Taaffe, and Captain Hay encountered an Italian dragoon, Sergeant-Major Stefano Masi, whose horse jostled theirs as he galloped past them toward the Porta della Piazza. While Teresa and Mary Shelley looked on from their carriage, the group of offended Englishmen pursued Masi and surrounded him at the city gate. Harsh words were exchanged, and Byron, mistakenly thinking the dragoon was an officer and a gentleman, threw down his card, demanding an apology or a duel. Masi in turn ordered the gate guards to arrest the insolent foreigners. Byron defiantly replied that they were welcome to try and spurred his horse through the gate, waving to the others to follow. In the confusion, Pietro Gamba struck Masi with his whip, Shelley was knocked from his horse, and Masi slashed Captain Hay across the nose and forehead with his sword. Masi then overtook Byron inside the city, where more insults were exchanged and Byron brandished his sword-stick. By now, darkness was falling and Byron returned home to the Palazzo Lanfranchi to check on his friends. Soon thereafter, somewhere nearby, Masi was stabbed in the side with a pitchfork, almost certainly wielded by Vincenzo Papi, one of Byron's servants. Masi fell from his horse and collapsed in the doorway of a jeweler's shop, and was not expected to survive the night.

Masi did recover, but, from the perspective of the Tuscan authorities, the damage had been done. They now had a solid pretext for pushing Byron and the Gambas out of the province, just as the Ravenna authorities had done. Over the next few months, everyone present was cross-examined and several servants were detained; Tita, the Venetian gondolier, was placed in solitary confinement, forced to shave off his signature black beard, and then exiled. Byron attempted to intervene via Edward Dawkins, the British consul in Florence, and much of his energy was spent in dealing with the fallout of what came to be known as "the Pisan affray." In his letters, Byron repeatedly calls Masi "the aggressor" who "sabred ...

unarmed people," and he shows no sign of remorse for his escalation of what began as a minor jostle. Relations between these privileged and high-handed English expatriates and the locals of Pisa had never been good, and now the city became especially unwelcoming. The Shelleys moved north to the coast of La Spezia and Byron relocated to Montenero, in the hills outside of Livorno – partly to avoid the coming summer heat but also to escape the disapproving looks of the locals, the rancor of the garrison guard, and the official harassment that the confrontation with Masi had sponsored. The Pisan colony was beginning to dissolve, and still Leigh Hunt had not arrived from England to begin work on the new journal they had planned. Forces had been set in motion that would result in the banishment of the Gambas within a few months, and when they went, Byron was bound to follow.

In the meantime, another blow fell. On April 9, Claire had written to Mary that she felt uneasy about Allegra, having not heard news of her in some time and fearing she was ill. With a mother's instinct, she had hit upon the truth: Allegra had contracted typhoid fever during an outbreak at the convent, and on April 20, she died. The mournful report came to Pisa by special messenger two days later, and it fell to Teresa to break the news to Byron. She describes his reaction: "A mortal paleness spread itself over his face, his strength failed him, and he sunk into a seat," remaining "immovable" for an hour, "and no consolation seemed to reach his ears, far less his heart." It was a quietly devastating loss, one that brought feelings of remorse to a father who had chosen to spend so little time with his daughter and who had consistently relegated her to the hands of others. As he remarked later, "While she lived, her existence never seemed necessary to my happiness; but no sooner did I lose her, than it appeared to me as if I could not live without her." Claire had quietly come to Pisa a week earlier and was about to move with the Shelleys to the Gulf of La Spezia for the summer. To prevent any scenes with Byron, the Shelleys kept Allegra's death a secret from her until they had relocated. Claire received the news in bewildered horror, seeing her worst fears fulfilled: as she had written to Byron in February, "I can no longer resist the internal inexplicable feeling which haunts me that I shall never see her any more." Now she sent him a letter of accusation and grief-stricken abuse, which Shelley tried but failed to intercept. Whatever his own feelings over Allegra's loss, Shelley continued in the role of conciliator, and soon wrote to reassure Byron: "Claire is much better: after the first shock she has sustained her loss with more fortitude than I had dared to hope." As Shelley told Trelawny, "Poor Clare has borne her [loss] with great fortitude, after the first shock; and I am persuaded that she will be happier than ever she could have been during the existence of a perpetual source of anxiety and suspense."

Allegra's embalmed body arrived at Livorno in a lead coffin, but Byron, in a state of grief-stricken denial, refused to see it or even admit the messengers who brought it. Instead, he had the coffin sent to his London publisher, the long-suffering John Murray, with a request that Allegra be buried in the Harrow Church, "Near the door – on the left as you enter," in a spot he recalled from his schooldays. He requested a marble tablet with the inscription,

> In memory of
> Allegra –
> daughter of G. G. Lord Byron –
> who died at Bagnacavallo

in Italy April 20th. 1822.

Aged five years and three months. –

"I shall go to her, but she shall not return to me. – "

2d. Samuel 12. – 23.–

But the church's officious rector, the Reverend John William Cunningham, refused to erect the plaque, calling it "an offence against taste and propriety" to have the illegitimate child memorialized so prominently. Apparently, Lady Byron sometimes worshipped at Harrow Church, and it was insinuated in the papers that Byron had chosen a memorial spot opposite her usual pew as a cruel reminder of their failed marriage. Byron responded, "God help me! I did not know that Lady B. had ever been in Harrow Church…. it has been my lot through life to be *never pardoned and almost always misunderstood.*" And so Allegra's story ends: she was placed somewhere unrecorded below the church, with no inscription of any kind to mark her presence or her loss.

Shelley and Williams received their new boat soon thereafter and began sailing up and down the coast, with the Shelleys' residence, Casa Magni, as a homebase (Figure 8.3). As Shelley wrote to Horace Smith, "like Anacreon's swallow, I have left my Nile, and have taken up my summer quarters here, in a lonely house close by the sea-side, surrounded by the soft and sublime scenery of the gulf of Spezzia." Regarding his own lack of poetic productivity during the past months, he added ruefully, "I do not write – I have lived too long near Lord Byron and the sun has extinguished the glow-worm." The relationship between the two poets had deteriorated, especially after the death of Allegra. Shelley wrote in June of his determination to "see little of Lord Byron … I detest all society – almost all, at least – and Lord Byron is the nucleus of all that is hateful and tiresome in it." Tellingly, the new boat was to have been named the *Ariel*, but Byron (at Trelawny's suggestion) had told Roberts to call it the *Don Juan*, which name was painted onto the sail. Annoyed, Shelley carefully cut out that portion of the canvas, but that little act of rebellion couldn't change his sense of Byron's overbearing presence. And while Byron himself had not been writing much poetry lately either – too distracted by the Pisan affray and Allegra's death – he was about to embark on a stunning episode of productivity. A year earlier, Teresa had made Byron promise to stop writing *Don Juan*, as she objected to its irreverence and indiscretion. When she lifted this ban that summer – knowing Byron needed something to raise his spirits – new stanzas came pouring out. When Byron wrote this chapter's letter, he had recently finished the Siege of Ismail cantos of *Don Juan* (and more), drafting Canto VII in June, Canto VIII in July, and Canto IX in August: as he writes here, "I have nearly (*quite three*) four new cantos of *Don Juan* ready.... There is a deal of war—a siege, and all that, in the style, graphical and technical, of the shipwreck in Canto Second." But Shelley would not live to read these new portions: his *Don Juan* would experience a shipwreck of its own.

Meanwhile, Byron had moved out to Montenero with Teresa and was summering in the spacious, salmon-colored Villa Dupuy (or Villa Rossa), where they could catch the breezes rolling across the hills above Livorno, "with the islands of Elba and Corsica visible from my balcony, and my old friend the Mediterranean rolling blue at my feet." He swam in the afternoons and, when the heat became particularly oppressive, would order "an avalanche of sherbets" for everyone, including the servants. That May, the

Mediterranean Squadron of the United States was at anchor at Livorno, and Byron (at his own request) was invited by the Commodore to visit the USS *Constitution* – "Old Ironsides" – which had famously defeated numerous British warships during the War of 1812. Always well disposed toward Americans, Byron was gratified by the warm reception he received on board, meeting everyone and offering the rose he wore in his buttonhole to an officer's wife as a memento. As he told Moore, he would "rather have a nod from an American than a snuffbox from an emperor." On board the *Ontario* that same day, he spotted a New York edition of his own poems and regarded it as a proof of his international fame.

As a further sign of his popularity among the Americans, Byron was visited by William Edward West of Kentucky, a painter who had been commissioned to take his portrait; as Byron tells Moore in this chapter's letter, "I sat for my picture to young West, an American artist" (Figure 8.4). According to West, Byron "was a larger man than I had fancied, rather fat and apparently effeminate – a delicate complexion[,] light blue or grey eyes – dark hair rather long and combed over his forehead with a few curls down about his neck." Byron would serve elaborate lunches of "fish, fowl, tongue, &c" but himself would eat only bread dipped in mustard, at least in front of his guest. West found Byron "a bad sitter," as he talked constantly or else assumed a false expression, but he was disarmed and delighted by Byron's manner, which he called "familiar and friendly." During one of their sessions, West recalled, "I observed at once the little window darken and heard a sweet voice say 'e troppo bello!' ["it's too beautiful!"]." It was Teresa, admiring West's work-in-progress; soon he was painting her portrait as well (Figure 8.5). West recalled that Byron "seemed very proud of her" and "was always playful towards her"; he also sat better – was more relaxed, less anxious – when she was in the room. Byron told West that there was nothing in the world he prized more than the love of beautiful women.

Northward along the coast near San Terenzo, ominous events were beginning to overtake the Shelley household. Standing on the balcony of the Casa Magni overlooking the wild coast of La Spezia by moonlight, haunted by the death of Allegra and his own children in Italy, Shelley twice glimpsed a naked child rise from the sea with clasped hands. Other visions followed, "as bad as in his worst times," as Mary reported. These included a night terror in which he woke Mary with his screams: he had seen Edward and Jane Williams, "their bodies lacerated – their bones starting through their skin, the faces pale yet stained with blood," stumbling into the room to warn him, "Get up Shelley the sea is flooding the house & it is all coming down." Earlier that week, while walking on the terrace, he had encountered his own ghostly double, who had asked him, "How long do you mean to be content?" Now, channeling the scene of Elizabeth's murder by the Creature in *Frankenstein*, he saw his own figure standing over the bed, strangling Mary. These latter visions seem to have been activated by Mary's near-fatal miscarriage, which she suffered in mid-June and only survived because Shelley had the presence of mind, as she bled uncontrollably, to fill a hip bath with ice – likely fetched from a *gelateria* in San Terenzo – for her to sit in. Shelley had grown increasingly estranged from Mary during this period, telling a friend she no longer understood him. He was distracted in part by Claire but mostly by Jane Williams, who would sail with him and her husband and play her guitar and sing, until, as Shelley wrote to his friend John Gisborne, "the earth appears another world."

Leigh and Marianne Hunt and their six young children arrived at Livorno in late June, and Shelley sailed with Williams on July 1 to meet them, racing down in the *Don Juan* which had been modified with new topmast rigging for increased speed: they covered 50 miles in little more than seven hours. After spending the night aboard ship, Shelley reunited gladly with his old friend Hunt, but things were in chaos. Out at Montenero, during one of West's portrait-painting sessions, Byron's servant Vincenzo Papi – the same man who had stabbed Sergeant-Major Masi with a pitchfork – had lost his temper after being ordered to fetch water from a nearby mountain spring. He had slashed Pietro Gamba in the arm and forehead, and Byron had gone for his pistols while also trying to calm the situation, as Hunt reported, "with his cool tones, and an air of voluptuous indolence." Fletcher was sent to notify the police, and, the next day – no doubt due to the fresh impetus of this outbreak of violence – the Gambas were officially banished from Tuscany. As Byron wrote, "Of course this is virtually my own exile, for where they go – I am no less bound by honour than by feeling to follow." Hunt had finally arrived to begin collaboration on the long-planned journal project, and now Byron was headed elsewhere. The Hunts moved into the ground floor of Byron's Casa Lanfranchi in Pisa, but everyone knew that this would only be temporary. Nevertheless, Shelley held on to hopes that the journal – which Byron had christened *The Liberal* – would somehow thrive amidst the upheavals. Thanks to Shelley's mediating efforts at "skrewing LB's mind to the sticking place about the journal," Byron agreed to contribute his satire *The Vision of Judgment* to the first issue. As this chapter's letter shows, Byron was also hoping to draw his old friend Thomas Moore into the Hunt project.

Eager to rejoin the women at Casa Magni, Shelley and Williams sailed north for Lerici on the afternoon of July 8, despite worrying storm clouds to the west. Trelawny later reported that his Genoese mate aboard the *Bolivar* said, "Look at those black lines and the dirty rags hanging on them out of the sky – they are a warning; look at the smoke on the water; the devil is brewing mischief." Ten days later, Shelley's body washed ashore near Viareggio. Because of local quarantine laws, all of the bodies – Shelley, Williams, and Charles Vivian – were buried in the sand where they were found, and could only be removed if they were cremated on the seashore. Trelawny took charge of the grisly operation, ordering an elevated iron frame, "five feet long, two broad," and, with Byron's help, procuring "incense, honey, wine, salt, and sugar" to assist in the rites of burning. Williams was first, his body so badly decomposed that Byron remarked in horror, "are we to resemble that? – why it might be the carcase of a sheep for all I can see." The next day, as the sun beat down upon them, they located Shelley's disfigured, blue-grey corpse by dragging through the sand with hooks, and managed to convey it to the frame for burning. As Byron describes the scene in this chapter's letter, "You can have no idea what an extraordinary effect such a funeral pile has, on a desolate shore, with mountains in the back-ground and the sea before, and the singular appearance the salt and frankincense gave to the flame." As Byron tells Moore, Shelley's heart miraculously refused to burn. Trelawny snatched it from the flames (though it may have been his liver, swollen with seawater) and eventually presented it to Mary as a keepsake.

As Trelawny fed the crematory furnace, Hunt retreated to the carriage and Byron swam off to the *Bolivar*, anchored at a distance of some 3 or 4 miles, "at mid-day, under a broiling sun." The result was a serious case of sun poisoning: "the consequence has been a feverish attack, and my whole skin's coming off, after going through the process of one large continuous blister, raised by the sun and sea together." The damage to his health was the last of a series of blows that had fallen on him in Pisa and its environs: Allegra's death, the affray with Masi, the exile of the Gambas, quarrels with Murray that would soon lead to a permanent break, and the drowning of Shelley and Williams. The expatriate experiment had fallen apart, and now Byron was stuck with Hunt, whom he tolerated, and Hunt's family, whom he cordially despised. As he worked on *Don Juan* through the August heat, he began thinking of escape – South America, perhaps, or Greece – while also pondering a more extreme conclusion. Haunted by the defleshed corpses on the seashore and his own broiled and flayed skin, Byron wrote in Canto ix, "Go ponder o'er the skeleton … / Death laughs at all you weep for: … / Mark! how its lipless mouth grins without breath!":

Mark! how it laughs and scorns at all you are!
    And yet *was* what you are: from *ear* to *ear*
It *laughs not* — there is now no fleshy bar
    So called; the Antic long hath ceased to *hear*,
But still he *smiles*; and whether near or far
    He strips from man that mantle (far more dear
Than even the tailor's) his incarnate skin,
White, black, or copper — the dead bones will grin.

9

—◇—

To Join the Greeks

[To John Cam Hobhouse]   *Genoa April 7th. 1823*

My dear H.—

I saw Capt. Blaquiere and the Greek Companion of his mission on Saturday.—Of course I entered very sincerely into the object of their journey—and have even offered to go up to the Levant in July—if the Greek provisional Government think that I could be of any use.— —It is not that I could pretend to anything in a military capacity—I have not the presumption of the philosopher at Ephesus—who lectured before Hannibal on the art of war*—nor is it much that an individual foreigner can do in any other way—but perhaps as a reporter of the actual state of things there—or in carrying on any correspondence ~~with~~ between them and their western friends—I might be of use—at any rate I would try.—Capt. Blaquiere (who is to write to you) wishes to have me named a member of the Committee in England—I fairly

---

* Phormio, a foolish philosopher who lectured on military leadership to the great Carthaginian general Hannibal when he was in Ephesus (*c*.194 BCE).

told him that my name in its present unpopularity there—
would probably do more harm than good—but of this you
can judge—and certainly without offence to me—for I have
no wish either to shine—or to appear officious;—in the
mean time he is to correspond with me.—I gave him a letter
to Ld. Sydney Osborne at Corfu*—but a mere letter of in-
troduction as Osborne will be hampered by his office in any
political point of view.—There are some obstacles too to my
own going up to the Levant—which will occur to you.—My
health—though pretty good—is not quite the same as when
it subdued the Olympian Malaria in 1810—and the unsettled
state of my lawsuit with Mr. Deardon—and the affairs still
in Hanson's hands—tend to keep me nearer home.—Also
you may imagine—that the "absurd womankind" as Monk-
barns† calls them—are by no means favourable to such an
enterprise.—Madam Guiccioli is of course—and naturally
enough opposed to my quitting her—though but for a few
months—and as she had influence enough to prevent my
return to England in 1819—she may be not less successful
in detaining me from Greece in 1823.—Her brother Count
Gamba the younger—who is a very fine spirited young fel-
low—as Blaquiere will tell you—is of a very different opin-
ion—and ever since the ruin of Italian hopes in 1820—has
been eager to go to Spain or to Greece—and very desirous to
accompany me to one or other of those countries—or at any
rate to go himself.—I wish you could have seen him—you
would have found a very different person from the usual run
of young Italians.—

---

* Lord Sydney Osborne was secretary to the government of the Ionian Islands, then controlled by the British.
† A phrase from Walter Scott, *The Antiquary* (1816).

With regard to my peculium [money] —I am pretty well off—I have still a surplus of three thousand pounds of last year's income—a thousand pounds in Exchequer bills in England—and by this time—as also in July—there ought to be further monies paid to my account in Kinnaird's bank.— From literary matters. I know not if any thing will be produced—but even out of my own—K[innair]d will I suppose furnish me with a further credit—if I should require it—since all my receipts will pass through his bank.—I have desired him not to pass further sums (except for the Insurances of Ly. B[yron]'s Life) to the payment of what remaining debts (and they are but few) may still be extant till the end of the year— when I shall know more precisely what I am to have—and what I may then still owe. You must be aware that it would not do to go without means into a country where means are so much wanted—and that I should not like to be an incumbrance—go where I would.— —Now I wish to know whether <u>there</u>—or (if that should not take place—) <u>here</u> I can do anything—by correspondence or otherwise to forward the objects of the Well-wishers to the Hellenic struggle.—Will <u>you</u> state this to them—and desire them to command me— if they think it could be of any service—of course—I must in no way interfere with Blaquiere—so as to give him umbrage—or to any other person.—I have great doubts—not of my own inclination but from the circumstances already stated—whether I shall be able to go up myself—as I fain would do—but Blaquiere seemed to think that I might be of some use—even <u>here</u>;—though <u>what</u> he did not exactly specify— —If there were any things which you wished to have forwarded for the Greeks—as Surgeons—medicines[,] powder—and swivels &c. of which they tell me that they were in want—you would find me ready to follow any

*directions—and what is more to the purpose—to contribute
my own share to the expence.— —Will you let me hear from
you—at any rate your opinion—and believe me*

Ever yrs.

N.B.

*P. S.—You may show this letter to D[ouglas] K[innair]d
—or to any one you please— —including such members of
the Committee as you think proper—and explain to them
that I shall confine myself to following their directions—if
they give me any instructions— —my uncertainty as to
whether I can so manage as to go personally—prevents me
from being more explicit—(I hear that Strangers are not
very welcome to the Greeks—from jealousy) except as far as
regards anything I might be able to do here—by obtaining
good information—or affording assistance.*

———•———

A return to Greece: the idea had been in Byron's mind for
over a decade, from the moment he had come back to England in 1811 after his youthful Childe Harold sojourn, through
all of his Italian wanderings, to his current perch in Genoa.
At first, that idea had been based in a desire to escape the
stifling atmosphere of the Regency *bon ton* and its gossipy
dramas, and to return to a place of bisexual freedom, the
home of the Maid of Athens and the sylph-like young men
of the monastery school. As time went on, layers of nostalgia
accumulated, so that Greece became for Byron a symbolic

region associated with youthfulness, health, and imaginative strength, a happy place to which his mind would turn as a refuge. He called it "a country replete with the *brightest* and *darkest*, but always most *lively* colours of my memory." In addition, Greece had been in many ways the making of him as a poet. Thanks to the success of *Childe Harold's Pilgrimage*, poetic tales such as *The Corsair* and *The Giaour*, and the early cantos of *Don Juan*, modern Greece was firmly associated with Byron's literary achievement. And underpinning all of this were the classical associations central to the intellectual and political history of the Western world, the works and deeds of the ancient Greeks that were deeply embedded in Byron's mind and culture. When he thought of going back to Greece, Byron was always charting a course to an equally real and imagined land (Figure 9.2).

By spring of 1823, events had brought a new urgency to Byron's meditations: the Greek War of Independence was under way. For centuries, at least since the fall of Constantinople in 1453, the Ottoman Empire had controlled much of the region that included Greece. But the revolutionary spirit of the age that had inspired national movements in the Americas, France, and Italy was now animating the Greeks, who were in open, if disorganized, revolt against Turkish rule. Byron had been slow to turn his attention to the developments in the Peloponnese, where the Revolution had been formally declared in March 1821. He had missed the chance, in 1822, to meet Alexander Mavrocordatos, the Greek patriot leader, who had been part of the Shelley circle in Pisa, tutoring Mary in the Greek language and inspiring Percy's narrative poem *Hellas*, with its famous prefatory statement, "We are all Greeks." And Byron had been too preoccupied with his own affairs – including the Guiccioli separation and the various dramas of both Ravenna and Pisa – to focus on the uprising. But after Shelley's death, he seemed to take on the philhellenism of his brother poet, telling Medwin as he prepared to leave Pisa, "I have formed a strong wish to join the Greeks." More practically, if rather uncertain as to his destination, he asked Kinnaird to obtain as much ready cash as possible: "My avarice – or cupidity – is *not* selfish … I want to get a sum together to go amongst the Greeks or Americans – and do some good." In Genoa, the Greek cause would eclipse the dream of South America, as Byron was drawn in by the proximity of the conflict, the ideals that it represented, and the appeals of men such as Captain Edward Blaquiere, who represented a newly formed political philanthropic association called the London Greek Committee. Significantly, Byron's old friends Hobhouse and Kinnaird were among its founding members.

In this 1823 letter to Hobhouse, Byron announces his readiness to join the Greek cause. He had just met with Blaquiere and Andreas Louriotis, who had visited him, on their way from London to Greece, with the express purpose of inviting Byron to join the new Committee. Inspired by their appeals, Byron took things a step further, offering to travel to Greece himself to do what he could to aid the Revolution. In so doing, he was reconnecting with the Greek national feeling he had first witnessed back in 1809, at Vostitsa on the Gulf of Corinth, when he and Hobhouse had stayed at the house of the Londos family, awaiting a change in the weather. Although the Londos clan had gained power and wealth by collaborating with the Ottomans under Veli Pasha, the son – Andreas Londos – would go on to become a hero of the Revolution. As the men talked with other visitors late into the night, someone mentioned the name of Rigas Pherraios, an early hero and martyr to the Greek cause, whereupon Andreas "jumped suddenly from the sofa, threw over the [chess]board, and clasping his hands, repeated the name of the patriot with a thousand passionate exclamations, the tears streaming down his cheeks." At that moment, Byron's eyes had been opened to the deep currents of Greek pride and resistance that lay beneath a superficial layer of cooperation with the Turks.

Soon thereafter, Byron composed his extensive notes for *Childe Harold's Pilgrimage*, in which he defends modern Greeks against their many critics:

> Where is the human being that ever conferred a benefit on Greece or Greeks? They are to be grateful to the Turks for their fetters, and the Franks for their broken promises and lying counsels: they are to be grateful to the artist who engraves their ruins, and to the antiquary who carries them away; to the traveller whose janissary flogs them, and to the scribbler whose journal abuses them! This is the amount of their obligations to foreigners.

With passages like this, the young Byron had begun his intermittent campaign to draw sympathetic British eyes to the Greek archipelago in the present day. Now he was ready to take up that task in earnest. As he says in this chapter's letter, he intends to go "perhaps as a reporter of the actual state of things there," a kind of war correspondent and celebrity influencer, and, most immediately, a philanthropist "affording assistance" to the Greek cause. As Blaquiere urged Byron in June, "your presence will operate as a Talisman – and the field is too glorious, – too closely associated with all that you hold dear, to be any longer abandoned."

Byron had been in the vicinity of Genoa since October of 1822, having relocated there after the banishment of the

Gambas from Tuscany. He moved into the Casa Saluzzo, a stately, sprawling sixteenth-century villa in the neighborhood of Albaro, about 60 miles north along the coast from the Shelleys' former residence on the Gulf of La Spezia. Byron's new villa had enough room for Teresa and her father and brother to occupy a suite of separate apartments, while Mary Shelley and the Hunt family took up residence nearby. But no one was happy in Genoa. Stricken by the loss of her husband, Mary Shelley wrote to Claire Clairmont of "this busy hateful Genoa where nothing speaks to me of him, except the sea, which is his murderer"; and, in early October, she confided in her journal, "I bear at the bottom of my heart a fathomless well of bitter waters." Leigh Hunt, also in deep mourning for Shelley, felt sidelined by Byron, who made clear both his lack of confidence in the journal project and his disdain for Hunt's awkward and high-handed neediness.

For his own part, Byron was still suffering from the effects of the "stupid long swim in the broiling Sun" during Shelley's beachside cremation. Six months afterwards, in the middle of the Genoa winter, he wrote, "I am far from well – have had various attacks – since last summer – when I was fool enough to swim four hours in a boiling Sun – after which all my skin peeled off – then a fever came on – and I have never been quite right from that time – August. – I am thin as a Skeleton." Even as spring arrived and the Greek Revolution called, Byron had to admit, "I have not been so robustious as formerly, ever since the last summer, when I fell ill after a long swim in the Mediterranean, and have never been quite right up to this present writing." The relentless physical energy that had propelled him through Venetian excesses and the first years of his affair with Teresa was flagging, and his spirits with it. He confessed, as he faced his thirty-fifth birthday, "I always looked to about thirty as the barrier of any real or fierce delight in the passions – and determined to work them out in the younger ore and better veins of the Mine – and I flatter myself (perhaps) that I have pretty well done so – and now the *dross* is coming."

In fact, Byron had been registering his sense of preternatural old age for much of his life, from his early laments over his lost boyhood, to his entry in the hotel registry at Secheron in 1816 ("age 100"), through to his present state of weariness in which he called himself "worn out in feelings"; only in his thirty-sixth year, he said, "I feel sixty in mind, and am less capable than ever of those nameless attentions that all women, but, above all, Italian women, require." In a similar vein, he remarked around this time, "I remember my youth, when my heart overflowed with affection ... ; and now ... I can scarcely, by raking up the dying embers of affection in that same heart, excite even a temporary flame to warm my chilled feelings." The passionate rebel felt himself flattening out, and a gray wind was blowing. He spoke with envy of those who are lucky enough to die young, before "the illusions that render existence supportable have faded away, and are replaced by experience, that dull monitress." After the deaths of Shelley and Allegra, there had crept upon Byron a sense that he too had passed beyond a horizon. The shades of middle age were gathering to remind him of all that had already faded away. In a stanza of *Don Juan* written in late 1822, he looked backward to his short season in Regency highlife:

Alas!
Where is the world of eight years past? 'T was there—
I look for it—'t is gone, a globe of glass!

Crack'd, shiver'd, vanish'd, scarcely gazed on, ere
   A silent change dissolves the glittering mass.
Statesmen, chiefs, orators, queens, patriots, kings,
   And dandies, all are gone on the wind's wings.

In Byron's eyes, the England – and the world – that he had known was gone, vanished, dissolved. Increasingly in a valedictory mood and beset by chronic illness, he was thinking of his endgame.

In an urgent rush of vitality that was perhaps a symptom of his decline, Byron wrote almost two-thirds of his masterpiece *Don Juan* in little more than a year, composing eleven cantos between the early months of 1822 and May 1823. He confessed in Canto xiv, "In youth I wrote, because my mind was full, / And now because I feel it growing dull." But this late outpouring amounted to over a thousand witty, agile stanzas, by turns sentimental and satiric, nostalgic and nasty, grim and gay. In those cantos, Juan goes from the erotic high jinks of a Turkish harem to the blood-soaked butchery of the Russian siege of Ismail, to the court of Catherine the Great, and finally to England, where he mingles with that "glittering mass" of Regency aristocrats that Byron remembered well, culminating in a series of country-house scenes at "Norman Abbey," closely modeled after his ancestral Newstead. Joining it all together was Byron's voice, which blends an extraordinary range of tones and registers within the ottava rima form, pushing forward into a modern poetic idiom that combines everyday speech, poetic cliché, cockney slang, epic rhetoric, professional jargon, and the fashionable prattle of aristocrats. During this same period, Byron also wrote a cultural satire (*The Age of Bronze*) and a romantic narrative set in the South Seas based on the mutiny on the *Bounty* (*The Island*). These months of productivity were to be his greatest, and final, tour de force.

But there was a complicating factor to this rush of poetic output: Byron's involvement with Leigh Hunt and his brother John, both radicals in the world of London journalism and publishing. The long and fruitful relationship Byron had shared with his conservative publisher John Murray, who had served as his advisor, manager, publicist, and friend for over a decade, was breaking down. Since leaving England, Byron had grown increasingly uncensored, ever more scornful of rules of propriety he thought hypocritical. By 1822, he had run out of patience with Murray's hesitancy to offend the powers-that-be. In contrast, the Hunts had long prided themselves on such offenses, and had been fined and jailed for publishing attacks on the king and his ministers. *The Liberal* had been designed accordingly as a fresh provocation against the Tories, powered in part by the radical political utopianism of Shelley. Murray warned Byron against being part of Hunt's plans, as did Thomas Moore and Hobhouse. For his own part, impatient with Murray's timidity, yet annoyed by Leigh Hunt's passive-aggressiveness, Byron fell into a kind of impulsive fatalism. He could only watch himself drifting angrily toward the Hunts, going so far as to admit to Murray in early October: "I am afraid the journal is a *bad* business – and won't do – but in it am sacrificing myself for others – I can have no advantage in it…. the *brothers* Hunt … pressed me to engage in this work – and in an evil hour I consented."

The first issue of *The Liberal* appeared on October 15, opening with *The Vision of Judgment*, Byron's scathing and uproarious satire on George III, George IV, and the royal laureate, Robert Southey. Predictably, the Tory press attacked: the *Literary Gazette* excoriated the poem's "heartless and beastly ribaldry," claiming there was "no language strong enough to declare the disgust and contempt which it inspires." Murray, in reporting to Byron the "universal outcry" that greeted *The Liberal* in London, wrote, "You see the result of being forced into contact with wretches who take for granted that every one must be as infamous as themselves – really Lord Byron it is dreadful to think upon your association with such outcasts from Society"; it was a connection that had created a "horrid sensation … in the mind of the public." He warned Byron, "My Company used to be courted for the pleasure of talking about you – it is totally the reverse now – &, by a re-action even your former works are considerably deteriorated in Sale." This is not a message a favorite author wants to receive from his publisher. Murray knew that, despite a superficial insouciance, Byron was very much invested in his popularity in England. Perhaps news of sad reversals and deteriorations would convince him to drop the Hunts and return to the Murray fold.

But Byron had by this time already sent his publisher an angry letter regarding the freshly written Cantos VI, VII, VIII, and IX of *Don Juan*. That letter is lost – perhaps one of a very few that Murray discarded in a rage – but we can judge its contents from the response he sent to Kinnaird, who was operating as a somewhat manipulative go-between. Murray said Byron's letter was so "particularly ungracious" that he outright refused to read the new cantos, stating "I will not be the publisher of any work that is accompanied by a condition so degrading to my feeling & character as that contained in Lord Byron's Letter." Byron claimed ignorance of any such "condition," but he nevertheless requested Murray put all of his unpublished poems into the hands of Kinnaird, to be delivered to John Hunt. Around this time, Byron wrote to bid "a final farewell" to Murray as a publisher on November 6, accusing him of "rude neglect" and discourtesy. Fortunately, Kinnaird never delivered this letter and relations between poet and publisher remained cordial, though they were forever changed. As our next chapter shows, Byron continued to write to Murray occasionally, but their working relationship had essentially ceased. Although Murray would publish *Werner* as a last gasp in 1823, all of the new cantos of *Don Juan* would appear from the house of Hunt. When you read Byron's epic, listen for that otherwise silent break that separates the fifth from the sixth canto, the moment when the Murray volumes give way to the Hunt sequels. Somewhere in that white space, you can hear an era – and one of the most important author–publisher relationships of the century – coming to an end.

In time, Genoa would become a place of final transitions for Byron: a city of last encounters and permanent farewells. He had already parted with Hobhouse, who had visited him in Pisa briefly in September 1822. The two friends had not seen one another since Venice, nearly five years earlier. Byron was sitting in the garden of the Palazzo Lanfranchi with Teresa, who was playing a melody on her guitar and talking with Byron "in a mood of serenity and sadness" of "his past life and his situation in Italy." It was a tender moment – serene and sad, nostalgic and quietly sensual, suffused with a sense of autumnal aftermath – and one that could serve well as an emblem for Byron's Italian existence after the deaths of Shelley and Allegra. He was telling Teresa, "if I had to begin my life over again, I wouldn't want anything changed in it," other than his marriage to Annabella and his current entanglement with Leigh Hunt. At that moment, Hobhouse burst into the garden, having given Byron no warning that he was on his way over from England. As Teresa reports, "the surprise was total"; she recalled Byron's face filling with "the liveliest joy … so great that it almost deprived him of strength. A fearful paleness came over his cheeks, and his eyes were filled with tears as he embraced his friend." It was as if Byron's reveries of his past life had summoned his most long-standing and loyal male companion to his side.

In keeping with their old habits, Byron and Hobhouse spent the days riding and the nights in conversation. They talked of England, of Lady Byron and Teresa, of Hobhouse's political career, and of the new cantos of *Don Juan*. As Hobhouse observed in his diary, "It seemed to us both that we had not been separated for more than a week – we talked over old times, & present times in the same strain as usual." On one of their rides through the countryside, perhaps to the old farm where Byron went shooting with his friends, they were caught in a thunderstorm and sought shelter in a cottage. Hobhouse noted that "an adventure occurred which gave me no high notion of the morals of the contadine" – perhaps a final fling with the pretty farm-keeper's daughter (a "contadina") whom Rogers had seen wearing bracelets that Byron had given her. When the two men parted a few days later, "on the most friendly terms," as Hobhouse noted, he registered that nevertheless "we were not as before quite": they had had "two or three mutual accusations half in joke" between them, and Hobhouse told Byron "that he should write less and not think the world cared so very much about his writing or himself." They still had their past in common, but they had taken very different paths since the time that Byron had grasped Hobhouse's hand through the window of his wedding carriage, as if for rescue. For his part, Byron had been both thrilled and dejected by the visit, writing mournfully to Kinnaird after Hobhouse's departure that "these glimpses of old friends for a moment are sad remembrancers" of old times, and of how much things had changed. He would never see Hobhouse again.

Later that autumn, now in Genoa, Byron wrote to Mary Shelley to disclaim his capacity for male friendship, a curious cutting of apparent ties:

> As to friendship, it is a propensity in which my genius is very limited. I do not know the male human being, except Lord Clare, the friend of my infancy, for whom I feel anything that deserves the name. All my others are men-of-the-world friendships. I did not even feel it for Shelley, however much I admired and esteemed him; so that you see not even vanity could bribe me into it, for, of all men, Shelley thought highest of my talents, – and, perhaps of my disposition.

Even the mutual admiration he shared with Shelley wasn't enough. Later in the same letter, Byron added Thomas Moore as a possible contender for the category of friend, but he compared his other many companions to "partners in the waltz of this world – not much remembered when the ball is over, though very pleasant for the time." The omission of Hobhouse from Byron's account is telling: rather than solidifying their friendship, Hobhouse's recent visit had left Byron dissatisfied and somewhat bewildered. He singled out instead the Earl of Clare, whom he knew at Harrow as a favorite among his "Theban band." He was drifting backward to friends whose absence allowed them to remain mostly ideal.

It's worth pausing to ask: could John Fitzgibbon, 2nd Earl of Clare, have been Byron's most important male friend

(Figure 9.1)? In 1821, as Byron composed his journal of "Detached Thoughts," he had maintained that his friendship with Clare began earliest and lasted longest, adding "I never hear the word 'Clare' without a beating of the heart – even *now*, & I write it – with the feelings of 1803-4-5–ad infinitum. – ." A few weeks later, the two men met briefly by chance on the road between Imola and Bologna, after eight years apart. Byron returned to his journal and wrote,

> This meeting annihilated for a moment all the years be-tween the present time and the days of *Harrow* – It was a new and inexplicable feeling like rising from the grave to me. – Clare too was much agitated … I could feel his heart beat to the fingers' ends…. We were but five minutes together – and in the public road – but I hardly recollect an hour of my existence which could be weighed against them.

Most startling here is Byron's sense of the priority of those five minutes with Clare over the wealth of moments in a life packed full of passion and sensation. Clare then visited Byron briefly in Pisa, leaving few traces to us except a version of the lament Byron would make again after Hobhouse's departure: "These transient glimpses of old friends are very painful … however agreeable they make the moment – They are like a dose of Laudanum – and its subsequent languor." Sadly, there is a huge archival gap as we approach the relationship of Byron and Clare: we know that the two men kept up a "very voluminous" correspondence throughout their lives, but lit-tle of it remains. Perhaps tellingly, Clare destroyed nearly all of Byron's letters. In one of the few that survives, sent shortly before the end in Messolonghi, Byron writes to Clare in a register mostly absent from his correspondence to men: "I hope that you do not forget that I always regard you as my dearest friend – and love you as when we were Harrow boys together – and if I do not repeat this often as I ought – it is that I may not tire you with what you know so well." It reads like a soulmate's greeting.

While Byron was in Genoa, other English friends and acquaintances circled through, offering reminders of the past. In November, James Wedderburn Webster turned up, carrying a load of debt and unsurprisingly separated from Lady Frances, whom Byron had seduced over that game of billiards at Aston Hall way back in 1813. Byron had "spared her" then, but he had prophesied her career of infidelity after hearing of her liaison with no less than the Duke of Wellington in the aftermath of his epochal victory at Waterloo. As Byron revealed to Lady Hardy, writing from Genoa about the Websters, there was a secret last stanza of his lyric, "When We Two Parted," written for Frances:

> Then – fare thee well – Fanny –
>   Now doubly undone –
> To prove false unto many –
>   As faithless to *One* –
> Thou art past all recalling
>   Even *would* I recall –
> For the woman once *falling*
>   Forever must *fall*. –

After Wellington, Lady Frances had gone on to other lovers, including Byron's old Trinity friend, the gambler Scrope Davies. In 1818, she had written to Davies in her characteristic, overwrought style (unwittingly duplicating Byron's judgment that she was "undone"), "I have loved thee to madness – to destruction – to Death – You have given me your heart – I will never part with it … I am lost – lost – undone." Meanwhile, Webster, whom Hobhouse called "a very strange creature, miraculously blind to his own defects," and "the greatest ass and cuckold in London," had gone through his own string of lovers. Now living on borrowed money (including £1,000 from Byron that he would never repay) and having been rejected by Lady Hardy, Webster was "moving Heaven and Earth – for reconciliation" with his wife. For a few months, Byron did his best to encourage the parted spouses, writing to Lady Frances in early 1823, "I still do not despair of your reunion," even as he observed privately, "She is very beautiful – and more romantic than wise…. the wonder is that they were not separated before." Webster's visit was essentially a comic interlude, and, in writing to Lady Hardy about it all, Byron was reprising his letters to Lady Melbourne of ten years earlier, playing the part of confidante to both Websters while gossiping behind the scenes (as we saw so vividly in the billiards letter of Chapter 3).

A more welcome visitor to Casa Saluzzo was Henry Edward Fox, the son of Lord Holland and scion of Holland House, where Byron had first met Lady Caroline Lamb in the heady days of fame in London. Byron had last seen him seven years ago, when Fox was only 14, "a pretty mild boy, without a neckcloth, in a jacket, and in delicate health" and, like Byron, afflicted with lameness. Byron had admired him immediately, calling him "an especial favourite of mine" and now found him to "have the softest and most amiable expression of countenance I ever saw, and manners correspondent." There's a hint of erotic attraction on Byron's side, born out of a nostalgia for his own involvement with the Holland circle, his typical attraction to young, good-looking men, and his sympathy with Fox's limping gait, which resembled his own.

As Byron told Moore, "But there is this difference: that *he* appears a halting angel, who has tripped against a star; whilst I am *Le Diable Boiteux*" – alluding to a novel by Le Sage subtitled, "The Devil on Two Sticks." Fox stayed only briefly and did not have a chance to meet Teresa. But if Byron and Fox could have glimpsed the near future, they would have stared at one another with greater intensity: after Byron's death, Teresa moved to London and took Fox as her lover, in an intermittent liaison of almost five years. Fox's gossipy, narcissistic private journal provides a fascinating glimpse of that relationship, and particularly of Fox's inability to understand his own feelings for the supremely deft and passionate Italian Countess: is she frank and sincere or affected and sentimental? Unattractive or pretty? Coarse and indelicate or passionate and sexually compelling? Clever or foolish? Generous and noble or a mere adventuress? Fox calls her all of these things by turns, amidst many evenings of pleasure and frequent "various quarrels and hysterics"; as he would write in the midst of their affair, "Poor Lord Byron! I do not wonder at his going to Greece." When Fox visited Genoa, Byron was only a few months away from that final departure.

According to Mary Shelley, Byron had spent his time in Genoa in a state of amused satisfaction with Teresa. Mary wrote to Jane Williams, "He is kept in excellent order, quarreled with & hen-pecked to his heart's content" – an echo of Byron's famous rhymed couplet in *Don Juan*: "But—Oh! Ye lords of ladies intellectual, / Inform us truly, have they not hen-peck'd you all?" Although they lived under the same roof, Byron and Teresa saw one another for only a few hours each day, dining together, going for late-afternoon walks, or visiting his menagerie of monkeys, rabbits, dogs, and several geese that Byron had spared from the butcher's cleaver and that now followed him everywhere. Sex was reserved for the evenings in Teresa's apartments, after which Byron would return to his own room to write letters and work on *Don Juan*. It was a relatively simple domestic rhythm that suited him, for a time. As he told a friend during this period, "I recommend solitude … a regular retirement, with a woman that one loves, and interrupted only by a correspondence with a man that one esteems." But Henry Fox remembered Byron telling him that "one of his reasons for going to Greece was to get rid of her and her family." Byron was beginning to chafe at his surroundings with the old restlessness of spirit that had kept him on the move, emotionally and geographically.

By spring 1823, Mary Shelley observed, "LB is fixed on Greece – he gets rid of two burthens; the G[uiccioli] & the Liberal – the first is natural, though I pity her." Once Teresa understood that a journey to Greece was inevitable, she pleaded to be included. Byron wrote to Kinnaird in May, "She wants to go up to Greece too! … of course the idea is ridiculous…. and if she makes a scene – (and she has a turn that way) we shall have another romance – and tale of ill usage and abandonment – and Lady Carolining – and Lady Byroning – and Glenarvoning." He observed ruefully and disingenuously, "there never was a man who gave up so much to women – and all I have gained by it – has been the character of treating them harshly." Remembered as someone "mad, bad, and dangerous to know," especially in regard to women, Byron saw himself as buffeted by female desires, altering his life to accommodate their wishes. Behind the breathtaking self-deception of that view lies a certain partial truth: Byron gave selfishly to women all his life, often to his own detriment, driven by impulses that sometimes partook of generosity. But he also hated confrontations, and, in the end, he had Teresa's brother Pietro, the "very fine spirited young fellow" who would accompany Byron to Greece, break the news of their journey to her. Conveniently, and thanks to the machinations of Count Guiccioli back in Ravenna, the banishment of the Gambas had just been lifted: the tide was dragging Teresa back to her native city, even as Byron's ship for Greece, the *Hercules*, made its way toward the harbor at Genoa.

During the same week that Captain Blaquiere and Andreas Louriotis met Byron and spurred him to action, three other visitors from England arrived at the Casa Saluzzo. The most important of these was the gorgeous, disreputable Marguerite, Lady Blessington (Figure 9.3), who arrived with her husband Lord Blessington and the sexually ambiguous dandy, Count Alfred D'Orsay. In Lady Blessington, Byron found his last female confidante: their conversations over the ensuing eight weeks ranged widely, amounting to a kind of mini-memoir, captured just before Byron was swallowed for good by Greece and its concerns. She was born Margaret Power in Tipperary, Ireland, to a poor family (though with some noble connections on her mother's side) and was married at 15 to an alcoholic English officer named Farmer, who would meet his death by falling out of the window of the Fleet debtors' prison. Margaret had left him after three months, living for several years under the protection of another officer, Captain Jenkins, becoming, as she herself put it, "that despised thing, a kept mistress." It was Jenkins who, in 1816, introduced her to Lord Blessington, then a widower, who took the vivacious and intelligent Margaret under his protection. Immediately after her husband's death in 1818, she became Lady Blessington, remarrying and altering her first name to Marguerite, and thereafter rising to the center of male aristocratic, artistic circles in London and abroad. Teresa Guiccioli, who both admired and disliked her, called Lady Blessington, "beautiful, witty, pleasant, and full of resources in society, but a little artificial," adding the observation that "she had points in her known and unknown past that were too vulnerable" for respectable Englishwomen to admit her to their circles. Like Byron, Lady Blessington was both outsider and insider, a figure with a scandalous past who compelled admirers, particularly of the opposite sex, with her looks, charm, and talents. She had come to Genoa to meet the famous poet whose works had captured her imagination.

At first, reality did not prove equal to Lady Blessington's expectations. On April 1, she wrote in her diary, "I have seen Lord Byron: and am disappointed." She was expecting the famous poet to be "dignified, cold, reserved, and haughty," a version of Childe Harold and the Byronic heroes of the Turkish tales, like Conrad from the *Corsair* with "his forehead high and pale" and "his dark eye-brow" that "shades a glance of fire." What she found instead was a rather smaller, gossipy, bantering, and mercurial person, feminine or boyish in some respects. Her description is worth quoting at length:

> I had fancied him taller, with a more dignified and commanding air.... His appearance is, however, highly prepossessing: his head is finely shaped, and the forehead open, high, and noble; his eyes are grey and full of expression, but one is visibly larger than the other; the nose is large and well shaped, but from being a little too thick, it looks better in profile than in front-face: his mouth is the most remarkable feature in his face, the upper lip of Grecian shortness, and the corners descending; the lips full, and finely cut. In speaking, he shows his teeth very

much, and they are white and even…. His chin is large and well shaped, and finishes well the oval of his face. He is extremely thin, indeed so much so that his figure has almost a boyish air; his face is peculiarly pale … and his hair (which is getting rapidly grey) is of a very dark brown…. His voice and accent are particularly agreeable, but effeminate – clear, harmonious, and so distinct, that though his general tone in speaking is rather low than high, not a word is lost…. But … were I to point out the prominent defect of Lord Byron, I should say it was flippancy, and a total want of … natural self-possession and dignity.

Lady Blessington's observations are particularly valuable as a record made by an astute, literary, largely unbiased woman of the world, of Byron's own age, with a similar trajectory from obscure origins to an aristocratic position impaired by sexual notoriety. She was fascinated by Byron while also very aware of his contradictions and shortcomings, and soon grew to feel a combination of attraction and pity toward what she called "this wayward, spoiled child of genius."

We have seen Byron as someone subject to mood swings and unpredictable changes of tone, a method-actor who took on various characters, each of which would become, for a time, the "real" him. Lady Blessington sensed this aspect of his personality immediately and was unsettled by it, remarking, "The mobility of his nature is extraordinary, and makes him inconsistent in his actions as well as his conversation." He would mercilessly ridicule "sentiment and romantic feelings" and then, the next day, would give himself over to tears in discussing his affections in a tremulous voice: "All this appears so inconsistent, that it destroys sympathy…. and certainly destroys in the minds of his auditors all confidence in his stability of character." Byron was well aware of his own mobile temperament. In stanzas of *Don Juan* written while the Blessingtons were visiting Genoa, he describes one character – Lady Adeline – in terms that reflect that knowledge:

> So well she acted, all and every part
>   By turns—with that vivacious versatility,
> Which many people take for want of heart.
>   They err—'tis merely what is called mobility,
> A thing of temperament and not of art,
>   Though seeming so, from its supposed facility;
> And false—though true; for surely they're sincerest,
> Who are strongly acted on by what is nearest.

In a footnote to the word "mobility" here, Byron defines it as "an excessive susceptibility of immediate impressions," calling it, in the voice of experience, "a most painful and unhappy attribute." Past a certain point, such mobility starts to dissolve the self altogether, fragmenting it into a kind of schizoid multiplicity. Lady Blessington noted, "Byron is a perfect chameleon … taking the colour of whatever touches him. He is conscious of this, and says it is owing to the extreme *mobilité* of his nature," a fact that has troubled his biographers, of which she would be one. She recorded him as saying, "I am such a strange mélange of good and evil, that it would be difficult to describe me. There are but two sentiments to which I am constant, – a strong love of liberty, and a detestation of cant."

On daily rides and at frequent dinners, Byron came to know the Blessingtons and the Count D'Orsay, the tall, perfectly dressed, elegant young man whom Byron called their "very handsome companion" with "all the air of a *Cupidon déchainé*," a Cupid on the loose. The Blessingtons called him their "young Lion," and relations among the three visitors were uncertain, with hints that D'Orsay was an erotic companion to either one or both of the couple. Byron was also charmed, and he enjoyed reading D'Orsay's sardonic journal of his experiences in fashionable London society, the same world he had conquered when he was D'Orsay's age. As he wrote to Lord Blessington, "there is scarcely a person mentioned whom I did not see nightly or daily – and was acquainted more or less intimately with most of them, but I never could have described it so well." Byron was particularly taken with D'Orsay's jaded depiction of "the *mystery of the English Ennui*," the particular brand of boredom that enveloped the leisured upper classes, who had no occupation other than socializing and hobbies. It was a similar target to the one he had just bullseyed in the English cantos of *Don Juan*. Byron also asked the talented "young Lion" to draw his portrait (Figure 9.4), which D'Orsay did several times at Genoa, producing what turned out to be our final clear images of the poet taken from life. Still handsome and slender, he looks older, with a slightly tentative air.

Greece was calling. Soon after the visit of Blaquiere and Louriotis, Byron wrote again to inform Hobhouse (and thus the London Greek Committee) that he had ordered gunpowder and medical supplies to be sent to Tripolitsa, at that time the seat of the Provisional Government of Greece. He also was developing his sense of purpose, which had a strong humanitarian tendency: he wrote less about acts of military glory and more about benevolent support. "I shall do my best to civilize their mode of treating their prisoners," he told Hobhouse, "and could I only save a single life – whether Turk or Greek – I should live 'mihi carior' ["dearer to myself"] – and I trust not less so to my friends." But, of course, what the

Greek leaders needed most was money. As his youthful passions and energy died down, Byron had hoped to cultivate avarice as a consolatory passion of middle age; but, he told Lady Blessington, the Greek Revolution had inspired "a new passion, – call it love of liberty, military ardour, or what you will, – to disgust me with my strong box, and the comfortable contemplation of my moneys, – nay, to create wings for my golden darlings that may waft them away from me for ever." Much of his correspondence of the spring of 1823 is devoted to securing as much financial liquidity as possible from his various estates and publications. As he told Kinnaird, "I wish to have as great a command of monies of mine as I can – that I might be of some use to the Cause," since "Cash is the Sinew of war."

On May 6, Byron finished the last canto of *Don Juan* he would complete (the sixteenth) amidst a gathering flurry of preparations for his departure. That same evening, he copied out a faltering lyric for Lady Blessington as a souvenir for her album. It reads in part,

> You have asked for a Verse:—the request
> In a rhymer 'twere strange to deny,
> But my Hippocrene was but my breast,
> And my feelings (its fountain) are dry.
>
> . . .
>
> I am ashes where once I was fire,
> And the bard in my bosom is dead,
> What I loved I *now* merely admire—
> And my heart is as grey as my head.

Byron presents his heart as an exhausted fount of inspiration: what he once loved in his hot youth he can now "merely admire" in grey-headed, ashy maturity. It's a poem of a burnt-out case, a farewell to his creative powers. He only had a few short lyrics – one of them a masterpiece, as we will see in the next chapter – left in him, along with a few more stanzas of an unfinished canto of *Don Juan* which begins with the haunting phrase, "The world is full of orphans." His attention turning fully toward the Greek cause, Byron was leaving poetry behind to become what he had always half-desired to be: a man of action. His desk, once covered with poetical manuscripts, was now heaped with books on modern Greece and maps of the territory. And yet, he promised, "*if I do* ... outlive the campaign, I shall write two poems on the subject – one an epic, and the other a burlesque, in which none shall be spared, and myself least of all," an intention he echoed to Trelawny as they parted in Greece later that year, "If things are farcical, they will do for *Don Juan*; if heroical, you shall have another canto of *Childe Harold.*" He still had hopes of renewing his vocation as a writer: but would Greece favor a burlesque farce or a heroic epic? The whole enterprise, and Byron's involvement in it, seemed poised between the two.

A flurry of details filled Byron's last weeks in Italy as everything was made ready for the journey. Byron had his mind set on stopping first at Zante (Zakynthos), one of the Ionian islands, which were a British Protectorate and thus a logical starting point for Byron in Greece. Leigh Hunt and Mary Shelley were both angry at Byron for what they saw as his careless desertion of them, despite his offers to pay for their return trips to England. Thanks mostly to the backbiting of Leigh and Marianne Hunt, the result was a series of terse or wounded letters that marked the conclusion of the *Liberal* project. Before the Blessingtons departed, Byron sold his yacht, the *Bolivar*, to Lord Blessington, and purchased Lady

Blessington's first-rate Arabian horse, named Mameluke, to take with him to Greece; but both negotiations were somewhat acrimonious, thanks in part to Byron's close-fisted way with money at this stage. Everything was being directed toward the Greek cause. From Genoa, Byron ordered scarlet and gold military uniforms for himself, Trelawny, and Pietro Gamba, along with three elaborate, classically styled helmets in black and gold, his own bearing the Byron family crest and motto (Figure 9.5). They suggest Byron's awareness of the importance of cutting a figure of command: he knew that any success he would have in Greece would be largely based on perception, on the iconography of leadership that might rally attention to the cause. Byron's banker, Charles Barry, was left to dispose of the contents of the Casa Saluzzo, including Byron's books and his well-traveled Napoleonic coach, the same one that had carried him away from his apartments in Piccadilly Terrace when he fled England so many years before. It would eventually end up, *circa* 1860, in South Australia, after it was presented as a wedding gift to Charlotte Harley, the daughter of Lady Oxford who had featured as the "Ianthe" of *Childe Harold's Pilgrimage*.

"Amid these perplexities and conflicts, the time of departure was looming," Teresa wrote in her memoir; and "when the day for leaving was decided upon, who could describe the anguish of that heart?" Unable to sleep, Teresa would stay up writing pleading love letters to Byron and then destroy them unsent, because she knew she needed to support him: he had given his word of honor that he would go to Greece. But, while visiting her apartment one evening, he saw and kept several of the fragmented letters, in which she had written "*a hand of iron weighs on my heart*" and had begged him to "cut short the horrible distance which will separate us…. If life and reason remain mine, give me this word of consolation: 'In winter we shall be side by side once again.'" In another, she offered a list of loving domestic commands that Byron would have done well to follow, urging him to "*take care of your health* – don't *dose yourself with medicines* – keep out of the burning sunlight … have cooling drinks – don't eat salt pork – take plenty of exercise – and stay in a place with *healthy air.*" The letter concluded with an endearing, heartbreaking apology: "Forgive me, my love, if I bother you with all this chatter. You will soon have a long rest from this kind of tedium!" Reading these letters, Byron tried to reassure Teresa, promising her that they would indeed reunite together soon, "and then nothing will be able to part us again." He then presented her with a large packet of his poetic manuscripts, what he called "my scribblings," for safekeeping, telling her to preserve them or burn them as she saw fit, while acknowledging, "It's possible that they'll be sought after, one day." To Teresa, it felt like a gesture of farewell.

On the day of his departure, July 13, Byron spent the last few afternoon hours alone with Teresa. She was leaving the next morning to begin her journey back to Ravenna with her father, and Byron would spend the night aboard the *Hercules*, in hopes of sailing at dawn. We are left to imagine their last conversation. Byron was parting from his most long-standing domestic partner, half-eager to escape her anguished pleading and yet tempted, even at the last, to give up the whole Greek plan, about which he had few illusions. Part of his regret centered on his feelings toward Italy itself, a place that had welcomed him and altered him profoundly – even more so than Greece, despite its influence early and late. For the past six years, he had "been of their families – and friendships and feuds – and loves – and councils – and correspondence in a part of Italy least known to foreigners – and have been amongst them of all classes – from the Conte to the Contadine." Now he was heading away from all of that, onto uncertain ground where he would be largely surrounded by strangers who wanted things from him: money, mostly, but also influence and connections. When the hour for his departure struck, Mary Shelley arrived by prior arrangement, so that Teresa would not have to be alone. There was a moment of awkward transition: Teresa sobbing, Mary pale and tender with her while attempting a farewell to Byron that could somehow do justice to everything they had been through, and Byron retreating into a businesslike manner, limping off rapidly after a few last words and a final look of pained affection at each of them. The world of men awaited aboard the *Hercules*.

That evening, Byron boarded the ship with his entourage, including Pietro Gamba, Trelawny, and an Italian physician named Francesco Bruno, along with eight servants, among them: Fletcher (who had been with Byron since his first journey to Greece); Tita Falcieri, the black-bearded Venetian gondolier; Lega Zambelli (Count Guiccioli's former steward who had become fiercely attached to Byron); and Vincenzo Papi, who had stabbed Masi with the pitchfork in Pisa. There were horses, dogs, and piles of luggage; supplies for Greece would be loaded into the hull when they arrived at Livorno, where they would also pick up a few more passengers sympathetic to the Greek cause, including James Hamilton Browne, who convinced them to travel first to Cephalonia rather than

Zante. But before the journey could get under way, they had to wait on the weather. Becalmed, and then damaged by a violent storm while still in sight of Genoa, the *Hercules* was brought back to the harbor for repairs on July 16. It was an anticlimactic beginning to the long-awaited adventure. Frustrated and melancholy, Byron met Charles Barry at the dock and, with Pietro, made his weary way back up the hill of Albaro to the empty Casa Saluzzo for a few hours' rest. Teresa and her father were long gone. Wandering aimlessly through the echoing rooms, Byron sank into dejection. He spoke frankly of the hopelessness of the Greek enterprise and wished that he were heading back to England instead. He retired alone to his bedroom, where he ate a simple dinner of cheese and figs, brooding until it was time to return to the ship. On the ascent to Albaro, Byron had wondered wistfully aloud to Pietro, "Where shall we be in a year?" Precisely one year later, his body was being lowered into the ground at Hucknall in Nottinghamshire.

On the day that Byron had confirmed arrangements for the *Hercules* to take him to Greece, he wrote a fragmentary poem urging himself to military glory:

> The Dead have been awakened – shall I sleep?
>   The World's at war with tyrants – shall I crouch?
> The harvest's ripe – and shall I pause to reap?
>   I slumber not – the thorn is in my Couch –
> Each day a trumpet soundeth in mine ear –
>   Its Echo in my heart – –

As the weather cleared over Genoa, the trumpet's echo began sounding louder. Byron spent the night back aboard the ship, and the next morning, as the wind blew fresh from the west, the *Hercules* set sail, carrying him back toward Greece and into the zone of war. The Earl of Clare had sent Byron what seems to have been a final letter, telling him, "wherever you go my dear Byron I shall never forget you … Farewell my dear friend." By the time it arrived in Genoa, Byron was already at anchor in Cephalonia.

10

◇

Pilgrim of Eternity

[To John Murray]   *Messolonghi.—Fy. 25th. 1824*

I have heard from Mr. Douglas K[innair]d that you state "a report of a satire on Mr. Gifford having arrived from Italy—<u>said</u> to be written by <u>me</u>!—but that you do not believe it."—I dare say you do not nor any body else I should think—whoever asserts that I am the author or abettor of anything of the kind on Gifford—lies in his throat.—I always regarded him as my literary father—and myself as his prodigal son; if any such composition exists it is none of mine— — <u>you</u> know as well as any body upon <u>whom</u> I have or have not written—and <u>you</u> also know whether they <u>do</u> or did not deserve that same— —and so much for such matters.—You will perhaps be anxious to hear some news from this part of Greece—(which is the most liable to invasion) but you will hear enough through public and private channels on that head.—I will however give you the events of a week—mingling my own private peculiar with the public for we are here jumbled a little together at present. On Sunday (the 15th. I believe) I had a strong and sudden convulsive attack which left me speechless though not motionless—for some strong men could not hold me—but whether it was epilepsy—

cataleps—cachexy—apoplexy—or what other <u>exy</u>—or <u>opsy</u>—the Doctors have not decided—or whether it was spasmodic or nervous &c.—but it was very unpleasant— and nearly carried me off—and all that—on Monday—they put leeches to my temples—no difficult matter—but the blood could not be stopped till eleven at night (they had gone too near the temporal Artery for my temporal safety) and neither Styptic nor Caustic would cauterize the orifice till after a hundred attempts.—

On Tuesday a Turkish brig of war ran on shore—on Wednesday—great preparations being made to attack her though protected by her Consorts—the Turks burned her and retired to Patras—on Thursday a quarrel ensued between the Suliotes and the Frank Guard at the Arsenal— —a Swedish Officer was killed—and a Suliote severely wounded—and a general fight expected—and with some difficulty prevented—on Friday the Officer buried—and Capt. Parry's English Artificers mutinied under pretence that their lives were in danger and are for quitting the country— —they may.— On Saturday we had the smartest shock of an earthquake which I remember (and I have felt thirty slight or smart at different periods—they are common in the Mediterranean) and the whole army discharged their arms—upon the same principle that savages beat drums or howl during an eclipse of the Moon—it was a rare Scene altogether—if you had but seen the English Johnnies who had never been out of a Cockney workshop before! or will again if they can help it—and on Sunday we heard that the Vizir is come down to Larissa with one hundred and odd thousand men.— —

In coming here I had two escapes, one from the Turks (one of my vessels was taken—but afterwards released) and the other from ship-wreck—we drove twice on the rocks near

*the Scrophes—(Islands near the Coast). I have obtained
from the Greeks the release of eight and twenty Turkish prisoners—men women and children—and sent them to Patras
and Prevesa—at my own charges—one little Girl of nine
years old—who prefers remaining with me—I shall (if I live)
send with her mother probably to Italy or to England—and
adopt her.—Her name is Hato—or Hatagée—she is a pretty
lively child—all her brothers were killed by the Greeks—and
she herself and her mother merely spared by special favour—
and owing to her extreme youth—she was then but five or
six years old. My health is now better and [I] ride about
again—My office here is no sinecure—so many parties—and
difficulties of every kind—but I will do what I can—Prince
Mavrocordato is an excellent person and does all in his power—but his situation is perplexing in the extreme—still we
have great hopes of the success of the contest.—You will hear
however more of public news from plenty of quarters—for I
have little time to write—believe me*

yrs. &c. &c.

N BN

———•———

Like Venice, Messolonghi is a place made of water. It nes-
tles beside a broad lagoon stretching from the Acheloos river
delta to the Gulf of Patras, and, in Byron's era, its streets were
essentially canalized: small flat-bottomed boats glided up to
the very doors of buildings encircled by the town's muddy

entrenchments. Byron observed ruefully, "The Dykes of Holland when broken down are the Deserts of Arabia for dryness in comparison," and speculated, "if we are not taken off with the sword – we are like to march off with the ague in this mud-basket," dying "*marsh*-ally" rather than "*mart*ially." From the upper window of the two-story Kapsalis house which fronted the lagoon, Byron could gaze out through the rain at the gray-brown Acarnanian mountains in the distance and watch herons and flamingos fishing in the shallow water (Figure 10.1). The walls of his sitting room were hung with rifles, pistols, swords, dirks, helmets, and other instruments of war, and the desk was strewn with maps and letters. His dog Lyon, a large Newfoundland retriever given to him in Genoa, sprawled on the floor, paws muddy. Byron had arrived in winter, the chilly, wet season that may have reminded him of the weather of his childhood in Scotland: he took to wearing a large tartan cloak to keep off the cold.

As Byron became more involved with the Greek Revolution, he sometimes saw himself as a character in a Walter Scott novel, perhaps the worthy scion of his warlike Scottish ancestors on his mother's side, the Gordons of Gight. Just before embarking for Messolonghi, he had stayed up all night eagerly finishing *Quentin Durward*, Scott's latest tale of military heroism, writing at the same time of his decision to support the Greeks using a phrase from *Redgauntlet*: "I shall 'cast in my lot with the puir Hill Folk.'" Aboard ship, Byron's doctor had noticed the poet rolling his Rs, pronouncing "Corinth" with a Scottish accent. Once on the mainland, Byron began operating something like a Highland chief, maintaining a company (he called them "clan or Sept or tribe or horde") of 500 Suliot soldiers, having admired their rough appearance and brave masculinity since his first visit to Albania and

Greece in 1809. To Pietro Gamba, he remarked, "Our wild troops here, which remind me of what our highlanders must have been, are more in my way, at least as a poet." In their Albanian kirtles and belts bristling with weapons, his Suliot troops looked almost like Scottish clansmen, lounging in the courtyard as the rain fell on Messolonghi.

When he wrote this letter to John Murray, Byron had been back in Greek lands for almost seven months, five of which he had passed on the island of Cephalonia (Figure 10.2). That time had been spent largely in attempts to determine how best he could be useful to the cause of Greek independence, while also securing as much ready cash as possible. Now on the mainland and outside of neutral territory, he found himself subject to various upheavals: an earthquake that "came and rocked the quivering wall – / And men and Nature reeled as if with wine" (as he wrote in a rare poetic effusion of this period); a "quarrel between the Suliots and the Frank guard" that ended in bloodshed and a fatality; the nearby wreck of a Turkish ship; and, most worrying, a "Strong and sudden convulsive attack," something like an epileptic fit, that left Byron weak and dizzy for days. And, in fact, Byron's convulsion had come in the immediate wake of his final disillusionment with the Suliots, who had refused to march on the fortress of Lepanto without more money. He had learned how difficult it was to find one's bearings while standing on shifting ground.

Byron was in Greece during a relative lull in the military conflict with the Turks, in the months before the Ottoman Empire gathered its strength against the revolutionaries in 1825. Instead of battles against Turkish forces, what he found was a bewildering scene of intramural struggle among the Greek leaders and their followers, featuring divided loyalties, misinformation, partisan maneuvering, power grabs, greed, and treachery. Intending to support the cause of Greek national independence, Byron soon became enmeshed in a civil war. Roderick Beaton calls it "a conflict between rival liberators, between bitterly contested assumptions of what it meant to be free" – nothing less than "the crucible in which the future political shape of independent Greece would be forged." Because Byron had come primarily as a benefactor to lend money and the power of his prestige, most of his time was spent in trying to determine which of the rival leaders he could trust. He was hoping to unite the Greeks, not realizing how deep-set the divisions were. From Cephalonia, he wrote to Hobhouse that he would "serve the *Cause* if the patriots will permit me – but it must be *the Cause* – and not individuals or *parties* that I endeavour to benefit." More simply, he proclaimed, "I did not come here to join a faction but a nation." Only after months of close observation did he realize that it was factions all the way down: there *was* no nation except the one that would emerge from that crucible.

Byron ends this letter to Murray with the observation, "Prince Mavrocordato is an excellent person and does all in his power—but his situation is perplexing in the extreme." This was Alexandros Mavrocordatos (Figure 10.2), the same man who had tutored Mary Shelley in the Greek language in Pisa: a wealthy, educated Phanariot politician who had risen to the head of the Legislative branch of the Provisional Government. By this time, Byron had thrown his lot in with Mavrocordatos (Figure 10.3), whom he called optimistically "the only *Washington* or *Kosciusko* kind of man amongst them." In so doing, Byron was allying himself with a vision of the Greek nation based on European Enlightenment models, featuring a strong central government and an active civic society. Mavrocordatos was opposed by powerful regional warlords such as Theodoros Kolokotronis, Petrobey Mav-romichalis, and Odysseus Androutsos, all of whom were fighting for independent, autocratic, clan-based territories of control – and all of whom sent emissaries to Byron, each assuring him that they were the true representatives of the Greek cause. It had taken months for Byron to admit that he had to make a choice, and now he was in Messolonghi, working alongside Mavrocordatos. That Byron wound up favoring the subtle political administrator over the romantic brigand-chiefs tells us something about his evolving vision of heroism. Greece had given him an advanced education in realpolitik, far beyond what he had learned during his brief time in the House of Lords.

Since leaving Italy the previous summer, Byron had passed through several stages of optimism and disillusion-ment regarding the Greek cause and his involvement in it. In part, these oscillations were driven by his own unstable health and frequent changes of mood. When we last saw him in the empty rooms of Casa Saluzzo, he was morbidly down-cast and hopeless. But once the *Hercules* was well embarked toward Greece, his spirits rose. On board, he cheerfully slept on the open deck, boxed with Trelawny and fenced with Gamba, played with his dogs, and practiced pistol shooting. He subsisted on modest lunches of cheese, pickles, and cider, joking with the sailors, clearly happy to be on his way. Yet his shipmate James Hamilton Browne noted that "in the midst of the greatest hilarity and enjoyment," Byron would some-times go ashen, and rapidly withdraw from the group with tears in his eyes. Some of his moodiness was likely neurolog-ical, a shadow of the depression and epilepsy that had begun to plague him. Some of it was surely the burden of his past, the many regrets and losses that returned like unpredictable but tenacious ghosts. And some may have been a sense of impending doom: was this a new beginning or just the end of it all? The trip to Greece wasn't a suicide mission, but then again, it wasn't *not* a suicide mission either. He had told Lady Blessington of his presentiment that he would die there, adding, "I hope it may be in action, for that would be a good finish to a very *triste* existence." Just before leaving Genoa, he wrote to Moore, "If any thing in the way of fever, fatigue, famine, or otherwise, should cut short the middle age of a brother warbler.... I pray you to remember me in your 'smiles and wine.'"

In sight of Cephalonia, Byron felt a powerful uplift of reconnection with the country where he had once been so happy: "I feel as if the eleven long years of bitterness I have passed through since I was here, were taken off my shoulders." They anchored in the harbor of Argostoli, the charming, well-kept capital of the island, with its jumble of Venetian-style buildings and hilltop castle in the distance. But Byron was initially wrongfooted by the absence of Edward Blaquiere, his supposed contact from the London Greek Committee on behalf of which Byron thought he was traveling. Blaquiere had unaccountably departed for England, and a bewildered Byron wrote to him on the night of his arrival in early August, "I write on the binnacle of a ship by the light of a lanthorn and a Squall blowing.... Here am I – but where are *you*?" His position was already a potentially awkward one: the Ionian Islands, including Cephalonia, had been a British Protectorate since 1815, and, under the unbending Lord High Commissioner Sir Thomas Maitland, the Islands had maintained strict neutrality in the conflict between the Greeks and the Turks. Byron was obviously not neutral: he intended to support the Greek Revolution, and his high profile and aristocratic position made this eminently visible. There he was, with a ship full of letters of credit, weapons, medical stores, and various philhellenic advisors and Greek patriots – and his main contact in Argostoli had fled back to London.

Fortunately, Browne had given Byron very good advice in encouraging him to choose Cephalonia as his initial landing point. The Governor there was Lt.-Col. Charles James Napier, a military hero of the Napoleonic wars, capable, enlightened, and deeply sympathetic to the Greek cause. He welcomed Byron to the community of Englishmen in Argostoli, while reporting to his superiors that Byron "only wants to look about him in Greece as a sort of Agent for the London Greek Committee," and that he "wishes to avoid giving any offence to the Ionian government." Byron and Napier liked one another immediately, each recognizing the other's talents and pragmatic powers of judgment. Both were realistic about the situation on the ground but also inspired by the idea that Greece might yet be free; and each saw in the other a potential leader. Recommending Napier to the London Committee, Byron wrote, "a better or a braver man is not easily to be found. – *He* is *our* Man to lead a regular force, or organize a national one for the Greeks." Soon after their meeting, Napier was telling Byron himself to assemble a force of Germans, Englishmen, and Greeks to "seize Napoli [Nafplio] and open the gates to all the people of Greece but exclude the warlike chiefs," and to send "forth troops under the constitutional banner" to plunder the warlords and expel the Turks. Inspired by Napier and Mavrocordatos, whom Napier trusted, Byron could glimpse possibilities for meaningful action. As he observed around this time, "it is better playing at Nations than gaming at Almacks [a gentleman's club] or Newmarket [the race track] or in piecing or dinnering."

Soon after anchoring off Argostoli, Byron learned that the Greek mainland was under Turkish blockade and that Mavrocordatos, threatened by the warlords, had withdrawn to Hydra, where the Greek fleet stood in need of cash to pay its soldiers and sailors. Byron's silver dollars were in high demand. But Byron proceeded with care, recognizing that "it will require much circumspection to avoid the character of a partizan." He told Hobhouse that "the Greeks appear in more danger from their own divisions than from the attacks of the Enemy. – There is a talk of treachery … a jealousy of strangers and a desire of nothing but *money*." But to whom should that money be given? For weeks, as he waited for further instructions from the London Greek Committee, Byron gathered information, most of which, when it came, only made the situation more uncertain. A case in point: he sent a message through the blockade to the mainland to Marcos Botsaris, the brave and effective Suliot chief who had been named General of Western Greece by the Provisional Government and was trusted and admired by many in Byron's circle. Botsaris composed an encouraging reply, but it arrived with a covering note informing Byron that, a few days after writing it, Botsaris had been killed at Carpenisi during a night raid on the Turkish camp.

Meanwhile, Teresa Guiccioli had never made it to Ravenna. En route, her father had been arrested by the Papal authorities on political charges and was now imprisoned in Ferrara. Teresa was residing in Bologna with her former tutor and cherishing the hope that Byron would give up his mission and return to Italy. In late July, she had written plaintively in her notebook, "Come and fetch me … if you still want to see me alive, or let me run away with you, at any cost." But Byron was focused elsewhere. Her brother Pietro kept Teresa informed on their travels and activities, and Byron would typically add a brief postscript. In these early days, he wrote to tell her, "be assured that there is nothing here that can excite anything but a wish to be with you again … I kiss your Eyes (*occhi*)"; and in late October, he was still reassuring her that they might be laughing together over amusing stories of his experiences "at no very remote period," and addressing her as "Ever my dearest T." But these were rare expressions of affection. He sent Teresa only a few letters from this point forward, having essentially closed that chapter of his existence. Byron was all for Greece now, come what may. As he wrote to her that autumn, "I was a fool to come here but being here I must see what is to be done."

A trip to nearby Ithaca in mid-August gave Byron the chance to follow in the footsteps of Homer's Odysseus – like him, a wanderer who returns to an uncertain home in Greece. After traveling by mules over the mountains to the small fishing village of Saint Euphemia on the east side of Cephalonia, Byron crossed the channel separating the two islands in a four-oared open boat with Gamba, Trelawny, Browne, Bruno, and their servants. They arrived in late evening, and Byron suggested they spend the night in the caves along the coast, probably thinking of the Cave of the Naiads described by Athena in the *Odyssey*. But Gamba, concerned for the poet's health, insisted they find better shelter. They wound up crowded on the floor of a merchant's small cottage nearby. The next morning, Byron wandered off to explore a steep, ivy-covered rock face rumored to be the remains of Odysseus's stronghold. When Gamba found him there, asleep under a wild fig tree, Byron scolded him, because (like the man from Porlock who interrupted Coleridge's vision of Xanadu) Gamba "had interrupted some beatific dream or vision he had been enjoying." The whole trip to Ithaca had a mythic shimmer, a sense of heightened reality. Met by the British Resident, Captain William Knox, the group visited the legendary Fountain of Arethusa, where they picnicked as Albanian goatherds played discordant music on rural pipes. Byron began calling Mrs. Knox "Penelope" and her son, "Telemachus." He felt himself becoming a literary character: part Odysseus, part Childe Harold, part Shakespeare's Prospero on his enchanted island, telling Trelawny, "If this isle were mine – 'I would break my staff and bury my book.'" He was almost ready to abjure the rough magic of poetry that had sustained him for so long.

Ithaca at the time was full of refugees from the Peloponnese: men, women, and children displaced by the ongoing conflict with the Turks. Knox was doing what he could to provide relief, and Byron entered generously into the effort, giving ready cash and arranging for regular payments for a group of families, widows, and orphans. He instructed his bankers "to furnish the Moreote refugees with every necessary for their decent subsistence at my expense," with more money "for the other families now in Ithaca." Knox particularly recommended the Chalandritsanos family, a disabled mother with three young daughters who had fled a prosperous life in Patras. Moved by their plight, Byron sent them to Cephalonia, where he found them housing and provided ongoing support. When the teenaged Chalandritsanos son, Loukas, heard the news, he returned from soldiering under Kolokotronis to join his mother and sisters, and Byron appointed him as his personal page. It was a pattern of generosity he would repeat in Messolonghi, as we have seen in this chapter's letter, telling Murray of his liberation of twenty-eight Turkish prisoners and his intention to adopt the girl Hato (or Hatadji) and "send [her] with her mother probably to Italy or to England." Byron may have indulged some egotistical dreams of finding glory as a hero of the Greek Revolution, but, on the ground, his actions were primarily humanitarian. Repeatedly, we see him using his fortune and influence to relieve local sufferings of Greeks and Turks alike.

On the return journey from Ithaca to Cephalonia, Byron initially seemed in good spirits, drinking gin and water aboard ship and swimming in the harbor, despite Dr. Bruno's warnings about the August sun's powerful rays. The group then toured the monastery at Samos on the east coast of Cephalonia: Byron climbed into an open sarcophagus and recited some lines from the gravedigger's scene in *Hamlet*. But, as the evening wore on, in the middle of the long-winded abbot's welcome address, he erupted in a furious rage, something approaching an apoplectic attack. Shouting "My head is burning; will no one relieve me from the presence of this pestilential madman?", he darted into a nearby room, tearing his clothes and raving incoherently. When the others tried to follow, they found him "half undressed, standing in a far corner like a hunted animal at bay." He hurled a chair at them, shouting, "Back! Out of my sight! Fiends, can I have no peace, no relief from this hell?" Finally, after several attempts, Browne persuaded Byron to take some of Dr. Bruno's pills, and he slept. He was calm and repentant the next morning, and apologized for his strange behavior, likely triggered by exhaustion, alcohol, and overexertion in the heat. But the paroxysm suggested that Byron's health was not at all stable: it was a worrying indicator of things to come.

Back in Argostoli, Byron and his entourage continued to reside aboard the anchored *Hercules* through August, despite Napier's offer of rooms in his official residence. During that time, he dined with Napier and mingled with the community of British soldiers and administrators that lived on Cephalonia. With Lt.-Col. John Duffie, he took frequent rides in the hills above the town, sometimes accompanied by a bodyguard, made up of exiled Suliots, part of a troop Byron had hired on arrival. Soon Duffie invited the famous poet to dine with the King's 8th Regiment, who cheerfully toasted the poet's health and the success of his cause. It was an emotional evening. Urged to address the assembled company, Byron apologized, saying he was unused to public speaking and his English was rusty after so many years among the Italians. But the upturned, smiling faces of the young soldiers made him realize that he was not the social pariah he often imagined. He later said that the reception he received that night from the regiment was "one of the brightest days in the tablet of a chequered life." Wavering between the roles of poet and soldier, he had felt welcomed on both counts by the King's 8th. And, this late in the game, after many years of self-exile and self-laceration, he had been given a rare chance to see his fame reflected in the admiring eyes of a British audience.

By early September, Captain Scott was ready to return to England with the *Hercules*, being unwilling to risk running the Turkish blockade. Byron accordingly rented a small ivy-covered cottage in the village of Metaxata, in the southeastern part of the island. There he had two rooms and a balcony overlooking the mountains and the sea; Gamba and Bruno shared a room, and the servants had the kitchen. Trelawny and Browne had departed for the Peloponnese with letters requesting information from the Provisional Government, which they believed to be in Tripolitsa. There they would meet the warlord Kolokotronis, who swayed them against Mavrocordatos and sent them on to Salamis, where they joined forces with the charismatic chief Odysseus Androutsos, "a really *great man* – a Grecian Bolivar," as Trelawny judged him. But Byron had his sights set on Mavrocordatos – his Grecian "*Washington* or *Kosciusko*." He continued to wait, both for the local bankers to make good on his letters of credit and for news from London. Meanwhile, there was a new regimen: rise at 9:00 a.m. and work several hours with Gamba on correspondence and matters relating to Greece, then tea, then ride horses into the afternoon. The main meal of cheese, olives, salad, and fruit was taken around 3:00 p.m., followed by pistol practice and reading. Many visitors came in the evenings, and conversation often lasted until midnight. Byron was also drinking fairly heavily, as well as taking daily doses of purgatives to keep his weight down, saying he was predisposed to "growing fat and growing mad" and wasn't sure which was worse.

Byron was happy in Metaxata: "I have found myself more comfortable, and my time passes more cheerfully than it has in a long time done." There he began a journal of his experiences in Greece, setting down the state of political and military affairs as best he could, and looking forward to a time "When the limbs of the Greeks" will be "a little less stiff from the shackles of four centuries," given that "at present … they are such d—d liars; – there never was such an incapacity for veracity shown since Eve lived in Paradise. But they may be mended by and bye." However, he kept the journal only fitfully and wrote little, other than letters of business. He even balked at correcting proofs for the remaining cantos of *Don Juan*, informing Hobhouse, "I wish [Hunt] to publish the remainder … and tell him to Correct the proofs from the M.S.S. and not be sending his lumbering packets up here

– where I have other matters to attend to." Although Byron would continue to send back corrections to Hunt, his mood made it clear how distant he felt from his vocation as a poet. You can hear an echo of that distance in this chapter's letter to Murray, as he briskly denies writing a satire on Gifford before turning to "news from this part of Greece." As he remarked to Gamba one morning over their paperwork and correspondence, "Poetry should only occupy the idle ... In more serious affairs it would be ridiculous."

While in Cephalonia, Byron had a series of conversations on religion with Dr. James Kennedy, an evangelical Scottish Presbyterian surgeon attached to the garrison at Argostoli. Byron had met him at the regimental dinner with the King's 8th and, along with Napier, Gamba, Browne, and several of the soldiers, had attended a kind of Bible study group held at Kennedy's quarters soon thereafter. Byron was charmed by Kennedy, both fascinated and amused by his strong resemblance to the notoriously atheistical Percy Shelley. As he told Kennedy, "I should have liked to have seen you argue together. You very much remind me of him, not only in countenance, but in your manner of speaking." Byron described him as the "zealous Dr. Kennedy – a very good Calvinist – who has a taste for controversy and conversion and thinks me so nearly a tolerable Christian that he is trying to make me a whole one." Though Byron was anything but a traditional believer, his wide-ranging discussions with Kennedy revealed a latent, unsettled faith. One night at Metaxata, after a lengthy sifting of his beliefs, Byron asked Kennedy, "What more do you wish of me, in order to reckon me a good Christian?" But when the doctor replied, "To kneel down, and pray to God," Byron demurred: "This is too much, dear doctor." Instead, in a characteristically pragmatic gesture, he presented Kennedy with a donation to the school for Greek women that his wife Mrs. Hannah Kennedy was working to establish.

Other visitors made the 5-mile journey from Argostoli to Byron's small villa perched near the shore amidst stands of cypress, olive, and orange trees. There was George Finlay, future historian of the Greek Revolution and fervent admirer of Byron's poetry, another Scotsman who looked so much like Percy Shelley that Byron told him, "I thought you were Shelley's ghost" when he first presented himself at Metaxata. There was Dr. Julius Millingen, a young medical student from Edinburgh, a "tall, rosy-cheeked dandy boy of simpering and affected manners," who had been sent by the London Greek Committee and who would travel to Messolonghi with Byron and attend during his last illness. There was Colonel Leicester Stanhope, an Irish liberal philhellene who brought a printing press with him, hoping to establish a free press in independent Greece. He would proceed Byron to Messolonghi, extolling the need for "books … newspapers, useful pamphlets, Greek Bibles," and "two schoolmasters." Doubtful of Stanhope's idealistic plans, Byron nicknamed him "the typographical colonel." There was Count Demetrio Delladecima, a local descendant of Italian nobility, who advised Byron on his dealings with the Provisional Government and who prefaced so many of his statements with the phrase "in ultima annalise" ("in the final analysis") that he was dubbed "Ultima Annalise." There was Dr. Stravelemo, who had been physician to the recently beheaded Albanian rebel chief Ali Pasha, and told highly colored tales of Albania that activated Byron's memories of his days as Ali's guest in Tepelene in 1809. There was Napier himself who sometimes rode out to the villa, as did Colonel Duffie. And so, the sitting room in Metaxata was full of lively voices each evening, as the wine was passed and the talk circled the great topic they all shared: the present and possible futures of Greece.

In November, Browne returned from the mainland with deputies of the Provisional Government, Andrea Louriotis and Jean Orlando, who were on their way to England hoping to secure a massive loan of £800,000 to fund the war effort. Byron wouldn't live to see the final outcome of those negotiations, whereby the Greeks were essentially compelled to mortgage "the whole of the national property of Greece" on usurious terms, netting only £300,000 but owing the whole amount. But the potential for a massive influx of funds spurred the Greek leaders to fresh activity. Still in Hydra, Mavrocordatos had set the loan appeal in motion and, after consulting with Trelawny and Browne, proposed a secondary aspect of the plan. Given the Turkish blockade and a gathering siege of Messolonghi, he asked, could Byron advance £6,000 immediately to fund the Greek fleet, an amount theoretically repayable out of the London loan? After some negotiation, Byron agreed to provide £4,000, the expectation of which was enough to launch sixteen ships, under the command of Admiral Miaoulis. At the end of November, they sailed from Hydra and Spetses toward Messolonghi, with Mavrocordatos on the corvette *Athena*. This had the triple effect of activating Greek forces to break the blockade, of involving Byron directly in the military course of the Revolution, and of reinforcing Mavrocordatos's standing among the rival Greek factions. It also removed barriers to Byron's own arrival on mainland Greece – both literally, in terms of raising the blockade, and figuratively, in that he would be joining Mavrocordatos now as the plausible leader not of a faction, but of a nation.

Mysteriously, even before the Greek fleet arrived, the greater part of the Turkish naval squadron melted away

and the Ottoman land forces near Messolonghi and Anato-
liko withdrew. Perhaps the local pashas had caught wind of
Byron's escalated involvement and decided to avoid a direct
confrontation with whatever force his wealth – rumored to
be immense – had set in motion. As the fleet entered the
Gulf of Patras, the Greeks managed to drive a solitary Turkish brig ashore on Ithaca, where they murdered the crew and
seized an immense amount of cash – something like £12,000,
three times the amount Byron had promised. This became
a huge problem later, not only because of the Greek viola-
tion of Ionian neutrality, but also because it emboldened the
Greek crews to announce they would only stay in the area
for two weeks before taking their bounty home. They arrived
on December 11, but Messolonghi was locked down with
bad weather for almost a week. When communication with
Cephalonia was possible, Mavrocordatos wrote immediately
to urge Byron to join him and bring the promised money:
"you will be received here as a saviour.... Be assured, My
Lord, that it depends only on yourself to secure the destiny
of Greece." He also offered the encouraging news that the
Ottoman garrisons guarding the strongholds at Patras and
Lepanto were "disaffected and mutinous," having not been
paid for over a year. Indeed, the Greek fleet had just taken
the cash representing their back salaries from the wrecked
Turkish brig on Ithaca. Mavrocordatos told Byron that the
time was ripe to sweep the Turks from the region, and the
clock was ticking.

Soon, Byron and his brigade of philhellenes at Cephalonia were on the move. Stanhope and Milligan had already
made the crossing to Messolonghi, with Stanhope informing
Byron that the Greeks "calculate ... on your aiding them with
resources for their expedition against Lepanto; they think

you will take 1000 or 1500 Suliotes into your pay for two or three months." Indeed, Byron had been making similar calculations in his journal, and his spirits were high with the possibilities. As he wrote excitedly to Kinnaird, asking him to send as much money as possible, "Why man! If we had but 100,000 sterling in hand, we should now be half-way to the city of Constantine" – that is, Constantinople, the Ottoman capital. Byron's use of "we" is telling, an indication that he increasingly saw himself as part of the Greek military force: it seemed that the mantle of leadership was falling on his shoulders. Mavrocordatos and others were encouraging him to go beyond fact-finding for the London Greek Committee, and even beyond aiding the cause with cash, to leading a troop against the fortress at Lepanto. Perhaps that war helmet would come in useful after all. In late December, Byron wrote to Kinnaird in a flush of optimistic fervor, echoing in the space of a few sentences Julius Caesar, a battle cry from the Napoleonic wars, and the rallying chant of his beloved Suliots: "I am embarking for Messolonghi…. I am passing 'the Rubicon' … the Gods give us joy! 'En avant', or as the Suliotes shout in their war cry – 'Derrah! Derrah!' … 'On – On – On!'"

Byron's journey to Messolonghi was the stuff of fiction, very much in the style of the seafaring and war cantos of *Don Juan*. Two boats carried the party: Pietro Gamba on the larger bombard yacht that held the servants, horses, Moretto the bulldog, and "all our implements of peace and war," and Byron on the smaller shallow-drafting mystico (the favored craft of pirates in the Mediterranean), along with Dr. Bruno, Fletcher, Loukas Chalandritsanos, and the dog Lyon. After a brief stop at nearby Zante to meet with Byron's banker, there was also money: 16,000 silver dollars with Byron and 8,000 with Gamba – altogether, the equivalent of about £5,000. Byron was thrilled to be finally in motion, eager as a young cadet given his first command, and energized to be (as he had put it in *Childe Harold*) "Once more upon the waters! yet once more!" Trelawny wrote, "as [Byron] sprang aboard the Mystico – and felt the salt spray dash over his face, he rubbed his hands joyously – and said – this is what I like – now hurrah for Greece." The boats departed Zante freshly laden with cash, and all were hoping for a rapid journey across the 40 or so nautical miles to the mainland. Soon the wind pulled the sleeker mystico ahead, and the crews, "full of confidence and spirits," shouted encouraging farewells to one another. Gamba recalled, "when the waves divided us, and our voices could no longer reach each other, we made signals by firing pistols and carbines," shouting, "To-morrow we meet at Missolonghi – to-morrow."

In fact, it would be another six eventful days before Byron and Gamba reunited. As Byron tells Murray in this chapter's letter, "In coming here I had two escapes, one from the Turks … and the other from ship-wreck." True to their threats, Admiral Miaoulis and the captains of the Hydra fleet had sailed home with their cash on Christmas Day, leaving the waterway open to Turkish patrols. As a result, Gamba's slower bombard was almost immediately spotted and challenged, and the crew feared the worst as the commander of the Turkish frigate boarded their vessel. Everyone knew that normally neither the Turks nor the Greeks took prisoners, except to torture them to death, and by now the Turkish leaders were well aware of the recent massacre of one of their crews on Ithaca. But, amazingly, the commander recognized the bombard's Greek captain, Spiro Valsamaki, as the man who had saved his life during a shipwreck some years earlier, and embraced him as a brother. Gifts of rum and a telescope to the Turkish authorities further smoothed the way, as did the fact that the ship was traveling under an Ionian flag of neutrality. Gamba and the crew spent several days cordially detained by Yusef Pasha in the Castle of the Morea, shooting woodcock and awaiting assistance from the British Vice Consul. They were soon released along with their ship and all of its contents, arriving in Messolonghi on the morning of January 4.

Meanwhile, Byron had several close calls of his own. Pursued by a Turkish brig in the darkness, the mystico escaped "by a miracle of the Saints," darting toward land and hiding among the shallow coastal waters near Skrofes. Fearing capture, Byron sent Loukas with another Greek on foot overland to Messolonghi, writing to Stanhope that he would "sooner cut [Loukas] in pieces and myself too than have him taken out by those barbarians." He requested that Mavrocordatos send ships to escort him in, meanwhile fuming in disbelief: "where the devil is the fleet gone?" The mystico crept "from Creek to Creek – as far as Dragomestri," keeping out of sight of the Turkish vessels until support from Messolonghi arrived. Even then, harsh squalls drove Byron's ship onto the rocks twice, and, as Byron put it ironically later, his "dollars had another narrow escape." If the mystico went down, he told Loukas (who had returned with the escort ships), he should climb onto Byron's back. As he wrote later in an unfinished lyric to his Greek page, "I watched thee in the breakers… / And bade thee cling to me through every shock – / This arm would be thy bark – or breast thy bier." Finally, on the evening of January 4, Byron sailed into the Gulf of Patras and the lagoon of Messolonghi, relieved to see Gamba's ship already there, safely at anchor.

The next morning, dressed for the occasion in a scarlet military jacket given to him by Colonel Duffie, Byron landed at Messolonghi to a savior's welcome (Figure 10.4). He was hailed by "salvos of artillery, firing of muskets, and wild music" and greeted warmly by Mavrocordatos, Stanhope, Gamba, and a crowd of soldiers and local citizens "of every rank, sex, and age." It was a peak moment, the top of the mark in Byron's transformation from scribbler to hero. Yet he also knew that the cheers were primarily directed at his barrels of silver dollars; that he was being maneuvered by Mavrocordatos; that the Greek and Suliot soldiers were unreliable and self-interested; and that he was, at some deep level, acting a part. He had told Duffie he would wear the scarlet jacket "in the mode of the ass in the lion's skin" in Aesop's fable, the moral of which is that a fool may deceive others by his dress and appearance, but only for a time. Any thoughts Byron had of himself as a hero were heavily colored with irony and self-deprecation. In the event, that realistic attitude helped him preserve his equanimity as the frustrations of his hundred days in Messolonghi unfolded. The author of *Don Juan* was well prepared to see everything that happened, including his own attempts at leadership and glory, as part of an ironic epic. As he observed after two months of frustration in Messolonghi, "This Greek business, its disasters and mismanagement, have furnished me with matter for a hundred cantos."

Money was much needed in Messolonghi, and Byron was immediately assailed with appeals from many quarters; as Trelawny put it, his house was "besieged, day and night, like a bank that has a run upon it." Within the first 48 hours, he began supporting a troop of 500 Suliots in arms, agreeing to supply them with a year's wages out of his own pocket. Another primary order of business was to pay the mariners from the Spetses fleet, who outraged Byron by sailing home as soon as the twenty barrels of silver were rolled aboard their ships, just as the Hydra sailors had done. Mavrocordatos made his own requests for further loans to support the defense of Euboea and Crete; Stanhope received money that Byron gave grudgingly to start printing a newspaper, the *Greek Chronicle*; and local chiefs of all descriptions climbed the stairs of the Kapsalis house to ask for a share of Byron's money. By this time, Byron had plenty of funds at his command, having finally sold his last property in England (the Rochdale coal mines in Lancashire) and in possession of something like £25,000, all of which he was prepared to commit to the Greeks. As Byron told his banker, if his loans were ever repaid, "I should still spend them in the Cause – and more to boot," though he hoped next time it would be "to better purpose than paying the arrears of fleets that sail away, and Soldiers that won't march." For Byron, the supply of money wasn't a problem, but the question of where to direct it to good effect remained.

The closest Byron came to military action in Greece was the plan to overthrow the fortress at Lepanto (or Nafpaktos), an ostensibly formidable target on a steep hillside overlooking a bay on the Gulf of Corinth. Encouraged by Mavrocordatos, Byron was to lead perhaps a thousand Suliot soldiers overland and capture the fortress, which was known to be lightly defended by a garrison of Albanians. In fact, it was all about money: the Albanians had made it clear that they would surrender the stronghold to the first force that would pay them their long-delayed wages. It was a good mission for Byron despite the theatricality of the putative assault: paying off the garrison, he could have seized an important military target on behalf of Mavrocordatos, strengthening the Greek leader's standing in Western Greece and demonstrating the power of his own purse against the Ottoman occupation. But Byron's beloved Suliots betrayed him. Their chiefs kept raising their demands, requiring higher pay, more promotions, and more cash in advance before they would agree to march on Lepanto. In this recalcitrance, they were in part motivated by the agitations of Nikolas Tzavellas, who had pretended to be one of Byron's most enthusiastic supporters. But Tzavellas was now operating as a double agent for the warlord Kolokotronis, who did not want Mavrocordatos to score any victories. In addition, the idea of Greek liberty meant little to the Suliots themselves: they had no motivation other than survival, which meant money. Byron was dismayed. His patience exhausted, he swore, "I will have nothing more to do with the Suliotes – they may go to the Turks or – the devil." The Lepanto plan was permanently shelved.

Hopes were briefly raised when the London Greek Committee sent naval "fire-master" William Parry with a small team of artificers to construct Congreve rockets to use against the Turks. Byron enjoyed Parry's rough-hewn manner and fondness for brandy and cider, and the two spent enjoyable evenings in storytelling, satiric imitations, drinking, and laughter, with Byron dubbing Parry "Falstaff" to his own Prince Hal. But the artillery project came to nothing because of lack of supplies, the indifference of the Greek leaders to this new technology, and a general revolt by the artificers, who felt unsafe in the town following the fatal "quarrel [that] ensued between the Suliotes and the Frank Guard at the Arsenal," as Byron reports to Murray in this chapter's letter. Parry remained loyal and would leave a vivid memoir of these days in Messolonghi, recalling that Byron's beloved dog Lyon accompanied the poet everywhere he went in Greece, becoming "perhaps his dearest and most affectionate friend" in his final months. Like Boatswain and his own namesake back at Newstead, Lyon presented Byron with a model of loyalty in striking contrast to his human associates. When Byron felt cheated or deceived, he would turn to the retriever and say, "Lyon, you are no rogue, Lyon" or "thou art an honest fellow, Lyon," as "the dog's eyes sparkled, and his tail swept the floor, as he sat with his haunches on the ground.... 'Lyon, I love thee, thou art my faithful dog!' and Lyon jumped and kissed his master's hand" (Figure 10.5).

Despite all of the setbacks and frustrations and his own deteriorating health, Byron remained engaged with the events on the ground in Messolonghi, planning with Mavrocordatos, dealing with local disputes, communicating with both Turkish and Greek authorities to arrange prisoner exchanges, spending money for the relief of families, paying soldiers, and corresponding with the London Greek Committee about the forthcoming loan. When, in mid-March, news spread that the loan had been approved, Odysseus Androutsos proposed a summit meeting of Greek leaders at Salona to formulate a plan to unite Eastern and Western Greece. He invited both Mavrocordatos and Byron to what surely was an attempted grab at the forthcoming cash. Warily, they agreed to go. But then ten days of heavy rain fell over the last two weeks of March, flooding the rivers and making the roads impassable. Meanwhile, among the warlords, other plots were developing to weaken Mavrocordatos and separate him from Byron before the London loan arrived; it was even thought for a time that one of the chieftains, George Karaiskakis, had betrayed Messolonghi to the Turks. All of these events, combined with the terrible weather, drove Byron into a depression. Gamba reports that "his temper was more irritable; he was frequently angry about trifles," and he complained "of not feeling himself well – of vertigo in the head – of a disposition to faint." As the spring came slowly to Messolonghi, Byron held on, operating on sheer nerve, determined to stay and be useful to the cause, despite the deep conflicts among the Greeks and his own deteriorating condition.

On April 9, letters from England arrived: one from Augusta, containing a silhouette of Byron's daughter Ada (now 6), and one from Hobhouse, who praised Byron for his many efforts and assured him that supporting the Greek cause was "doing something worth living for." That afternoon, the sky lightened above the lagoon, and Byron, buoyed in spirits, urged Gamba to ride with him in the hills above the town. They had been cooped up too long. But the pair of riders had only gone a few miles when the heavy rains began to fall again. They returned home, cold and soaked to the skin. Byron was feverish that night, rode again the next day, and the fever returned, along with various pains. Byron told Millingen he had spent the day reflecting on a prediction made by a Scottish fortune-teller when he was a boy: beware your thirty-seventh year. From that point forward, Byron's descent began: he might well have survived his immediate illness – probably malaria or rheumatic fever – but Drs. Bruno and Millingen were determined to bleed and purge Byron, despite the poet's vehement objections. He had told Lady Blessington "All that I have seen of physicians has given me a dread of them," and had ordered Trelawny, "don't let the blundering blockhead doctors bleed me." But Trelawny wasn't there.

Byron resisted the leeches and the lancet as long as he could, but his doctors pressured him so vehemently that he eventually gave up, saying, "Come; you … damned set of butchers; take away as much blood as you will; but have done with it." Altogether, they would remove over two liters of Byron's blood, while also giving him emetics and purgatives – castor oil, epsom salt, enemas – until he was fatally dehydrated and exhausted. Given the treatment, it is a wonder he survived for as long as he did. A violent storm raged outside and "the rain was falling with almost tropical violence," while in the apartment all felt "the calm of coming death." Byron's final words are disputed: he seems to have mentioned Hobhouse, Lady Byron, Ada, Augusta, and the Earl of Clare. In Italian, he said "Io lascio qualche cosa di caro nel mondo (I leave behind me something precious in the world)," and then, in English, "For the rest, I am content to die." All agree on the simple declarative sentence he uttered before losing consciousness for the last time, on the night before he died: "I want to sleep now" (Figure 10.6). *Implora pace.*

Earlier that year, on his birthday in January, Byron had written his final poetic masterpiece, a valedictory lyric headed, "January 22nd 1824. Messolonghi. On this day I complete my thirty-sixth year." Its immediate, somewhat embarrassing inspiration was the romantic indifference of his page Loukas Chalandritsanos. Since meeting Loukas on Cephalonia, Byron had been hoping for mutual erotic attraction and more, writing elsewhere that it was his fate "To strongly – wrongly – vainly – love" the 15-year-old with a passion he had thought extinct. He was likely drifting back in time to his affair with Nicolo Giraud in Athens in 1810, hoping to recapture the magic of his youth. Loukas was having none of it, though he was casually willing to accept the wealthy Englishman's gifts and money. And so, on the wrong side of his mid-thirties, Byron begins the poem in rueful resignation: "'Tis time this heart should be unmoved, / Since others it has ceased to move." It's a version of the plea for stoic calm with which Byron concluded his lines "To the Po" written for Teresa Guiccioli in the tempestuous opening weeks of their relationship: the desire for an immovable heart. Back then, it was the power of shared passion that threatened Byron's mental stability; now it was failure of his charms, a mere fizzle where he used to count on fireworks.

On the journey to Cephalonia, the *Hercules* had spent a clear night sailing in sight of Stromboli, a lonely volcano on an island in the Tyrrhenian Sea. Trelawny described it as "shrouded in the smoke from its eternal volcanic fires" and struck by booming waves that could be heard in the distance like "the bellowings of imprisoned demons." The men told ghost stories while Byron gazed at Stromboli, storing away the imagery that would shape this Messolonghi poem:

> The fire that on my bosom preys
> Is lone as some volcanic isle,
> No torch is kindled at its blaze
> A funeral pile!

So much is crowded into that stanza: Byron's night view of the "volcanic isle" Stromboli as he sailed away from Teresa and Italy; his memories of Caroline Lamb's "little volcano" of a heart during his years of fame in London; the eruption of Tambora that led to the "haunted summer" at Geneva in 1816; Shelley's cremation on the beach at Viareggio, "a funeral pile"; the burning pyre of the Assyrian king Sardanapalus, "a light / To lesson ages, rebellious nations, and / Voluptuous princes," lit by a lover's torch at the conclusion of Byron's play; and Byron's own inflammable mind, full of poetry that he called "the lava of the imagination," and that Stanhope had recently compared to "a volcano ... full of fire, wealth, and combustibles; ...when this matter comes to be strongly agitated, the explosion is dreadful."

But then the poem turns, mirroring Byron's own turn from a life of poetry and sensual pleasures in Italy toward the privations and exertions of wartime Greece. He upbraids himself for his self-pity: "But 't is not *thus* – 't is not *here* / Such thoughts should shake my soul." The poem shifts into the second-person, becoming an urgent letter to himself: snap out of it, wake up, and remember where you are.

> The Sword – the Banner – and the Field,
>   Glory and Greece, around us see!
> The Spartan borne upon his shield
>   Was not more free!
>
> Awake! (*not* Greece – She *is* awake!)
>   Awake my spirit – think through *whom*
> Thy life blood tracks its parent lake
>   And then strike home!

A different kind of longing echoes through this call to arms. You can feel the undertow of Byron's past, the last pull of England as he urges himself to "strike home," with echoes of "strike *for* home," back to the "parent lake" at Newstead, "our own dear lake, / By the old Hall" as he wrote in a poem for Augusta, the hall of those "barons of old" that he addressed in one of his earliest lyrics, "On Leaving Newstead Abbey":

> Shades of heroes farewell! your descendant departing,
>   From the seat of his ancestors, bids ye adieu!
> Abroad, or at home, your remembrance imparting
>   New courage, he'll think upon glory, and you.

The Messolonghi poem thus connects across Byron's career back to its very beginnings, to the aristocratic vision of heroism he embraced when, as George Gordon, not much older than Loukas, he gazed at the Crusaders and Saracens carved on the mantelpiece of Newstead Abbey and wondered what being Lord Byron would require of him.

The previous April, Lord Blessington had suggested that Byron might become emperor of the Greeks, if he so desired. But Byron demurred, saying,

> My notions on that score are limited to getting away with a whole skin, or sleeping quietly with a broken one, in some of my old Glens where I used to dream in my former excursions.... A lease of my "body's length" is all the land which I should covet in that quarter.

Byron had spent most of his life on the move: he had been a pilgrim and a wanderer, a more or less temporary resident of country houses, college rooms, city flats, monasteries, casas, villas, inns, cottages, sailing ships, and more. But his comment to Lord Blessington suggests a desire to stop roaming and return to "my old Glens where I used to dream," a reference to his first journey to Greece but also a double invocation, both of his early childhood haunts in Scotland and of the tombstone under the elm tree at Harrow where Byron "frequent mus'd the twilight hours away," as he wrote in a lyric of 1807. In that poem, he had imagined that "'twould soothe my dying hour / ... To know, some humbler grave, some narrow cell, / Would hide my bosom where it lov'd to dwell; / ... Here might I sleep, where all my Hopes arose, / Scene of my youth, and couch of my repose." Byron concludes his Messolonghi poem with a similar acceptance of a humble resting place in Greece, another scene of his youth. And even though he wouldn't officially be buried here, part of him – his heart, or maybe it was his lungs, removed for embalming – remains in Messolonghi, interred in a spot marked by his statue in the Garden of Heroes:

> If thou regret thy youth, – why live? –
>   The land of honourable death
> Is here – up to the field, and give
>   Away thy breath!

> Seek out – less often sought than found –
>   A soldier's grave, for thee the best.
> Then look around, and choose thy ground,
>   And take thy rest.

In the end, after all that Byron had done and suffered and dreamed since first catching sight of Cephalonia from the deck of the *Spider* with Hobhouse on that clear morning in 1809, Greece had become this orphan's final adopted home.

AFTER BYRON

Odysseus Androutsos joined forces with the Ottomans and offered to deliver the Acropolis in exchange for regional power. He was captured by the Greek revolutionaries, tortured, and executed in 1825. His body was thrown from the Acropolis.

Lady Blessington lived with Count Alfred D'Orsay for twenty years following the early death of her husband, Lord Blessington. Her home remained a fashionable literary salon. She became a popular novelist, editor, and journalist, dying in Paris of a burst heart at age 60.

Lady Byron (Annabella Milbanke) devoted herself to social causes including prison reform, abolition, and female education. Before her death, she told Harriet Beecher Stowe the history of her marriage to Byron, including his incest with his half-sister. The resulting exposé, *Lady Byron Vindicated*, caused shockwaves throughout Victorian England and America.

Loukas Chalandritsanos took a cache of money from Byron's room soon after his death, claiming, when discovered, that Byron had told him that he wanted him to have it.

Claire Clairmont turned down a marriage proposal from Trelawny and lived in Russia, Dresden, England, Paris, and Italy as a governess, housekeeper, companion, and teacher, eventually receiving an inheritance of £12,000 from Percy Shelley. She died unmarried in Florence, aged 80.

The Earl of Clare married the Hon. Elizabeth Burrell in 1826, but the couple lived apart: he in Limerick and, for several years, in Bombay, and she on the Isle of Wight with a beloved female companion, Miss Charlotte Elliot.

Margarita Cogni remained in Venice. Arsène Houssaye in his *Voyage a Venise* (1850) says that he met her, and that she had become an oyster seller, apparently at some kind of stall or buffet, and that, as long as she talked about Byron, he and his friend went on eating oysters.

Alfred D'Orsay married Harriet Gardiner, the 15-year-old daughter of Lord and Lady Blessington, in 1827. She paid £100,000 of his debts when they separated less than a decade later. He lived with Lady Blessington until her death.

Scrope Davies had affairs with Lady Frances Webster and Lady Caroline Lamb. Before leaving England to escape his gambling debts, Scrope hastily packed a trunk of manuscripts and letters written by Byron and Shelley and deposited it with his bankers via Douglas Kinnaird. The trunk was rediscovered in 1976 and hailed as the literary find of the century.

Giovanni "Tita" Falcieri traveled to England with Byron's body and remained there briefly to serve as a valet to Hobhouse. In 1825, he went back to Greece to fight in the revolution.

William Fletcher partnered with Lega Zambelli to establish a pasta-making business in London. After it failed, he was supported irregularly by Augusta Leigh until his death in 1839.

Henry Edward Fox, 3rd Lord Holland, became the lover of Teresa Guiccioli. In a wonderful vertigo-inducing moment, circa 1830, Fox called on Lord Fitzharris, Teresa's new lover, and found him "slightly clothed, reading [Teresa's] copy of *Gle-narvon*," which had been Byron's own copy of Caroline Lamb's scandalous *roman-à-clef.*

Pietro Gamba published *A Narrative of Lord Byron's Last Journey to Greece* in 1825. He died of typhus, still fighting for the Greek cause, in 1827.

Teresa Guiccioli returned to her husband, and, following his death, traveled to London and had affairs with Henry Fox and Lord Fitzharris. Later in life, she married the Marquis de Boissy, who would proudly introduce her as "the former mistress of Lord Byron." She remained Byron's most loyal supporter, defending his memory and legacy until the end of her days.

John Cam Hobhouse remained involved with the government as a Member of Parliament, Privy Councillor, and First Commissioner of Woods and Forests, among other roles. He became Baron Broughton in 1831 and later was one of the founders of the Royal Geographical Society. His close friendship with Byron remained the most important facet of his life.

Lady Caroline Lamb formally separated from her husband William Lamb in 1825 amidst a losing struggle with mental illness, worsened by drinking and drugs. She died, with her long-suffering husband by her side, in 1828.

Augusta Leigh, in failing health and after decades of silence between them, met with Lady Byron one last time at the White Hart in Reigate in 1851. Augusta hoped for absolution and Annabella demanded confessions. Neither got what she wanted. Augusta died a few months later, receiving on her deathbed a two-word message from Annabella: "Dearest Augusta."

Ada Lovelace (née Byron) became a mathematician and worked with Charles Babbage on his Analytical Engine. She is remembered as the world's first computer programmer, having published an algorithm for the machine to calculate Bernoulli numbers. In 1835, she married William, 8th Baron King, and had three children. She died of uterine cancer at 36, the same age as her famous father.

Teresa Macri, "The Maid of Athens," married the Englishman James Black and had four children by him. The couple lived in impoverished circumstances but were visited regularly by Byron fans. One journalist remarked that nineteenth-century tourists in Athens would no more fail to see Teresa than to miss viewing the Acropolis by moonlight.

Alexandros Mavrocordatos went into temporary retirement after the Fall of Messolonghi in 1826, but eventually returned to become a key figure in the Greek government, serving as minister of finance and prime minister, among other roles. Later in life, he represented Greece as ambassador to Bavaria, Britain, and the Ottoman Empire. He died in 1865.

Dr. Julius Millingen entered the service of the Ottomans and lived in Constantinople for many decades as the physician to five successive sultans.

Thomas Moore published the first full biography of Byron in 1830, based on the poet's letters and journals, on conversations with Mary Shelley and others, and on Moore's memories of the burned memoir. He outlived all five of his children, dying a broken man in 1852. He is remembered today as one of Ireland's most important national poets.

John Murray continued to publish significant books of the era, including Charles Lyell's *Principles of Geology*. His firm remained in family hands into the new millennium and his descendants down through John Murray VII have welcomed and aided Byron scholars for generations.

Mary Chaworth Musters had returned to her husband but was traumatized in 1831 when their home, Colwick Hall, was sacked by rioters who were angry at the failure of the Second Reform Bill. She hid all night outside in the rain with her daughter and watched the house burn. She died a few months later, at the age of 40.

Charles James Napier became Major General of the Bombay Army, and eventually the British Commander-in-Chief in India. In 1842, when he conquered the entire Sindh Province after having been ordered merely to put down an uprising, newspapers reported that Napier sent to his superiors a one-word, punning dispatch: "*Peccavi*," Latin for "I have sinned" (Sindh).

William Parry published a memoir, *The Last Days of Lord Byron*, which Leigh Hunt's *Examiner* attacked, calling Parry an "exceedingly ignorant, boasting, bullying, and drunken individual." Parry sued and won a token, pyrrhic victory that blackened his character. He retreated into alcohol and ended up spending the last seventeen years of his life in the Hanwell Lunatic Asylum.

Elizabeth Pigot never married. Engaged once in 1807, she had accidentally sent a letter meant for Byron to her fiancé, who broke off the engagement. She aided Moore in writing his biography of Byron. Some years later, Teresa Guiccioli sent her a lock of her own hair, which Elizabeth kept carefully next to a lock of Byron's own.

Mary Shelley wrote novels, aided feminist causes, edited her husband's works, and raised their surviving child. When she died at age 53 of a brain tumor, Percy Shelley's heart was found among her things, wrapped in silk between the pages of her copy of *Adonais*.

Edward John Trelawny threw in his lot with the Greek warlord Odysseus Androutsos, going so far as to marry Odysseus's 13-year-old sister, Tarsitsa. Soon after Odysseus's arrest and execution, Trelawny was shot in the back as part of an assassination plot, possibly arranged by Mavrocordatos. Trelawny recovered, divorced Tarsitsa, and returned to England to write memoirs of his experiences with the Byron and Shelley circles. He survived them all, and well into his eighties remained a living memory of the Romantic age.

ILLUSTRATIONS

ACKNOWLEDGMENTS

This book is dedicated to Jerry McGann, who has been talking with me about Byron for thirty years now and remains an ongoing source of wisdom and inspiration, for me and for the field of literary studies. Jerry's scholarship gave us Byron's poetry in the forms we know it today and has helped us appreciate its complexity and power. I count myself extraordinarily lucky to have been his student, and even luckier to count him as a colleague and a friend.

I began this biography while Jonathan Sachs and I were editing Byron's selected writings, and that collaborative project spurred this one on. Jonathan should be thought of as another presiding spirit in these pages: his ways of thinking and writing about Byron have deeply informed my own. Peter Graham encouraged me to write this book and read and commented on most of it in manuscript, for which he has my heartfelt thanks. I also am indebted to Peter for introducing me to the larger world of Byron societies and the terrific people who inhabit them, particularly the Byron Society of America. The Byron Research Center in Messolonghi, directed by the generous force of nature that is Rodanthi-Rosa Florou, has been one of the most vibrant of these. I want to thank Rosa and the members of the Messolonghi Byron Society for their hospitality and assistance, and thank the many students, scholars, curators, and visitors who have been part of my experiences in Greece that influenced this book, with particular thanks to Maria Schoina. Stephen Minta and Roddy Beaton have been unfailingly kind advisors; their work has been a model for my own. David McClay has helped guide my steps on the Byron trail, and he has my thanks as well.

Special thanks go to Geoffrey Bond, Charlie Carter, Liz Denlinger, Doucet Devin Fischer, Piya Pal-Lipinski, and Jack Wasserman for their generous assistance in my research. I relied on Lindsey Eckert, Alice Levine, and Jonathan Mulrooney and for their encouragement, friendship, and deep knowledge of Byron and his circles. For similar reasons, Omar Miranda and Kaila Rose have been inspirational throughout, as have Jonathan Gross, Marsha Manns, and Julia Markus. Devoney Looser and Jane Stabler have influenced this project in any number of happy ways, and they have my admiration and gratitude.

I owe a deep debt to my colleagues at the University of Virginia, most profoundly to Steve Arata, Bruce Holsinger, John Parker, and Jim Seitz, who read and helped me revise large portions of the book, and whose collegiality is only equaled by the shining example of their own work. Thanks also go to Steve Cushman, Mark Edmundson, and Siva Vaidhyanathan, who advised me as I developed the book; to Tom Williams, who read and responded to drafts with generosity and insight; to Regan Schadl, whose editorial skills improved the book immensely; and to Tochi Eze, for assistance with the illustrations. I want to thank Merve Emre, Austin Graham, Mike St. Clair, and Jim Wamsley for advice, both personal and professional, that allowed me to see this project through.

Thanks go to my editor at Cambridge University Press, Bethany Thomas, for believing in the book and helping me make it a reality. I also want to thank George Laver, Leigh Mueller, and Sarah Starkey for their assistance, and my anonymous readers for their edits and enthusiasm.

A final word of thanks to my family: my children, Clay and Layth, who, along with my parents, George and Libby, talked with me about Romantic poetry when the pandemic kept us apart and have been my champions all along; and Megan, *mia amica amante*, whose love and encouragement mean more than to me she knows.

ABBREVIATIONS

BB   Leslie A. Marchand, *Byron: A Biography*, 3 vols.
            (New York: Alfred A. Knopf, 1957)
BLJ   *Byron's Letters and Journals*, 11 vols. & suppl., ed.
            Leslie A. Marchand (Cambridge, MA: Harvard
            University Press, 1973–1994)
BLL   Fiona MacCarthy, *Byron: Life and Legend* (New
            York: Farrar, Straus, and Giroux, 2002)
Bulldog   *Byron's Bulldog: The Letters of John Cam Hobhouse
            to Lord Byro*n, ed. Peter Graham (Columbus:
            Ohio State University Press, 1984)
C   *The Works of Lord Byron: Poetry*, ed. E. H. Coler-
            idge (London: John Murray, 1898–1905)
CHP   *Childe Harold's Pilgrimage*
CPW   *Lord Byron: The Complete Poetical Works*, 7 vols.,
            ed. Jerome J. McGann (Oxford: Clarendon Press,
            1980–1993). The texts of Byron's poems are
            quoted from this edition.
HD   John Cam Hobhouse, *Diary*, ed. Peter Cochran:
            www.petercochran.wordpress.com/hobhouses-
            diary
HVSV   *His Very Self and Voice: Collected Conversations
            of Lord Byron*, ed. Ernest J. Lovell, Jr. (New York:
            Macmillan, 1954)
LBCLB   *Lady Blessington's Conversations of Lord Byron*, ed.
            Ernest J. Lovell, Jr. (Princeton University Press,
            1969)

LJ	*The Works of Lord Byron: Letters and Journals,* ed. Rowland Prothero (London: John Murray, 1898–1905)
LJM	*The Letters of John Murray to Lord Byron,* ed. Andrew Nicholson (Liverpool University Press, 2007)
LMWS	*The Letters of Mary Wollstonecraft Shelley,* 3 vols., ed. Betty T. Bennett (Baltimore: Johns Hopkins University Press, 1980)
LPBS	*Letters of Percy Bysshe Shelley,* 2 vols., ed. Frederick L. Jones (Oxford: Clarendon, 1964)
Medwin	Thomas Medwin, *Conversations of Lord Byron,* ed. Ernest J. Lovell, Jr. (Princeton University Press, 1966)
Moore	Thomas Moore, *The Letters and Journals of Lord Byron, with Notices of His Life,* 2 vols. (London: John Murray, 1830)
Origo	*The Last Attachment: The Story of Byron and Teresa Guiccioli* (New York: Scribner's, 1949)
Prose	*Byron: The Complete Miscellaneous Prose,* ed. Andrew Nicholson (Oxford University Press, 1991)
SC	*Shelley and His Circle, 1773–1822,* 10 vols., ed. Donald Reiman, Kenneth Neill Cameron, and Doucet Devin Fischer (Cambridge, MA: Harvard University Press, 1961–2002)
Vie	Teresa Guiccioli, *Vie de Lord Byron en Italie (Lord Byron's Life in Italy),* trans. Michael Rees, ed. Peter Cochran (Newark: University of Delaware Press, 2005)

NOTES

INTRODUCTION

Page 1 "world…darkened": Hallam Tennyson, *Alfred Lord Tennyson: A Memoir*, 2 vols. (London: Macmillan, 1897), vol. I, p. 4; Henry Van Dyke, *The Poetry of Tennyson* (New York: Scribner's, 1889), p. 12.

Page 1 "great luminary of Heaven": Walter Scott, "Character of Lord Byron," *The Mirror of Literature, Amusement, and Instruction* (London), 3, 87 (June 5, 1824), p. 377.

Page 1 "dreary blank in creation": *The Love Letters of Thomas Carlyle and Jane Welsh*, ed. A. Carlyle (London: John Lane, 1909), vol. I, p. 369.

Page 1 "bright sun was extinguished": Byron, "Darkness," line 2.

Page 2 "astonish the latter days": Moore, 2.273.

Page 3 "great monuments": *Byron's Letters and Journals: A New Selection*, ed. Richard Lansdown (Oxford University Press, 2015), p. xi.

Page 3 "brilliance, charm, and wit": *BLJ*, vol. I, pp. 1–2.

Page 3 "mirror himself": letter to John Murray, January 19, 1830. *Selected Letters of Mary Wollstonecraft Shelley*, ed. Betty T. Bennett (Oxford University Press, 1994), p. 224.

Page 4 "no pan-ecumenical service": Dwight Garner, "Mourning the Letters That Will No Longer Be Written, and Remembering the Great Ones That Were," *New York Times*, June 17, 2020.

Page 4 "ten individuals": *LBCLB*, p. 72.

Page 4 "the more the merrier": *LBCLB*, p. 220.

Page 5 *"praise* as well as *censure"*: *BLJ*, vol. IX, p. 68.

Page 5 "my land's language": *CHP*, Canto IV, stanza 9.

Page 5 "battle must be fought": *BLJ*, vol. IX, p. 191.

Page 6 generations of Black writers: Matt Sandler, "Black Byronism," *The Byron Journal* 45:1 (2017), pp. 39–53; and *The Black Romantic Revolution* (New York: Verso, 2020).

Page 6 pan-European influence: *The Reception of Byron in Europe*, 2 vols., ed. Richard Cardwell (London: Theommes Continuum, 2004).

Page 6 "thing of dark imaginings": *Lara*, Canto I, lines 313–317.

1 A SPICE OF EVERY THING

Page 16 *"Super*excellent rooms": *BLJ*, vol. I, p. 79.

Page 16 "sedgy banks": Byron, "Thoughts Suggested by a College Examination," line 51.

Page 17 "remember him perfectly": Medwin, p. 57.

Page 17 "born for his own ruin": Medwin, p. 55.

Page 17 "all his foibles": *LJ*, vol. XIII, p. 232.

Page 18 "a curse, chaining": Edward John Trelawny, *Recollections of the Last Days of Shelley and Byron* (London: Moxon, 1858), p. 244.

Page 18 "a better *pair of legs"*: *BLJ*, vol. II, p. 98.

Page 19 "half a Scot": Byron, *Don Juan*, Canto X, stanza 17.

Page 19 "crags that are wild": Byron, "Lachin Y Gair," lines 39–40.

Page 19 "play tricks": *BB*, vol. I, p. 139.

Page 20 "Abbey had been stripped": W. W. Pratt, *Byron at Southwell: The Making of a Poet* (Austin: University of Texas, 1948), p. 1.

Page 20 "cracks in these battlements": Byron, "On Leaving Newstead," lines 1–4.

Page 20 "thorough bachelor's mansion": *BLJ*, vol. III, p. 96.

Page 21 "never *seen* reading": *BLJ*, vol. IX, p. 42.

Page 22 "friendships were form'd": Byron, "On a Distant View of Harrow," line 4.

Page 22 "nothing to learn": John Cam Hobhouse (Lord Broughton), *Recollections of a Long Life, with Additional Extracts from His Private Diaries*, ed. Lady Dorchester, 4 vols. (London: John Murray, 1910), vol. IV, p. 5.

Page 23 *"beau ideal"*: Medwin, p. 59.

Page 23 "Even as a brother": Byron, "The Dream," lines 45–64.

Page 23 "that lame boy": Moore, vol. I, p. 34.

Page 23 "his hopes for family": *BLL*, pp. 34–35.

Page 24 "principal Southwell belles": *BLJ*, vol. I, p. 48.

Page 24 "a thousand *dolls*": *BLJ*, vol. I, p. 131.

Page 24 *"rational* companion": *BLJ*, vol. I, p. 131.

Page 24 "fat, bashful boy": Moore, vol. I, p. 65.

Page 25 "love's *extatic posture*": Byron, "To Mary," lines 45–47.

Page 26 "blind anger": Byron, draft dedication to *CHP*, Canto IV; *CPW*, vol. II, p. 122.

Page 26 "Christmas stories": Byron, *English Bards and Scotch Reviewers*, lines 245–260.

Page 26 "a correct taste": *BLJ*, vol. I, p. 147n5.

Page 27 "a dull stupidity": *The Satirist* (October 1807), rpt. in *The Romantics Reviewed: Contemporary Reviews of British Romantic Writers*, ed. Donald Reiman, part B, vol. II, p. 2102.

Page 27 "stagnant water": *Edinburgh Review* (January, 1808), rpt. in *The Romantics Reviewed*, part B, vol. II, pp. 835, 833.

Page 27 "young tyrants": Byron, *English Bards and Scotch Reviewers*, lines 84–85.

Page 27 "born for opposition": Byron, *Don Juan*, Canto XV, stanza 22.

Page 27 "unsocial as a wolf": *BLJ*, vol. VII, p. 230.

Page 27 "no longer a boy": *BLJ*, vol. VIII, p. 37.

Page 28 "Hermit, midst of crowds": Byron, "Childish Recollections," lines 235–242.

Page 28 "at heart a child": Byron, "To E.N.L., Esq," lines 43–46.

Page 28 "4 Dozen of Wine": *BLJ*, vol. I, p. 78.

Page 28 "covered with invitations": *BLJ*, vol. I, p. 81.

Page 29 "*endless variety*": *BLJ*, vol. I, p. 81.

Page 29 "the heart—is lonely still": Byron, "Stanzas [I would I were a careless child]," lines 25–32.

Page 29 "gradations in the vices": *BLJ*, vol. IX, p. 37.

Page 30 "Out, hunchback!": Byron, "The Deformed Transformed," part 1, scene 1.

Page 30 "My poor mother": *LBCLB*, pp. 80–81.

Page 30 "*diabolical* disposition": *BLJ*, vol. I, pp. 93–94.

Page 30 "Highlander's heel-piece": *BLJ*, vol. I, p. 180.

Pages 30–31 "a true Byronne": *BLJ*, vol. I, p. 56.

Page 31 "her *hospitable* mansion": *BLJ*, vol. I, p. 80.

Page 31 "collegiate pastor": *BLJ*, vol. VII, p. 230.

Page 31 "those singing-boys": *The Journal of Thomas Moore*, ed. W. S. Dowden, 6 vols. (Newark: University of Delaware Press, 1983–1991), vol. IV, p. 1540.

Page 31 "voice whose tones inspire": Byron, "Stanzas to Jessy," lines 9–10.

Page 31 "blushes as modest": Byron, "The Cornelian," line 4.

Page 31 "a downcast look": Byron, "The Cornelian," lines 9–10.

Page 32 "Both were young": *CPW*, vol. I, pp. 181–182.

Page 32 "the glance none saw": Byron, "To Thyrza [Without a stone to mark the spot]," lines 29–36.

Page 32 "the most romantic period": *BLJ*, vol. VII, p. 24.

Page 32 "claret in my *head*": *BLJ*, vol. I, p. 124.

Page 33 "swam in the Thames": *BLJ*, vol. I, p. 32.

Page 33 "most important confidants": Richard Holmes, *Sidetracks: Explorations of a Romantic Biographer* (New York: Harper Collins, 2000).

Page 34 "*bear* to Grantchester": E. N. Long to Byron (John Murray Archive, National Library of Scotland), folder MS43514, letter 135: November 18, 1807.

Page 34 "*felt by a* BEAR!": "The Cantab. No. III," *The Satirist* 2 (June, 1808), p. 368.

Page 34 "unequivocal disavowal": *BLJ*, vol. I, p. 167.

Page 34 "some low Lampoon": Byron, *English Bards and Scotch Reviewers*, lines 974–977.

Page 35 "cursedly dipped": *BLJ*, vol. I, p. 163.

Page 35 "an abyss of Sensuality": *BLJ*, vol. I, pp. 157–158.

Page 35 "systematic profligacy": *BLJ*, vol. I, p. 165.

Page 35 "young gentleman miscarried": *BB*, vol. I, p. 51.

Page 36 "my jealous heart": Byron, "[Well! Thou art happy]," lines 9–22; see *CPW*, vol. I, p. 222.

Page 37 "noble Newfoundland dogs": *The Life, Writings, Opinions, and Times of... Byron*, 3 vols. (London: Matthew Iley, 1825), vol. I, p. 60.

Page 37 "wiped away the slaver": Moore, vol. I, p. 119.

Page 37 "Boatswain is dead!": *BLJ*, vol. I, p. 176.

Page 37 "Beauty without Vanity": *CPW*, vol. I, pp. 391–392.

Page 38 "here he lies": Byron, "Inscription on the Monument of a Newfoundland Dog," lines 7–26, quoted from the original monument; see Andrew Stauffer, "Byron's Monumental Epitaph to His Dog," *The Byron Journal* 26 (1998), pp. 82–90.

Page 38 "Hobhouse – a Pig": *BLJ*, vol. VII, p. 225.

Page 39 "evening diversions": *BB*, vol. I, p. 174.

Page 39 "Paphian girls": *CHP*, Canto I, stanza 7.

Page 39 "skull-bearing Lordship": *Letters of William and Dorothy Wordsworth III: The Middle Years (Part 2: 1812–1820)*, second edition, ed. Ernest de Selincourt, Mary Moorman, and Alan G. Hall (Oxford University Press, 2000), p. 176.

Page 39 "buffooning all around the house": *BLJ*, vol. VII, p. 231.

Page 40 "set of monkish dresses": Moore, vol. I, p. 174.

Page 40 "tight little island": *BLJ*, vol. V, p. 136, with reference to a song by Thomas Dibdin, "The Sung Little Island" from *The British Raft* (1797).

Page 41 "world is all before me": *BLJ*, vol. I, p. 206.

Page 41 "thus ends my first chapter": *BLJ*, vol. I, p. 211.

2 THE AIR OF GREECE

Page 48 "through the bridges": *BLJ*, vol. I, p. 132.

Page 49 "coxcombs & *virtuosos*": *BLJ*, vol. I, p. 134.

Page 49 "a-pleasuring": *BLJ*, vol. I, p. 215.

Page 49 "buffoonery and fine prospects": *BLJ*, vol. I, p. 240.

Page 49 "fair ... sweet Florence": *CHP*, Canto I, stanzas 30–32.

Page 50 "written as if by a man": *BLJ*, vol. IX, p. 40.

Page 51 "thou Parnassus!": *CHP*, Canto I, stanza 60.

Page 52 "dreamlike quality": *BLL*, p. 93.

Page 52 "the air of Greece": Edward John Trelawny, *Records of Shelley, Byron, and the Author* (London: Routledge, 1878), p. 27.

Page 53 "I've the ague": Byron, "Written after swimming from Sestos to Abydos, May 9, 1810."

Page 54 "vast realm of wonder": *CHP*, Canto II, stanza 88.

Page 54 "white minarets": HD, entry for May 13, 1810.

Page 54 "triple battlements": *BLJ*, vol. I, p. 251.

Page 55 "glittering in their decay": *BLJ*, vol. 3, p. 180.

Page 55 "one of the first books": Moore, vol. I, p. 38.

Page 55 "a handsome Bouquet": *BLJ*, vol. I, p. 207.

Page 56 "sherbet and sodomy": *BLJ*, vol. VI, p. 207.

Page 56 "most cultured city in Greece": Stephen Minta, *On A Voiceless Shore: Byron in Greece* (New York: Henry Holt, 1998), p. 29.

Page 56 "a little war": *BB*, vol. I, p. 204.

Page 56 "painted complexions": *BLJ*, vol. I, pp. 230–231.

Page 57 "most horrible cruelties": *BLJ*, vol. I, pp. 227–228.

Page 58 "juniors and favourites": *BLJ*, vol. III, p. 130; Moore, vol. I, p. 38.

Page 58 "in friendship and mischief allied": Byron, "On a Distant View of Harrow," stanza 2.

Page 59 "*rabies* for rhyming": Byron, "Preface" to *English Bards and Scotch Reviewers*.

Page 59 "the scourge of satire": review of *English Bards and Scotch Reviewers* in *The Poetical Register* (1808–1809); rpt. in *The Romantics Reviewed: Contemporary Reviews of British Romantic Writers*, ed. Donald Reiman, part B, vol. II p. 1965.

Page 60 "better not read": *Critical Review* (December 1809), p. 384.

Page 60 "tenderness and real feeling": *Critical Review* (December 1809), p. 389.

Page 60 "My heart, untravelled": Oliver Goldsmith, "The Traveller" (1765), stanza 1.

Page 60 "My hate, untraveled": *CPW*, vol. I, p. 319.

Page 61 "Sunium's marbled steep": Byron, "The Isles of Greece" from *Don Juan*, Canto III.

Page 61 "Greece might still be free": Byron, "The Isles of Greece" from *Don Juan*, Canto III.

Page 62 "Maid of Athens": Byron, "Song [The Maid of Athens]," lines 1–6.

Page 62 "to be deflowered": HD, entry for March 3, 1810.

Page 62 "30,000 piastres": *BLJ*, vol. II, p. 46.

Page 63 "better amusement": *BLJ*, vol. II, p. 13.

Page 63 "little nosegay of flowers": HD, entry for July 17, 1810.

Page 63 "Green earth's end": *BLJ*, vol. XI, p. 157.

Page 63 "ambrosial curls": *BLJ*, vol. II, p. 6.

Page 63 "an unbroken colt": *BLJ*, vol. II, p. 6.

Page 63 "These Sylphs": *BLJ*, vol. II, p. 12.

Page 63 "peltings and playings": *BLJ*, vol. II, p. 13.

Page 64 "above two hundred": *BLJ*, vol. II, p. 23.

Page 64 "we may be *two*": *BLJ*, vol. VII, p. 92.

Page 65 "interposition of foreigners": Byron, notes to *CHP*, Cantos I–II; *CPW*, vol. II, p. 202.

Page 66 "almost without a desire": *BLJ*, vol. II, p. 54.

Page 66 "severe": *BLJ*, vol. XI, p. 159.

Page 66 "some 4000 lines": *BLJ*, vol. II, p. 55.

Page 66 "stupid from the shock": *BLJ*, vol. II, pp. 69, 77.

Pages 66–67 "my friends the Turks": *BLJ*, vol. II, p. 75.

Page 67 "England & all its clouds": *BLJ*, vol. II, p. 85.

Page 67 "makers and unmakers of beds": *BLJ*, vol. II, pp. 105–6.

Page 68 "nothing carnal": *CHP*, Canto I, stanza 7; *BLJ*, vol. II, p. 131.

Page 68 "raising a Monument": *LJM*, p. 3.

Page 68 "loved a living thing": *BLJ*, vol. II, p. 110.

Page 68 "loved and lovely one!": *CHP*, Canto II, stanza 96.

Page 68 "pulse to pulse responsive": Byron, "Stanzas to Jessy," stanzas 5–7.

Page 69 "found myself famous": Moore, vol. I, pp. 346–347.

3 MAD, BAD, AND DANGEROUS TO KNOW

Page 77 "the political coin": *Byron's "Corbeau Blanc": The Life and Letters of Lady Melbourne*, ed. Jonathan D. Gross (College Station: Texas A&M University Press, 1997), p. 2.

Page 77 "cleverest of women": *BLJ*, vol. III, p. 209.

Page 77 "my influence over you": Gross, *Byron's "Corbeau Blanc"*, p. 145.

Page 78 "celebrated but banal": Clara Tuite, *Lord Byron and Scandalous Celebrity* (Cambridge University Press, 2015), p. 20.

Page 79 "like real life": *BLJ*, vol. III, p. 145.

Page 79 "worthy of Faublas!": Medwin, p. 217.

Page 79 "pale beautiful face": *BB*, vol. I, pp. 328, 331.

Page 80 "new and rare": *LJ*, vol. II, p. 451.

Page 80 "Master of my soul": *BLL*, p. 172.

Page 80 "tiresome enough": *BLJ*, vol. II, p. 170.

Page 80 "fascinating little being": *BLJ*, vol. II, p. 171.

Page 81 "obstinate little heart": Elizabeth Jenkins, *Lady Caroline Lamb* (Boston: V. Gollancz, 1932), p. 61.

Page 81 "wild antelope": Caroline Lamb to Byron, August 9, 1812, Dep. Lovelace Byron 155, folio 81; quoted in Tuite, *Lord Byron and Scandalous Celebrity*, p. 20.

Page 81 "unfortunate drama": *BLJ*, vol. II, pp. 187–188.

Page 81 "give up all": *BLJ*, vol. II, p. 186.

Page 81 "fly with you": *BLJ*, vol. II, p. 186.

Page 82 "Mothers for confidantes!": Mabell, Countess of Airlie, *In Whig Society 1775–1818* (London: Hodder and Stoughton, 1921), p. 131.

Page 82 "cuckolding": Peter Cochran, "The Byron–Lady Melbourne Correspondence, 1812–1813," (petercochran.files .wordpress.com/2011/08/byron-and-lady-melbourne-1. pdf).

Page 82 "on every table": *BB*, vol. I, p. 335.

Page 83 "who dares look": *BB*, vol. I, p. 337.

Page 83 "lone being": *BB*, vol. II, p. 337.

Page 83 "I wished to forget": *BLJ*, vol. II, p. 208.

Page 84 *"lobster sallad & Champagne"*: *BLJ*, vol. II, p. 208.

Page 84 "Queen Mothers": *BLJ*, vol. III, pp. 87–88; Tuite, *Lord Byron and Scandalous Celebrity*, p. 20.

Page 84 "bewitch'd the whole family": Airlie, *In Whig Society*, p. 131.

Page 85 "all night scribbling": *BLJ*, vol. IV, p. 29.

Page 86 "partly by bribery": *BLJ*, vol. II, p. 311.

Page 86 "deeply interested": Medwin, p. 86.

Page 87 "it is *icy*": *BLJ*, vol. III, p. 230.

Page 87 "a Georgian page": Byron, *The Giaour*, lines 1067, 456.

Page 87 "AEtna's breast": Byron, *The Giaour*, lines 1101–1102.

Page 87 "Scorpion girt by fire": Byron, *The Giaour*, lines 422–438.

Page 88 "bowers of Armida": *BLJ*, vol. II, p. 238.

Page 88 "Young Peri": Byron, "To Ianthe," lines 19–22.

Page 88 "snowing perfect Avalanches": *BLJ*, vol. III, p. 13.

Page 88 "gods of Lucretius": *BLJ*, vol. III, p. 210.

Page 89 "you will *'ruin me'*": *BLJ*, vol. III, p. 43.

Page 89 "a scene occurred": Medwin, p. 217.

Page 89 "I clasped a knife": *BB*, vol. I, pp. 399–400.

Page 90 "cursed scarification": *BLJ*, vol. III, p. 72.

Page 90 "a great villain": *BLJ*, vol. III, p. 157.

Page 90 "'Remember me!'": Medwin, p. 217.

Page 90 "unhallowed thirst": *CPW*, vol. II, p. 18.

Page 90 "thou fiend to me!": C, vol. III, p. 60.

Page 91 "dreadful legacy": *Lady Morgan's Memoirs* (London: Allen, 1862), vol. II, p. 207.

Page 91 "she will never rest": *BLJ*, vol. IV, p. 24.

Page 91 "shoot myself": Paul Douglass, *Lady Caroline Lamb: A Biography* (New York: Palgrave Macmillan, 2004), p. 165.

Page 92 "good & diabolical": *BLJ*, vol. IV, pp. 110–111.

Page 92 "my proper woe": Byron, "Epistle to Augusta," lines 23–24.

Page 92 "snake of a poem": *BLJ*, vol. III, p. 100.

Page 93 "vanquish my demon": *BLJ*, vol. III, p. 124.

Page 93 "*hers* was not guilt!": Byron, *The Giaour*, lines 1141–1144.

Page 93 "cherished madness of my heart!": Byron, *The Giaour*, lines 1182–1191.

Page 94 "The man is insane": *The Letters of William and Dorothy Wordsworth: The Middle Years*, vol. II, ed. Ernest de Selincourt (Oxford: Clarendon, 1939), p. 734.

Page 94 "ridiculed dandy": John Stewart, *Byron and the Websters* (Jefferson, NC: McFarland, 2008), p. 1.

Page 94 "his cap & bells": *BLJ*, vol. III, p. 145.

Page 94 "kisses her hand": *BLJ*, vol. III, pp. 116, 129.

Page 94 "speculate upon his spouse": *BLJ*, vol. III, p. 133.

Page 95 "perfectly *convulsed*": Stewart, *Byron and the Websters*, p. 80.

Page 95 "foolish nymph": *BLJ*, vol. III, p. 116.

Page 95 "he attacked both the girls": *BLJ*, vol. III, p. 144.

Pages 95–96 "at your *mercy*": *BLJ*, vol. III, p. 146.

Page 96 "the death of Alexander": *BLJ*, vol. III, p. 145.

Page 96 "cursed situation": *BLJ*, vol. III, p. 147.

Page 96 "stans pede in uno": *BLJ*, vol. III, p. 162.

Page 96 "eating my own heart": *BLJ*, vol. III, pp. 205, 208.

Page 96 "still my Selim?": Stewart, *Byron and the Websters*, p. 77.

Page 96 "cherished madness": Stewart, *Byron and the Websters*, p. 75.

Page 97 "a thousand farewells": letter from Byron to Augusta Leigh, November 24 or 25, 1813. Pforzheimer Collection, NYPL. B0126; Adam Friedgen and Andrew Stauffer, "Fourteen New Byron Letters," *Keats–Shelley Journal* 66 (2017), p. 47.

Page 97 "written *con amore*": *BLJ*, vol. III, p. 243.

Page 97 "wives of my acquaintances": *BLJ*, vol. III, p. 241.

Page 97 "her whimsical romance": *BLJ*, vol. IV, p. 22.

4 FARE THEE WELL!

Page 100 "unhappily your disposition": Miranda Seymour, *In Byron's Wake* (New York: Pegasus Books, 2018), p. 115.

Page 101 "Now I have *her*": Malcolm Elwin, *Lord Byron's Wife* (Harcourt, Brace, and World, 1962), p. 293.

Page 101 "tempted to throw myself": Julia Markus, *Lady Byron and Her Daughters* (New York: W.W. Norton, 2015), p. 79.

Page 102 "thy most loving, Pippin": Peter Quennell, *Byron: The Years of Fame*, new edition (Hamden, CT: Archon, 1967), p. 227.

Page 102 "when I was yours": Quennell, *Byron: The Years of Fame*, p. 229.

Page 103 "*reclaiming* of him": Seymour, *In Byron's Wake*, p. 117.

Page 104 "I *esteemed* so much": *BLJ*, vol. II, p. 195.

Page 104 "a clever woman": *BLJ*, vol. II, p. 199.

Page 105 "touch my heart": Malcolm Elwin, *Lord Byron's Wife* (London: Macdonald, 1962), p. 109.

Page 105 "very bad, very good man": Elwin, *Lord Byron's Wife*, p. 109.

Page 105 "perpetual war": *BLJ*, vol. IV, p. 182.

Page 106 "Strengthened by longer observation": Elwin, *Lord Byron's Wife*, p. 153.

Page 106 "misery of restless inconsistency": Elwin, *Lord Byron's Wife*, p. 119.

Page 107 "two parallel lines": *BLJ*, vol. II, p. 231.

Page 107 "hot suppers": *BLJ*, vol. II, p. 246.

Page 107 "a thousand crimes": Byron, *The Corsair*, line 695.

Page 109 "men like scarecrows": *Prose*, pp. 22, 26.

Page 109 "barbarity to neglect": *Prose*, p. 27.

Page 109 "happiest effects": George Pellew, *The Life and Correspondence of the Right Honorable Henry Addington, First Viscount Sidmouth*, 3 vols. (London: John Murray, 1846), vol. III, p. 93.

Page 109 "grand old father": *Prose*, p. 312.

Page 110 "dull, stupid old system": *BLJ*, vol. III, p. 218.

Page 110 "Weep, daughter": Byron, "Lines to a Lady Weeping," lines 1–2.

Page 110 "most important personage": *BLJ*, vol. IV, pp. 62, 53.

Page 110 "especially for Mr. Darcy": *Jane Austen: The Critical Heritage*, vol. I: *1812–70* (London, Routledge, 1968), p. 8.

Page 110 "declined me as a lover": *BLJ*, vol. III, p. 108.

Page 111 "object of life is Sensation": *BLJ*, vol. III, p. 109.

Page 111 "No craving void": Alexander Pope, "Eloisa to Abelard," lines 88–94.

Page 111 "I can't *stagnate*": *BLJ*, vol. III, p. 119.

Page 112 "the language of Passion": Mabell, Countess of Airlie, *In Whig Society 1775–1818* (London: Hodder and Stoughton, 1921), pp. 161–162.

Page 112 "odd situation and friendship": *BLJ*, vol. III, p. 227.

Page 112 "perfectly unprecedented": *LJM*, p. 72.

Page 113 "the year of revelry 1814": *BLJ*, vol. IX, p. 168.

Page 113 "She walks in beauty": Byron, "She Walks in Beauty," lines 1–2.

Page 113 "I am not well": *BLJ*, vol. III, p. 246.

Page 113 "a little feverish": *BLJ*, vol. IV, p. 66.

Page 113 "six hundred in heart": *BLJ*, vol. IV, p. 67.

Page 114 "No more rhyme": *BLJ*, vol. IV, p. 92.

Page 114 "not an *Ape*": *BLJ*, vol. IV, p. 104.

Page 114 "I hate civilization": *BLJ*, vol. IV, pp. 21–22.

Page 114 "indifference has frozen": *BLJ*, vol. IV, p. 121.

Page 114 "the 'objections'": *BLJ*, vol. IV, pp. 155, 169.

Page 115 "a moment of joy": *BB*, vol. I, p. 474.

Page 115 "never rains but it pours": Seymour, *In Byron's Wake*, p. 58.

Page 115 "new existence": *BLJ*, vol. IV, p. 173.

Page 115 "reform thoroughly": *BLJ*, vol. IV, pp. 175, 178.

Page 116 "reply was hardly articulate": *BLL*, pp. 229–230.

Page 116 "*caressable* into kindness": *BLJ*, vol. V, p. 231.

Page 117 "these long blank days!": Elwin, *Lord Byron's Wife*, p. 237.

Page 117 "never married at all": *BLJ*, vol. IV, p. 239.

Page 117 "my abominable parrot": *BLJ*, vol. IV, p. 240.

Page 117 "there shall not be any delay": Elwin, *Lord Byron's Wife*, p. 231.

Page 117 "more *less* impatient": HD, entries for December 26 and 27, 1814.

Page 117 "*absit omen*": HD, entry for January 1, 1815.

Page 118 "things reel'd around him": Byron, "The Dream," lines 145–158.

Page 118 "buried a friend": HD, entry for January 2, 1815.

Page 119 "his countenance changed": Elwin, *Lord Byron's Wife*, p. 250.

Page 119 "on the sofa before dinner": HD, entry for May 15, 1824.

Page 120 "surely in hell": Samuel Rogers, *Recollections of the Table Talk of Samuel Rogers* (New York: Appleton, 1856), p. 236.

Page 120 "softer pillow than my heart": Quennell, *Byron: The Years of Fame*, p. 208.

Page 120 "*poor B*": Quennell, *Byron: The Years of Fame*, p. 207.

Page 120 "mischief in private": Elwin, *Lord Byron's Wife*, p. 275.

Page 120 "She don't ever bore me": *BLJ*, vol. IV, pp. 251, 255.

Page 121 "mine's the guilt": Byron, "Herod's Lament for Mariamne," lines 21–24.

Page 121 "lava of the imagination": *BLJ*, vol. III, p. 179.

Page 121 "Dearest, first, and best": Benita Eisler, *Byron: Child of Passion, Fool of Fame* (New York: Knopf, 1999), p. 452.

Page 122 "We don't want *you*": *BB*, vol. II, p. 524.

Page 122 "leave me and go to her": Eisler, *Byron*, p. 459.

Page 122 "her affectionate care": Eisler, *Byron*, p. 460.

Page 123 "keep them innocent": Elwin, *Lord Byron's Wife*, p. 299.

Page 123 "adulteries and indecencies": Seymour, *In Byron's Wake*, p. 117.

Page 124 "'whores and fiddlers'": *BLJ*, vol. IV, p. 260.

Page 124 "implement of torture": Harriet Beecher Stowe, *Lady Byron Vindicated* (Boston: Fields Osgood, 1870), p. 306.

Page 124 "child of love": *CHP*, Canto III, lines 1094–1095.

Page 125 "perish in its depth": *BLJ*, vol. V, p. 26.

Page 125 "dregs of my memory": *BLJ*, vol. V, pp. 26–27.

Page 125 "ladies of fashion": Quennell, *Byron: The Years of Fame*, p. 308.

Page 126 "managed you better": Quennell, *Byron: The Years of Fame*, p. 308.

Page 126 "so he talks of me": Elwin, *Lord Byron's Wife*, p. 448.

Page 127 "I scarce can die": Byron, "Fare Thee Well!," lines 1–60.

Page 127 "talent for equivocation": Elwin, *Lord Byron's Wife*, p. 394.

5 HAUNTED SUMMER

Page 131 "very pretty villa": *BLJ*, vol. V, p. 80.

Page 131 "darken'd Jura": *CHP*, Canto III, lines 806–810.

Page 133 "Ada! sole daughter": *CHP*, Canto III, lines 1–4.

Page 133 "cunning in mine overthrow": Byron, "Epistle to Augusta," lines 21–24.

Page 133 "dearest & deepest": *BLJ*, vol. IV, p. 69.

Page 134 "to herd with Man": *CHP*, Canto III, lines 100–101.

Page 136 "free & unknown": *The Clairmont Correspondence: 1808–1834*, ed. Marion Kingston Stocking (Baltimore: Johns Hopkins University Press, 1995), p. 36.

Page 136 "offer you *that*": *The Clairmont Correspondence: 1808–1834*, p. 40.

Page 136 "prancing to you at all hours": *BLJ*, vol. V, p. 162.

Page 137 "comet of a season": Byron, "Churchill's Grave," lines 1–2.

Page 137 "Glory and the Nothing": Byron, "Churchill's Grave," line 43.

Page 137 "a gallant spirit": HD, entry for April 25, 1816.

Page 137 "Once more upon the waters!": *CHP*, Canto III, lines 10–13.

Page 137 "fell like a thunderbolt": *The Diary of John William Polidori*, ed. William Michael Rossetti (London: Elkin Mathews, 1911), p. 33.

Page 138 "French passports": *BLJ*, vol. V, p. 77.

Page 138 "place of skulls": *CHP*, Canto III, lines 145–155.

Page 138 "reviving Thraldom": *CHP*, Canto III, lines 175–177, 165–168.

Page 138 "politics and slaughters": *BLJ*, vol. IV, p. 302.

Page 138 "chiefless castles": *CHP*, Canto III, lines 411–413.

Page 139 "A thousand battles": *CHP*, Canto III, lines 451, 433, 554.

Page 139 "magnificently stern array": *CHP*, Canto III, line 248.

Page 139 "the great of old": Byron, *Manfred*, act 3, scene 4, line 39.

Page 140 "your venerable age": *The Clairmont Correspondence: 1808–1834*, p. 46.

Page 140 "bashful, shy, consumptive": *Diary of John William Polidori*, p. 99.

Page 141 "float by your window": *BB*, vol. II, p. 618.

Page 141 "victim of a happy passion": *The Clairmont Correspondence: 1808–1834*, pp. 240–241.

Page 142 "almost perpetual rain": Mary and Percy Shelley, *History of a Six Weeks' Tour* (London: Hookham and Ollier, 1817), p. 99.

Page 142 "stupid mists": *BLJ*, vol. v, p. 86.

Page 142 "Tambora's eruption": Gillen D'Arcy Wood, *Tambora: The Eruption that Changed the World* (Princeton University Press, 2014), p. 8.

Page 142 "Das Hungerjahr": Wood, *Tambora*, pp. 45, 61.

Page 142 "the making of white bread": *SC*, vol. vii, p. 34.

Page 143 "a ghost story": Mary Shelley, "Introduction" to *Frankenstein* (London: Colburn and Bentley, 1831), p. viii.

Page 143 "eyes instead of nipples": *Diary of John William Polidori*, p. 128.

Page 143 "corpse would be re-animated": "Introduction," *Frankenstein*, p. x.

Page 143 "pale student of unhallowed arts": "Introduction," *Frankenstein*, p. x.

Page 144 "little baby came to life": *The Journals of Mary Shelley 1814–1844*, ed. Paula Feldman and Diana Scott-Kilvert, 2 vols. (Oxford: Clarendon, 1987), vol. i, p. 170.

Page 144 "as vampire sent": Byron, *The Giaour*, lines 755–762.

Page 145 "feeding upon the life": *The Vampyre: A Tale* (London: Sherwood, Neely, and Jones, 1819), p. 42.

Page 145 "a celebrated dark day": Estill Curtis Pennington, "Painting Lord Byron: An Account by William Edward West," *Archives of American Art Journal*, 24, 2 (1984), p. 20.

Page 146 "bright sun was extinguished": Byron, "Darkness," lines 2–6.

Page 146 "pall of a past world": Byron, "Darkness," lines 28–30.

Page 146 "crowd was famish'd": Byron, "Darkness," line 55.

Page 146 "chaos of hard clay": Byron, "Darkness," lines 69–72.

Page 146 "their mutual hideousness": Byron, "Darkness," lines 66–67.

Page 146 "Universal Darkness buries All": Alexander Pope, *Dunciad*, Canto IV, lines 653–656.

Page 146 "She was the universe": Byron, "Darkness," lines 81–82.

Page 146 "thunder storms that visit us": Mary and Percy Shelley, *History of a Six Weeks' Tour*, p. 99.

Page 147 "The sky is changed!": *CHP*, Canto III, lines 860–877.

Page 148 "sheathing it as a sword": *CHP*, Canto III, lines 905–913.

Page 149 "serene and glowing evening": Mary and Percy Shelley, *History of a Six Weeks' Tour*, p. 112; see also *LPBS*, vol. I, p. 480.

Page 149 "nearly wrecked": *BLJ*, vol. V, p. 81.

Page 149 "looks of wonder": *LPBS*, vol. I, p. 484.

Page 149 "inhuman tyranny": *LPBS*, vol. I, p. 485.

Page 149 "seven pillars": Byron, *The Prisoner of Chillon*, line 27.

Page 149 "sea of stagnant idleness": Byron, *The Prisoner of Chillon*, lines 249–260, 274.

Page 150 "dark slavery": Percy Shelley, "Hymn to Intellectual Beauty," lines 13, 69–70.

Page 150 "wonderfully peopled": *LPBS*, vol. I, p. 485.

Page 150 "greatest man": *LPBS*, vol. I, p. 494.

Page 150 "wild Rousseau": *CHP*, Canto III, lines 725–727, 740–744.

Page 150 "birth-place of deep Love!": *CHP*, Canto III, line 923.

Page 150 "sublime capacity": *CHP*, Canto III, Byron's note to line 923.

Page 151 "Undying love ... bees and birds": *CHP*, Canto III, lines 950, 933.

Page 151 "blown my brains out": *BLJ*, vol. V, p. 165.

Page 151 "thy crystal sea": Byron, "Sonnet to Lake Leman," lines 1–11; see *CPW*, vol. IV, pp. 16–17.

Page 152 "light of an enchantment": *LPBS*, vol. I, p. 583.

Page 152 "mad as the winds": *LPBS*, vol. I, p. 489.

Page 152 "continue to like Shelley": *BLJ*, vol. v, p. 107.

Page 152 "to finish Chillon for you": *The Clairmont Correspondence: 1808–1834*, p. 52.

Page 153 "a very plain woman": *BLJ*, vol. IV, p. 241.

Page 153 "Me. de Stael has been particularly kind": *BLJ*, vol. v, p. 109.

Page 154 " – – and publish": *BLJ*, vol. v, p. 85.

Page 154 "God damn!": *BLJ*, vol. v, p. 187.

Page 154 "moral Clytemnestra": Byron, "Lines on Hearing that Lady Byron was Ill," lines 37, 23–24.

Page 155 "Mary & Shelley's friendship": *The Clairmont Correspondence: 1808–1834*, pp. 69–70.

Page 155 "is the brat mine?": *BLJ*, vol. v, p. 162.

Page 157 "4 hours rain": *BLJ*, vol. v, p. 102.

Page 157 "the ocean of hell": *BLJ*, vol. v, p. 106.

Page 157 "like a cloud of incense": S. T. Coleridge, "Hymn before Sun-rise, in the vale of Chamouni," lines 80–85.

Page 157 "huge sea of mist": William Wordsworth, *The Prelude*, Book 13, lines 67–72.

Page 157 "tail of a white horse": *BLJ*, vol. v, p. 101.

Page 157 "*woods of withered pines*": *BLJ*, vol. v, p. 102.

Page 158 "Why are ye beautiful?": *Manfred*, Act 1, scene 2, lines 8–9.

Page 158 "my own wretched identity": *BLJ*, vol. v, pp. 104–105.

Page 159 "paradise of exiles": Percy Shelley, "Julian and Maddalo," line 57.

6 THE GREENEST ISLE OF MY IMAGINATION

Page 170 "some little Account": *LJM*, p. 276.

Page 172 "fairy city of the heart": *CHP*, Canto IV, lines 154–158.

Page 172 "haunted me most": *BLJ*, vol. v, p. 132.

Page 172 "gloomy gaiety": *BLJ*, vol. v, pp. 129, 132.

Page 172 "her day of woe": *CHP*, Canto IV, lines 160–161.

Page 173–174 "thrice as many to boot": *BLJ*, vol. VI, p. 92.

Page 174 "what I get by my brains": *BLJ*, vol. VI, p. 92.

Page 174 "several thousand pounds": *BLJ*, vol. VI, p. 66.

Page 174 "sex orgy": Peter Cochran, "Byron and Shelley: Radical Incompatibles," *Romanticism on the Net* 43:6 (August 2006), paragraph 6.

Page 175 "liveliest & happiest looking man": *LPBS*, vol. II, p. 42.

Page 175 "Countesses smell so of garlick": *LPBS*, vol. II, p. 57.

Page 175 "worst inhabitants of Venise": *LMWS*, vol. I, pp. 92, 96.

Page 175 "associates with wretches": *LPBS*, vol. II, p. 57.

Page 176 "confess – you dog": *BLJ*, vol. VI, p. 232.

Page 177 "devil of a mannerist": *BLJ*, vol. V, p. 185.

Page 177 "habit of osculation": *BLJ*, vol. V, p. 193.

Page 177 "pretty as an Antelope": *BLJ*, vol. V, pp. 133–135.

Page 178 "Heaven above – & woman beneath": *BLJ*, vol. V, p. 141.

Page 179 "pair of great black eyes": *BLJ*, vol. V, p. 186.

Page 179 "*forbirsi i scarpi*": *BLJ*, vol. V, p. 189.

Page 179 "sixteen slaps": *BLJ*, vol. V, p. 166.

Page 179 "told the affair": *BLJ*, vol. V, p. 167.

Page 179 "the Armenian language": *BLJ*, vol. V, p. 130.

Page 180 "tête brûlante": G. B. Rizzoli, "Byron's Unacknowledged Armenian Grammar and a New Poem," *Keats-Shelley Journal* 64 (2015), pp. 43–71; 55.

Page 180 "sobbing and weeping": Rizzoli, "Byron's Unacknowledged Armenian Grammar," p. 55.

Page 181 "the terrestrial Paradise": *BLJ*, vol. IX, p. 31.

Page 181 "fiddling, feasting, dancing": Byron, *Beppo*, lines 4–8.

Page 182 "roaring, humming": Byron, *Beppo*, lines 15–18.

Page 182 "turned the corner of twenty-nine": *BLJ*, vol. V, p. 176.

Page 182 "no more a roving": *BLJ*, vol. V, p. 176.

Page 183 "Westminster abbey of Italy": *BLJ*, vol. V, p. 218.

Page 184 "the marble mart": *CHP*, Canto IV, lines 442–448.

Page 184 bread made from grass: *BLJ*, vol. V, p. 217.

Page 184 "A ruin amidst ruins": *CHP*, Canto IV, lines 218–219.

Page 184 "it beats Greece": *BLJ*, vol. V, p. 221.

Page 184 "Rome! my country": *CHP*, Canto IV, lines 694–696.

Page 184 "many-nation'd spoilers": *CHP*, Canto IV, lines 383–384.

Page 185 "barbarism at last": *CHP*, Canto IV, lines 966–967.

Page 186 "a little bark of hope": *CHP*, Canto IV, lines 928–942.

Page 186 "beings of the mind": *CHP*, Canto IV, lines 37–44.

Page 186 "A being more intense": *CHP*, Canto III, lines 46–49.

Page 186 "black-eyed Venetian girl": *BLJ*, vol. V, p. 251.

Page 187 "careless and relaxed realism": *BB*, vol. II, p. 709.

Page 187 "more charming every day": HD, entry for October 14, 1819.

Page 187 "I pitched my staff": *BLJ*, vol. VI, p. 17.

Page 188 "little darling": Doris Langley Moore, *Lord Byron: Accounts Rendered* (New York: Harper and Row, 1974), p. 309.

Page 188 "a little Queen in Creation": Moore, *Accounts Rendered*, p. 310.

Page 189 "something in my old age": *BLJ*, vol. V, p. 228.

Page 190 "Good Night to you dammee!": Byron, "My Dear Mr. Murray," lines 1–84; *CPW*, vol. IV, pp. 161–164.

Page 190 "first Gonorrhea": *BLJ*, vol. VI, p. 14.

Page 190 "good place for women": *BLJ*, vol. VI, p. 17.

Page 190 "fair Venice!": *CHP*, Canto IV, lines 167–169.

Page 190 "prettiest Bacchante in the world": *BLJ*, vol. VI, p. 40.

Page 191 "Poor Arpalice!": *SC*, vol. VII, p. 336.

Page 191 "most bizarre man in the world": *SC*, vol. VII, pp. 323, 325.

Page 191 "a *piece* in the forenoon": *BLJ*, vol. VI, p. 55.

Page 191 "damme it's life!": *BLJ*, vol. VI, p. 48.

Page 192 "my ragamuffins": *BLJ*, vol. VI, p. 248.

Page 192 "devil of a Spirit": *BLJ*, vol. VI, p. 62.

Page 193 "beautiful as ever": *LPBS*, vol. II, p. 36.

Page 193 "no right to the child": *LPBS*, vol. II, p. 36.

Page 193 "I rode one evening": Shelley, "Julian and Maddalo," lines 1–4, 28–31.

Page 194 "You talk Utopia": Shelley, "Julian and Maddalo," lines 175–179.

Page 194 "conversation consisted": *LPBS*, vol. II, pp. 36–37.

Page 194 "stanzas of great energy": *LPBS*, vol. II, pp. 36–37.

Page 194 "a windless bower": Shelley, "Lines Written Among the Euganean Hills," lines 343–352.

Page 195 "given up Concubinage": *BLJ*, vol. VI, p. 93.

7 STRICTEST ADULTERY

Page 198 "Nothing so difficult": Byron, *Don Juan*, Canto IV, lines 1–2.

Page 199 "sell *my chattels*": *BLJ*, vol. VI, p. 255.

Page 199 "sad ... unbearable": *BLJ*, vol. VI, p. 241.

Page 199 "I now quit Italy": *BLJ*, vol. VI, p. 241.

Page 199 "all dressed for travel": *SC*, vol. VII, p. 593.

Page 200 "because they are pretty": *Vie*, p. 123.

Page 200 "melodiousness of his voice": *Vie*, p. 123.

Page 200 "that mysterious fellow feeling": *Vie*, p. 125.

Page 200 "destiny of their hearts": *Vie*, p. 122.

Page 200 "too overwhelmed": *Vie*, p. 124.

Page 201 "I felt attracted to him": *SC*, vol. VII, p. 387.

Page 201 "*tua Amica Amante*": *SC*, vol. VII, p. 389.

Page 201 "I have fallen in love": *BLJ*, vol. VI, p. 107.

Page 201 "fair as Sunrise": *BLJ*, vol. VI, p. 114.

Page 202 "sacrifice to Wealth": *BLJ*, vol. VI, p. 115.

Page 203 "damned cutting & slashing": *BLJ*, vol. VI, p. 105.

Page 204 "stiletto in my gizzard": *BLJ*, vol. VI, p. 163.

Page 204 "She has no tact": *BLJ*, vol. VI, pp. 107–108.

Page 204 "Italian Caroline Lamb": *BLJ*, vol. VI, p. 115.

Page 205 "promiscuous concubinage": *BLJ*, vol. VI, p. 108.

Page 205 "sailed across the lagoon": *Vie*, p. 130.

Page 205 "be content with your Naiads": *Bulldog*, pp. 65–67.

Page 205 "entangled you in her nets": Origo, 103–104.

Page 206 "you have a geni for war": *Bulldog*, p. 273.

Page 206 "Leave the bitches": *Bulldog*, p. 274.

Page 206 "where would Paradise be?": *BLJ*, vol. VI, p. 112.

Page 207 "my last adventure": *BLJ*, vol. VI, p. 175.

Page 208 "utterly incapable of *real* love": *BLJ*, vol. VI, p. 129.

Page 208 "considered a *Maniac*": Ralph Milbanke, Earl of Lovelace, *Astarte: A Fragment of Truth* (London: Christophers, 1921), p. 84.

Page 208 "dripping like a Triton": *BLJ*, vol. VI, p. 133.

Page 209 "not the father": *BLJ*, vol. VI, p. 141.

Page 209 "woman making herself miscarry": *BLJ*, vol. VII, p. 138.

Page 209 "River that rollest": Byron, "To the Po," lines 1–8.

Page 210 "The Land where I was born": *CPW*, vol. VII, p. 58.

Page 210 "My blood is all meridian": Byron, "To the Po," lines 45–52.

Page 210 "tendest wildly": Byron, "To the Po," lines 19–20.

Page 211 "*implora pace*": *BLJ*, vol. VI, p. 149.

Page 211 "an English grave": *BLJ*, vol. VI, p. 149.

Page 212 "more ravished myself": *BLJ*, vol. VI, p. 236.

Page 212 "tears come from the heart": *BLJ*, vol. VI, p. 154.

Page 212 "solitude terrifies me": *BLJ*, vol. VI, pp. 158–159.

Page 213 "Sweet hour of twilight!": Byron, *Don Juan*, Canto III, stanza 105.

Page 213 "she can't guide her horse": *BLJ*, vol. VI, p. 186.

Page 213 "is it not *life*": *BLJ*, vol. VI, p. 232.

Page 213 "every body reads": *LJM*, p. 285.

Page 214 "immoral turn of the whole": *Bulldog*, pp. 258, 256.

Page 214 "infamous publication": *Letters of William and Dorothy Wordsworth III: The Middle Years (Part 2: 1812–1820)*, second edition, ed. Ernest de Selincourt, Mary Moorman, and Alan G. Hall (Oxford University Press, 2000), vol. II, p. 549.

Page 214 "never drenched & scorched": letter in John Murray Archive, rpt. in Peter Cochran, "Francis Cohen, *Don Juan*, and Casti," *Romanticism* 4:1 (1998), pp. 120–124.

Page 214 "paradise of sherbet and sodomy": *BLJ*, vol. VI, p. 207.

Page 215 "nothing further for immortality": *LJM*, pp. 280–281.

Page 215 "the Public are astonished": *LJM*, p. 281.

Page 215 "Juan's are a child's play": *BLJ*, vol. VI, p. 206.

Page 215 "The fools think": *BLJ*, vol. VI, p. 206.

Page 215 "our unlawful loves": *BLJ*, vol. VI, p. 163.

Page 216 "a hundred times Victor": *BLJ*, vol. VI, p. 199.

Page 216 "threw me into convulsions": *BLJ*, vol. VI, p. 206.

Page 216 "Alfieri's Mirra": *BLJ*, vol. VI, p. 217.

Page 216 "perfectly *convulsed*": John Stewart, *Byron and the Websters* (Jefferson, NC: McFarland, 2008), p. 80.

Page 217 "sobbing and weeping": G. B. Rizzoli, "Byron's Unacknowledged Armenian Grammar and a New Poem," *Keats-Shelley Journal* 64 (2015), pp. 43–71; p. 55.

Page 217 "cistern of Gold fishes": *BLJ*, vol. VI, p. 214.

Page 217 "I will nurse you": *Bulldog*, p. 279.

Page 218 "My dearest Teresa": *BLJ*, vol. VI, p. 216.

Page 218 he refused: *Vie*, p. 169.

Page 218 "strictest adultery": *BLJ*, vol. VI, p. 238.

Page 218 "flatterer of fiddlers": *BLJ*, vol. VI, p. 226.

Page 219 "Allegra is here with me": *BLJ*, vol. VI, p. 223.

Page 219 "pitch my tent": *BLJ*, vol. VI, p. 226.

Page 219 "found a *house* and family": *BLJ*, vol. VI, p. 226.

Page 219 "no freedom in Europe": *BLJ*, vol. VI, pp. 226–227.

Page 220 "No tooth-brushes": Samuel Smiles, *A Publisher and His Friends: Memoir and Correspondence of John Murray*, 2 vols. (London: John Murray, 1891), vol. I, p. 409.

Page 220 "solemnity of their pilgrimage": *Vie*, p. 178.

Page 221 "happiest hours of our life": *Vie*, p. 178.

Page 221 "heard her talking": *Vie*, p. 196.

Page 221 "another Eden": Byron, *Don Juan*, Canto IV, stanza 10.

Page 221 "true love's antithesis": Byron, *Don Juan*, Canto III, stanza 8.

Page 221 "like vinegar from wine": Byron, *Don Juan*, Canto III, stanza 5.

Page 222 "consume his life": *BLJ*, vol. VI, p. 214.

Page 222 "curious foreign cap": *BB*, vol. II, p. 820.

Page 222 "eminently handsome": *BB*, vol. II, p. 820.

Page 222 "a sad place": *BLJ*, vol. VI, p. 238.

Page 222 "an ugly, ill-made girl": *BLL*, p. 369.

Page 222 "very merry and tipsy": *BLJ*, vol. VI, p. 238.

Page 223 "damned modest": *BLJ*, vol. VI, p. 232.

Page 223 "stronger than *Cunt*": *BLJ*, vol. VI, p. 232.

Page 223 "my Life in M.S.": *BLJ*, vol. VI, p. 235.

Page 223 "world at large": *Vie*, p. 186.

Page 223 "dark secrets": *Vie*, p. 188.

Page 224 "in high discussion": *BLJ*, vol. VI, p. 239.

Page 224 *"any visitor who may come"*: Origo, p. 157.

Page 224 "the eve of exploding": *BLJ*, vol. VI, p. 240.

Page 224 "chiefly weariness": Origo, p. 158.

Page 225 "feel the degradation": *BLJ*, vol. VI, p. 226.

Page 225 "all over now": *BLJ*, vol. VI, p. 241.

Page 225 "gloomy Venetian palace": *BLJ*, vol. VI, p. 245.

Page 225 "to hear & to tell": *Bulldog*, p. 283.

Page 226 "Chain'd and lotted out": Byron, *Don Juan*, Canto IV, stanzas 91, 94.

Page 226 "love a season": Byron, "[Stanzas ('Could Love For Ever')], lines 14–15; see *CPW*, vol. IV, pp. 242–246.

Page 226 "Mylord is leaving Venice": Origo, p. 164.

Page 227 "arrange my future life": *BLJ*, vol. VI, p. 255.

Page 227 "Love has won": *BLJ*, vol. VI, pp. 258–259.

Page 227 "game at hearts": *BLJ*, vol. VII, p. 43.

Page 227 "a mystery about these things": *BLJ*, vol. VII, pp. 20–21.

Page 228 "two Cats, six dogs": *BLJ*, vol. VII, pp. 208–209.

Page 228 "ill conduct of the Count": marginalia in Teresa Guiccioli's copy of Byron's *Works* (1832–1833), Pforzheimer Collection, New York Public Library, TG0213, vol. IV, p. 319.

Page 229 "the heart of their houses": *BLJ*, vol. VII, pp. 170–171.

8 A FUNERAL PILE

Page 233 "singing birds": *LMWS*, vol. I, p. 209.

Page 234 "windless bower": Shelley, "Lines Written Among the Euganean Hills," lines 343–352.

Page 235 "quasi in the fact": *BLJ*, vol. VII, p. 102.

Page 235 "pepper his ragamuffins": *BLJ*, vol. VII, pp. 112, 103.

Page 235 "fool or a rogue": *BLJ*, vol. VII, p. 112.

Page 235 "his unhappy bride": *Vie*, p. 224.

Page 236 "ill treated her!": marginalia in Teresa Guiccioli's copy of Byron's *Works* (1832–1833), Pforzheimer Collection, New York Public Library, TG0213, vol. IV, p. 319.

Page 236 "dotardly caresses": *BLJ*, vol. VII, p. 92.

Page 236 "custom of the country": *BLJ*, vol. VII, p. 126.

Page 236 "and his alimony": *BLJ*, vol. VII, p. 134.

Page 237 "them as a nation": *BLJ*, vol. VII, p. 77.

Page 237 "by money, means, or person": *BLJ*, vol. VIII, p. 49.

Page 237 "Cardinal glares pale": *BLJ*, vol. VII, p. 84.

Page 238 "leading revolutionary in Ravenna": Origo, p. 272.

Page 238 "Kill'd by five bullets": Byron, *Don Juan*, Canto V, stanza 34.

Page 238 "five bits of lead": Byron, *Don Juan*, Canto V, stanzas 38–39.

Page 239 "a free Italy!!": *BLJ*, vol. VIII, p. 47.

Page 239 "the whole nation": *BLJ*, vol. VIII, pp. 48–49.

Page 239 "Italians are always lost": *BLJ*, vol. VIII, p. 49.

Page 240 "return to making operas": *BLJ*, vol. VIII, p. 105.

Page 240 "take a run *alone*?": *BLJ*, vol. VIII, p. 104.

Page 240 "he keeps her": *CPW*, vol. IV, p. 532.

Page 241 "nurs'd in effeminate arts": Byron, *Sardanapalus*, Act 1, scene 1, line 42; Act 3, scene 1, line 222.

Page 241 "Eat, drink, and love": Byron, *Sardanapalus*, Act 1, scene 2, line 252.

Page 241 "in deep voluptuousness": Byron, *Sardanapalus*, Act 1, scene 1, lines 9–13.

Page 241 "put more love": *BLJ*, vol. VIII, p. 26.

Page 241 "strictest adultery": *BLJ*, vol. VI, p. 232.

Page 242 "very slave of circumstance": Byron, *Sardanapalus*, Act 4, scene 1, lines 330–334.

Page 242 "Nothing – except thirty three": *BLJ*, vol. VIII, p. 32.

Page 242 "smoked glasses": *BB*, vol. II, p. 873.

Page 242 "*le beau sang* of the family": *BB*, vol. II, p. 870.

Page 243 "obstinate as a Mule": *BLJ*, vol. VIII, p. 66.

Page 243 "Have they *reared* one?": *BLJ*, vol. VII, p. 80.

Page 243 "*my damn'd Brute*": *The Journals of Claire Clairmont*, ed. Marion Kingston Stocking (Cambridge, MA: Harvard University Press, 1968), p. 145.

Page 244 "rail against learned women": Doris Langley Moore, *Lord Byron: Accounts Rendered* (New York: Harper and Row, 1974), p. 294.

Page 244 "Gunpowder & fire": *LPBS*, vol. II, p. 323.

Page 244 "melancholy and degrading habits": *LPBS*, vol. II, p. 330.

Page 244 "barbarous & wild": *LPBS*, vol. II, p. 323.

Page 245 "this Circean Palace": *LPBS*, vol. II, pp. 330–331.

Page 245 "a virtuous man": *LPBS*, vol. II, p. 322.

Page 245 "Lord Byron gets up at two": *LPBS*, vol. II, p. 330.

Page 246 "terrible & degrading consequences": *LPBS*, vol. II, p. 336.

Page 247 "stamp of immortality": *LPBS*, vol. II, p. 322.

Page 247 "venture to prophesy": *LPBS*, vol. II, p. 357.

Page 247 "a sort of chameleon": *LPBS*, vol. II, p. 358.

Page 247 "loud in his praise": *LPBS*, vol. II, p. 345.

Page 247 "rage and fury": *BLJ*, vol. IX, p. 54.

Page 248 "apocalyptic ... a revelation": *LPBS*, vol. II, p. 388.

Page 248 "paradise of a decaying body": *LPBS*, vol. II, p. 376.

Page 248 "demon of mistrust": *LPBS*, vol. II, p. 324.

Pages 248–249 "skipping so fast": *LPBS*, vol. II, p. 334.

Page 249 "excessive vivacity": *LPBS*, vol. II, p. 334.

Page 249 "*dreams* of Paradise & angels": *LPBS*, vol. II, p. 335.

Page 249 "agonies of packing": *BLJ*, vol. VIII, p. 190.

Page 249 "depression of Spirits": *BLJ*, vol. IX, p. 47.

Page 250 "mountain of lead": *BLJ*, vol. VIII, p. 230.

Page 250 "the *future* Lady B": *BLJ*, vol. VIII, p. 234.

Page 250 "My dear Papa": *BLJ*, vol. VIII, p. 403.

Page 250 "paternal Gingerbread": *BLJ*, vol. VIII, p. 226.

Page 251 "respectable private families": *LPBS*, vol. II, p. 347.

Page 251 "sunshine and good humour": *Journal of Edward Elleker Williams*, ed. Richard Garnett (London: Elkin Mathews, 1902), p. 22.

Page 251 "spirit of the place": David Crane, *Lord Byron's Jackal: A Life of Trelawny* (New York: Harper Collins, 2012), p. 39.

Page 251 "constant companions": *LPBS*, vol. II, p. 373.

Page 252 "full of *Ghosts*": *BLJ*, vol. IX, p. 74.

Page 252 "large, gloomy ... throughout the evening": Moore, vol. II, p. 612.

Page 252 "English household comforts": *BLJ*, vol. IX, p. 82.

Page 252 "vats of claret": *LPBS*, vol. II, p. 379.

Page 252 "good cavaliers flock together": letter to Marianna Hunt, March 5, 1822, *LMWS*, vol. I, p. 221.

Page 253 "nice pretty girl": *The Journals of Mary Shelley 1814–1844*, ed. Paula Feldman and Diana Scott-Kilvert, 2 vols. (Oxford: Clarendon, 1987), vol. I, p. 378.

Page 253 "pretty, sentimental, innocent, superficial Italian": *LPBS*, vol. II, p. 363.

Page 253 "a devil of a noise!": *BLL*, p. 410.

Page 254 "farm-keeper's daughter": *BB*, vol. III, p. 947.

Page 256 "unarmed people": *BLJ*, vol. IX, p. 134.

Page 256 "no consolation": *Vie*, p. 440–441.

Page 256 "While she lived": *LBCLB*, pp. 71–72.

Page 257 "feeling which haunts me": *The Clairmont Correspondence: 1808–1834*, ed. Marion Kingston Stocking (Baltimore: Johns Hopkins University Press, 1995), p. 169.

Page 257 "Claire is much better": *LPBS*, vol. II, p. 420.

Page 257 "source of anxiety and suspense": *LPBS*, vol. II, p. 422.

Page 257 "In memory of / Allegra": *BLJ*, vol. IX, pp. 163–164.

Page 258 "*almost always misunderstood*": *BLJ*, vol. X, pp. 54–55.

Page 258 "like Anacreon's swallow": *LPBS*, vol. II, p. 423.

Page 258 "extinguished the glow-worm": *LPBS*, vol. II, p. 423.

Page 258 "I detest all society": *LPBS*, vol. II, p. 434.

Page 259 "rolling blue at my feet": *BLJ*, vol. IX, p. 173.

Page 260 "a nod from an American": *BLJ*, vol. IX, p. 171.

Page 260 "rather fat and apparently effeminate": Estill Curtis Pennington, "Painting Lord Byron: An Account by William Edward West," *Archives of American Art Journal* 24:2 (1984), p. 19.

Page 260 "familiar and friendly": Pennington, "Painting Lord Byron," p. 19.

Page 260 "e troppo bello!": Pennington, "Painting Lord Byron," p. 19.

Page 260 "very proud of her": Pennington, "Painting Lord Byron," p. 19.

Page 261 "his worst times": *LMWS*, vol. I, p. 245 (August 15, 1822).

Page 261 "Get up Shelley": *LMWS*, vol. I, p. 245 (August 15, 1822).

Page 261 "mean to be content?": *LMWS*, vol. I, p. 245 (August 15, 1822).

Page 261 "earth appears another world": *LPBS*, vol. II, p. 435.

Page 262 "voluptuous indolence": Leigh Hunt, *Lord Byron and Some of His Contemporaries,* second edition, 2 vols. (London: Henry Colburn, 1828), vol. I, p. 17.

Page 262 "virtually my own exile": *BLJ,* vol. IX, p. 179.

Page 262 "skrewing LB's mind": *LMWS,* vol. I, p. 248.

Page 263 "black lines and the dirty rags": Edward Trelawny, *Recollections of the Last Days of Shelley and Byron* (London: Moxon, 1858), p. 116.

Page 263 "incense, honey, wine, salt, and sugar": *Letters of Edward John Trelawny,* ed. H. Buxton Forman (Oxford University Press, 1910), p. 3.

Page 263 "carcase of a sheep": *Letters of Edward John Trelawny,* p. 8.

Page 264 "the dead bones will grin": Byron, *Don Juan,* Canto IX, stanzas 11–12.

9 TO JOIN THE GREEKS

Page 269 "most *lively* colours": *BLJ,* vol. III, pp. 230–231.

Page 269 "We are all Greeks": Percy Shelley, "Preface" to "Hellas."

Page 270 "join the Greeks": Medwin, p. 223.

Page 270 "My avarice – or cupidity": *BLJ,* vol. IX, pp. 207–208.

Page 271 "tears streaming down his cheeks": John Cam Hobhouse, *Journey through Albania and other provinces of Turkey* (London: Cawthorn, 1813), vol. I, pp. 225–229.

Page 271 "their obligations to foreigners": *CPW,* vol. II, p. 201.

Page 271 "operate as a Talisman": Roderick Beaton, *Byron's War: Romantic Rebellion, Greek Revolution* (Cambridge University Press, 2013), p. 132.

Page 272 "this busy hateful Genoa": *LMWS,* vol. I, p. 258 (September 15, 1822).

Page 272 "fathomless well of bitter waters": *The Journals of Mary Shelley 1814–1844,* ed. Paula Feldman and Diana Scott-Kilvert, 2 vols. (Oxford: Clarendon, 1987), vol. II, p. 433.

Page 272 "stupid long swim": *BLJ*, vol. x, p. 56.

Page 272 "thin as a Skeleton": *BLJ*, vol. x, p. 112.

Page 272 "robustious as formerly": *BLJ*, vol. x, p. 137.

Page 273 "the *dross* is coming": *BLJ*, vol. x, p. 87.

Page 273 "I feel sixty in mind": *LBCLB*, p. 49.

Page 273 "warm my chilled feelings": *LBCLB*, p. 103.

Page 273 "that dull monitress": *LBCLB*, p. 163.

Page 274 "gone on the wind's wings": Byron, *Don Juan*, Canto xi, stanza 76.

Page 274 "growing dull": Byron, *Don Juan*, Canto xiv, stanza 10.

Page 275 "the journal is a *bad* business": *BLJ*, vol. x, p. 13.

Pages 275–276 "heartless and beastly ribaldry": *Literary Gazette* (October 19, 1822), pp. 655–656.

Page 276 "such outcasts from Society": *LJM*, p. 455.

Page 276 "works are considerably deteriorated": *LJM*, p. 456.

Page 276 "a condition so degrading": *LJM*, p. 459.

Page 277 "rude neglect": *BLJ*, vol. x, p. 28.

Page 277 "mood of serenity and sadness": *Vie*, p. 488.

Page 277 "wouldn't want anything changed": *Vie*, p. 488.

Page 278 "he embraced his friend": Moore, vol. ii, pp. 613–614.

Page 278 "talked over old times": *BB*, vol. iii, p. 1031.

Page 278 "morals of the contadine": *BB*, vol. iii, p. 1031.

Page 278 "mutual accusations half in joke": HD, entry for September 20, 1822.

Page 279 "sad remembrancers": *BLJ*, vol. ix, p. 211.

Page 279 "Shelley thought highest of my talents": *BLJ*, vol. x, p. 34.

Page 279 "partners in the waltz": *BLJ*, vol. x, p. 34.

Page 280 "hear the word 'Clare'": *BLJ*, vol. viii, p. 44.

Page 280 "but five minutes together": *BLJ*, vol. x, p. 49.

Page 280 "transient glimpses of old friends": *BLJ*, vol. ix, p. 201.

Page 281 "my dearest friend": *BLJ*, vol. xi, p. 148.

Page 281 "fare thee well – Fanny": *BLJ*, vol. x, p. 198.

Page 282 "lost – lost – undone": John Stewart, *Byron and the Websters* (Jefferson, NC: McFarland, 2008), p. 130.

Page 282 "greatest ass and cuckold": HD, entry for January 29, 1820.

Page 282 "moving Heaven and Earth": *BLJ*, vol. x, p. 102.

Page 282 "I still do not despair": *BLJ*, vol. x, pp. 106–107.

Page 282 "more romantic than wise": *BLJ*, vol. x, pp. 101–102.

Page 282 "a pretty mild boy": *BLJ*, vol. x, p. 136.

Page 282 "an especial favourite of mine": *BLJ*, vol. x, p. 174.

Page 282 "softest and most amiable expression": *BLJ*, vol. x, p. 135.

Page 283 "*Le Diable Boiteux*": *BLJ*, vol. x, p. 136.

Page 283 "Poor Lord Byron!": *The Journal of the Hon. Henry Edward Fox*, ed. The Earl of Ilchester (London: Thornton Butterworth, 1923), p. 216.

Page 283 "hen pecked to his heart's content": *LMWS*, vol. i, p. 295.

Page 283 "lords of ladies intellectual": Byron, *Don Juan*, Canto i, stanza 22.

Page 284 "I recommend solitude": *LBCLB*, p. 210.

Page 284 "to get rid of her": *Journal of the Hon. Henry Edward Fox*, p. 298.

Page 284 "LB is fixed on Greece": *LMWS*, vol. i, p. 341.

Page 284 "Lady Byroning – and Glenarvoning": *BLJ*, vol. x, p. 178.

Page 284 "treating them harshly": *BLJ*, vol. x, p. 178.

Page 285 "a kept mistress": *LBCLB*, p. 12.

Page 286 "but a little artificial": *Vie*, pp. 523, 535.

Page 286 "and am disappointed": Lady Blessington, *The Idler in Italy*, 2 vols. (London: Henry Colburn, 1839), vol. i, p. 393.

Page 286 "dignified, cold, reserved, and haughty": *LBCLB*, p. 7.

Page 286 "a glance of fire": Byron, *The Corsair*, lines 203, 196.

Page 286–87 "I had fancied him taller": *LBCLB*, pp. 5–7.

Page 287 "wayward, spoiled child of genius": *LBCLB*, p. 35.

Page 287 "The mobility of his nature": *LBCLB*, pp. 49, 47.

Page 287 "All this appears so inconsistent": *LBCLB*, p. 33.

Page 288 "strongly acted on by what is nearest": Byron, *Don Juan*, Canto XVI, stanza 97.

Page 288 "excessive susceptibility of immediate impressions": Byron, *Don Juan*, Canto XVI, note to stanza 97.

Page 288 "Byron is a perfect chameleon": *LBCLB*, p. 71.

Page 288 "strange mélange of good and evil": *LBCLB*, p. 220.

Page 288 "the air of a *Cupidon déchaîné*": *BLJ*, vol. X, p. 136.

Page 289 "scarcely a person mentioned": *BLJ*, vol. X, p. 139.

Page 289 "*mystery* of the English Ennui": *BLJ*, vol. X, p. 139.

Page 289 "mode of treating their prisoners": *BLJ*, vol. X, p. 152.

Page 290 "wings for my golden darlings": *LBCLB*, p. 182.

Page 290 "Cash is the Sinew of war": *BLJ*, vol. X, p. 154.

Page 290 "my heart is as grey as my head": *CPW*, vol. VII, pp. 75–76.

Page 291 "two poems on the subject": *LBCLB*, p. 183.

Page 291 "If things are farcical": *HVSV*, p. 434.

Page 292 "the anguish of that heart": *Vie*, p. 571.

Page 293 "side by side once again": *Vie*, p. 572.

Page 293 "*take care of your health*": *Vie*, p. 573.

Page 293 "this kind of tedium": *Vie*, p. 573.

Page 293 "nothing will be able to part us": *Vie*, p. 574.

Page 293 "my scribblings": *Vie*, p. 574.

Page 294 "from the Conte to the Contadine": *BLJ*, vol. VII, p. 180.

Page 295 "Where shall we be in a year?": *Vie*, pp. 577–578.

Page 295 "The Dead have been awakened": *CPW*, vol. VII, p. 77.

Page 296 "Farewell my dear friend": *BLL*, p. 516; National Library of Scotland, MS 43424.

10 PILGRIM OF ETERNITY

Page 300 "the ague in this mud-basket": *BLJ*, vol. XI, p. 107.

Page 300 "the puir Hill Folk": *BLJ*, vol. XI, p. 82.

Page 300 "clan or Sept or tribe or horde": *BLJ*, vol. XI, p. 35.

Page 301 "Our wild troops here": Pietro Gamba, *A Narrative of Lord Byron's Last Journey to Greece* (London: John Murray, 1825), p. 122.

Page 301 "reeled as if with wine": *CPW*, vol. VII, p. 82.

Page 302 "shape of independent Greece": Roderick Beaton, *Byron's War: Romantic Rebellion, Greek Revolution* (Cambridge University Press, 2013), pp. 147, 149.

Page 302 "it must be *the Cause*": *BLJ*, vol. XI, p. 42.

Page 302 "I did not come here": *BLJ*, vol. XI, p. 32.

Page 302 "the only *Washington* or *Kosciusko*": *BLJ*, vol. XI, p. 44.

Page 303 "greatest hilarity and enjoyment": James Hamilton Browne, "Voyage from Leghorn to Cephalonia with Lord Byron," *Blackwood's Edinburgh Magazine* 35:117 (August 1834), pp. 56–67; 59.

Page 304 "a very *triste* existence": *LBCLB*, p. 221.

Page 304 "in your 'smiles and wine'": *BLJ*, vol. XI, pp. 84–85.

Page 304 "eleven long years of bitterness": Edward Trelawny, *Recollections of the Last Days of Shelley and Byron* (London: Moxon, 1858), p. 201.

Page 304 "on the binnacle of a ship": *BLJ*, vol. XI, p. 15.

Page 305 "avoid giving any offence": *BLL*, p. 468.

Page 305 "*He* is *our* Man": *BLJ*, vol. XI, p. 73.

Page 305 "seize Napoli [Nafplio]": *The Life and Opinions of General Sir Charles James Napier*, 4 vols. (London: John Murray, 1857), vol. I, pp. 336–337.

Page 305 "playing at Nations": *BLJ*, vol. XI, p. 80.

Page 306 "avoid the character of a partizan": *BLJ*, vol. XI, p. 32.

Page 306 "desire of nothing but *money*": *BLJ*, vol. XI, p. 24.

Page 306 "Come and fetch me": *Vie*, p. 609.

Page 307 "I kiss your Eyes": *BLJ*, vol. XI, p. 21.

Page 307 "Ever my dearest T.": *BLJ*, vol. XI, p. 57.

Page 307 "what is to be done": *BLJ*, vol. XI, p. 43.

Pages 307–308 "some beatific dream or vision": *HVSV*, p. 412.

Page 308 "break my staff": Trelawny, *Recollections of the Last Days of Shelley and Byron*, p. 209.

Page 308 "furnish the Moreote refugees": *BLJ*, vol. XI, p. 19.

Page 309 "My head is burning": *HVSV*, p. 424.

Page 309 "a hunted animal at bay": *HVSV*, p. 424.

Page 309 "Back! Out of my sight!": *HVSV*, p. 424.

Page 310 "one of the brightest days": *HVSV*, p. 429.

Page 311 "a Grecian Bolivar": *BLL*, p. 476.

Page 311 "growing fat and growing mad": *BLL*, p. 479.

Page 311 "time passes more cheerfully": James Kennedy, *Conversations on Religion, with Lord Byron* (London: John Murray, 1830), p. 214.

Page 311 "such d—d liars": *BLJ*, vol. XI, pp. 32–33.

Page 311 "his lumbering packets": *BLJ*, vol. XI, p. 24.

Page 312 "only occupy the idle": Gamba, *A Narrative of Lord Byron's Last Journey to Greece*, p. 48.

Page 312 "You very much remind me": Kennedy, *Conversations*, p. 197.

Page 312 "zealous Dr. Kennedy": *BLJ*, vol. XI, p. 56.

Page 312 "kneel down, and pray to God": Kennedy, *Conversations*, p. 380.

Page 313 "Shelley's ghost": Leicester Stanhope, *Greece in 1823 and 1824* (London: Sherwood, Gilbert, and Piper, 1825), pp. 512–513.

Page 313 "tall, rosy-cheeked dandy boy": *Letters of Edward John Trelawny*, ed. H. Buxton Forman (Oxford University Press, 1910), p. 149.

Page 313 "two schoolmasters": William Parry, *The Last Days of Lord Byron* (London: Knight and Lacey, 1825), p. 270.

Page 314 "national property of Greece": William St. Clair, *That Greece Might Still Be Free: The Philhellenes in the War of Independence* (Oxford University Press, 1972), p. 209.

Page 315 "received here as a saviour": *BB*, vol. III, p. 1140.

Page 315 "disaffected and mutinous": Harold Nicolson, *Byron: The Last Journey* (London: Constable, 1924), p. 174.

Page 316 "1000 or 1500 Suliotes": Nicolson, *Byron: The Last Journey*, p. 178.

Page 316 "100,000 sterling in hand": *BLJ*, vol. XI, p. 86.

Page 316 "I am embarking for Messolonghi": *BLJ*, vol. XI, p. 86.

Page 316 "implements of peace and war": *BLJ*, vol. XI, p. 89.

Page 317 "Once more upon the waters!": *CHP*, Canto III, line 10.

Page 317 "now hurrah for Greece": Beaton, *Byron's War*, p. 204.

Page 317 "firing pistols and carbines": Moore, vol. II, p. 704.

Page 318 "a miracle of the Saints": *BLJ*, vol. XI, p. 87.

Page 318 "sooner cut [Loukas] in pieces": *BLJ*, vol. XI, p. 87.

Page 318 "where the devil is the fleet gone?": *BLJ*, vol. XI, p. 87.

Page 318 "from Creek to Creek": *BLJ*, vol. XI, p. 90.

Page 318 "another narrow escape": *BLJ*, vol. XI, p. 92.

Page 318 "I watched thee in the breakers": *CPW*, vol. VII, p. 81.

Page 319 "salvos of artillery": Gamba, *Narrative*, p. 84.

Page 319 "ass in the lion's skin": *BLJ*, vol. XI, p. 43.

Page 319 "matter for a hundred cantos": Parry, *Last Days*, p. 192.

Page 319 "besieged, day and night": Trelawny, *Recollections*, p. 222.

Page 320 "Soldiers that won't march": *BLJ*, vol. XI, p. 140.

Page 321 "nothing more to do with the Suliotes": *BLJ*, vol. XI, pp. 111–112.

Page 322 "you are no rogue, Lyon": *BB*, vol. III, p. 1192.

Pages 322–323 "temper was more irritable": John Cam Hobhouse (Lord Broughton), *Recollections of a Long Life, with Additional Extracts from His Private Diaries*, ed. Lady Dorchester, 4 vols. (London: John Murray, 1910), vol. III, p. 367.

Page 323 "something worth living for": *Bulldog*, p. 343.

Page 323 "a dread of them": *LBCLB*, p. 208.

Page 323 "blundering blockhead doctors": Nicolson, *Byron: The Last Journey*, p. 113.

Page 324 "damned set of butchers": Nicolson, *Byron: The Last Journey*, p. 258.

Page 324 "calm of coming death": Parry, *Last Days*, p. 124.

Page 324 "I am content to die": Gamba, *Narrative*, pp. 264–265.

Page 324 "I want to sleep now": *BB*, vol. 3, p. 1128.

Page 324 "To strongly – wrongly – vainly – love": *CPW*, vol. VII, p. 82.

Pages 324–325 "'Tis time this heart": Byron, "January 22nd 1824. Messalonghi. On this day I complete my thirty sixth year," lines 1–2.

Page 325 "bellowings of imprisoned demons": Trelawny, *Recollections*, p. 184.

Page 325 "A funeral pile!": Byron, "January 22nd 1824," lines 9–12.

Page 325 "a light / To lesson ages": Byron, *Sardanapalus*, act 5, scene 1, lines 440–42.

Page 325 "lava of the imagination": *BLJ*, vol. III, p. 179.

Page 326 "the explosion is dreadful": Beaton, *Byron's War*, p. 257.

Page 326 "And then strike home!": Byron, "January 22nd 1824," lines 21–28.

Page 326 "our own dear lake": Byron, "Epistle to Augusta," lines 73–74.

Page 326 "Shades of heroes farewell!": Byron, "On Leaving Newstead Abbey," lines 21–24.

Page 327 "lease of my 'body's length'": *BLJ*, vol. X, p. 157.

Page 327 "frequent mus'd": Byron, "Lines Written Beneath an Elm in the Churchyard of Harrow," line 10.

Page 327 "couch of my repose": Byron, "Lines Written Beneath an Elm in the Churchyard of Harrow," lines 19–26.

Page 328 "And take thy rest": Byron, "January 22nd 1824," lines 33–40.

INDEX

Index

Index

Index